PATERNOSTER BIBLICAL MON

On I'net

Your Father the Devil?

A full listing of titles in this series appears at the end of this book.

Paternoster Biblical Monographs

At the present time we are experiencing a veritable explosion in the field of biblical and theological research with more and more academic theses of high quality being produced by younger scholars from all over the world. One of the considerations taken into account by the examiners of doctoral theses is that, if they are to be worthy of the award of a degree, then they should contain material that needs to be read by other scholars; if so, it follows that the facilities must exist for them to be made accessible. In some cases (perhaps more often than is always realized) it will be most appropriate for the distinctive contribution of the thesis to be harvested in journal articles; in others there may be the possibility of a revision that will produce a book of wider appeal than simply to professional scholars. But many theses of outstanding quality can and should be published more or less as they stand for the benefit of other scholars and interested persons.

Hitherto it has not been easy for authors to find publishers willing to publish works that, while highly significant as works of scholarship, cannot be expected to become 'best-sellers' with a large circulation. Fortunately the development of printing technology now makes it relatively easy for publishers to produce specialist works without the commercial risks that would have prevented them from doing so in the past.

The Paternoster Press is one of the first publishers to make use of this new technology. Its aim is quite simply to assist biblical and theological scholarship by the publication of theses and other monographs of high quality at affordable prices.

Different publishers serve different constituencies. The Paternoster Press stands in the tradition of evangelical Christianity and exists to serve that constituency, though not in any narrow way. What is offered, therefore, in this series, is the best of scholarship by evangelical Christians.

PATERNOSTER BIBLICAL MONOGRAPHS

Your Father the Devil?
A New Approach to John and 'the Jews'

Stephen Motyer

PATERNOSTER PRESS

First published 1997 in Paternoster Biblical and Theological
Monographs by Paternoster Press
Paternoster Press is an imprint of Authentic Media
PO Box 300, Carlisle, Cumbria, CA3 OQS, U.K.
and PO Box 1047, Waynesboro, GA 30830-2047, USA

03 02 01 00 99 98 97   7 6 5 4 3 2 1

British Library Cataloguing in Publication Data

A record for this book is available from the British Library.

ISBN 0-85364-832-8

This book was prepared for publication and typeset at London Bible
College, Northwood, U.K., using a Macintosh Performa 6200 and the
WriteNow 4.0 word-processing software from Softkey International.
Printed and bound in Great Britain for
Paternoster Press
by Nottingham Alpha Graphics.

*To my Colleagues at London School of Theology,
in gratitude for their friendship, encouragement, inspiration and
partnership in the Gospel and in Christ.*

Contents

Preface

This study was first submitted to London University as a Ph.D. thesis, in 1992, and I am delighted that it now appears in published form. Various delays have held it up since then, and in revising it for publication it has not proved possible to engage extensively with the technical johannine literature published in the intervening period. However I do not think that anything has appeared which would compel me substantially to revise the thesis defended in this book.

I believe that, in two vital respects, John's Gospel needs a 'new look' comparable to that announced by J.A.T. Robinson in 1959, when he discerned various "straws in the wind" which seemed to him to herald the break-up of the fifty-year-old consensus on the background and origins of the Gospel.[1] He was quite right, and the expression 'new look' has passed into the coinage of New Testament scholarship. Over the course of the following decade, the face of johannine scholarship changed beyond recognition, and a new consensus emerged.

That consensus, now thirty years old, needs challenging in turn. I think I discern one straw in the wind which might herald a second 'new look', and that is the recent interest in the relevance of the first century Jewish apocalypses for the interpretation of John. Part of Robinson's 'new look' was to see John as related to first century Judaism rather than the world of Greek thought, but for Robinson the impetus for this arose chiefly from the Qumran literature, then recently published. Only in the last few years has the relevance of the apocalypses been recognised. When they are taken seriously, the foundations begin to shift, I believe ...

Are there any other straws in the wind? Perhaps a hint here and there. But maybe I will float a few with this book. In two related respects, as I say, the current consensus needs to be questioned:

(1) *In relation to John's anti-Judaism.* From its inception with the work of J. Louis Martyn, this new consensus has regarded the Fourth Gospel as fundamentally anti-Jewish in motivation and content. Whereas other parts of the New Testament can be called anti-Jewish just in that they regard Christian faith as a *successor* which *replaces* Jewish faith and life, in the Fourth Gospel opposition seems to take

---

1   Robinson "New Look" 94

the form of downright *hostility*. It is not surprising that many writers, both Christian and Jewish, have expressed deep discomfort over the way "the Jews" are apparently 'demonised' in John.

This study takes its starting-point from the most offensive statement of all, Jesus' charge in John 8:44 that the Jews are "of your father the devil". But I shall argue that, *far from 'demonising' the Jews, this charge is part of a strategy, rooted in the conditions of late first-century Judaism, which is designed to appeal to Jews to see Jesus as the Messiah, and is motivated by a deep commitment to the good of Israel.*

(2) *In relation to John's purpose.* I use the word 'purpose' here in a special sense, intended just to denote its function among late first-century Jews. The dominant consensus maintains that the Fourth Gospel uses a kind of private Christian language, related to the language of Judaism but 'relexicalized', to use Bruce Malina's expression: that is, the Fourth Gospel attempts to bolster the faith of Christians by turning traditional Jewish language into the technical terms of a new *Christian* faith from which Jews are excluded. Like Nicodemus, they ought to be able to understand (3:10), but of course they cannot, because the words have been redefined. So, like Nicodemus, they are effectively mocked.

I think that this consensus needs seriously to be challenged. Far from reinforcing Christian sectarianism, *the Fourth Gospel is deeply aware of the traumas and needs of late first-century Judaism, and seeks to address them not as a fugitive from the fold, but as a member of the flock.*

These are the issues which this study seeks boldly to explore. From it emerges a 'new look', I believe, not just on "the Jews" of the Fourth Gospel, but on the whole Gospel and its environment. Whether others will be convinced to 'look' in this way, of course, I do not know. But I can hope. And pray. Modesty, however, and realism, forbid me to use the word 'look' in the subtitle of the book! 'New approach' will do nicely and claims enough.

I am very grateful to numerous people who have had a hand in the production of this book. To Professor Graham Stanton, of King's College London, who was the supervisor of the original research: I was so appreciative of his self-sacrificial help and advice. To the management at London Bible College, first for allowing me study-leave in 1991-2 to write the original Ph.D. thesis, and more recently for a sabbatical term (autumn 1996) which has afforded space to revise it and prepare it for publication. To Dr Bruce Winter and his colleagues at Tyndale House, Cambridge, who granted me free accommodation for four weeks there in 1991-2 to enable access to some less available corners of the scholarly literature. Looking further back, to Professor Peter Stuhlmacher of Tübingen University, who kindly welcomed a young lecturer into his post-graduate seminar in 1981-2 and encouraged him, although I was then pursuing a different Ph.D. topic. More than all, I owe a huge debt of gratitude to my wife and family, who over many years have nobly put up with the distraction and absences caused by my commitment to this work.

And the dedication expresses my gratitude to a group of colleagues with whom it has been an enormous privilege to work for ten years. They have rekindled my love for God and my commitment to the disciplined use of the mind in biblical scholarship, and are a prize bunch!

London Bible College
January, 1997

Introduction

This book wants to understand John 8:31-59, and the relation-ship between Jesus and "the Jews" in that passage. Throughout the Fourth Gospel, "the Jews" are (on the whole) portrayed as unbel-ieving and hostile towards Jesus, and these attitudes crystallise into the confrontation in 8:31-59, where Jesus accuses them of being "of your father the devil" (8:44), and they respond by accusing him of demon-possession (8:48).

The language of this passage has been roundly condemned as antisemitic, both in intent and more importantly in *effect:* for "You are of your father the devil" (8:44) was grist to the Nazi mill, at the end of a long history of occasions on which this passage was used to fuel opposition to Jews. Günter Reim recalls seeing a photograph of a sign at the entrance to a Franconian village, proclaiming "Der Vater der Juden ist der Teufel".[1] Richard Lowry spares no punches: there is, he says,

> an unbroken epigenous line of development from John's portrayal of the Jews as spawn of the devil, eagerly doing their 'father's desires'; through the medieval flowering of antisemitic tracts illustrated with woodcuts of 'the Jews and their father, the devil'; up to a little children's picture-book, published in 1936 by the Nazi's [sic] Stürmer-Verlag, whose first page is headed by the slogan: 'Der Vater der Juden ist der Teufel'[2]

The Jewish scholar Lillian Freudmann writes,

> John especially has been labeled 'the father of anti-Semitism'. John gave the word 'Jews' a specially abusive meaning. He designated Jesus' adversaries — elders, scribes, priests, Pharisees — as *the* Jews. In his writing Jews literally reached the depth of hell as they become descendants of the devil.[3]

She calls 8:31-59 a "tirade against the Jews",[4] and quotes

---

1   Reim "Teufelskinder" 619
2   Lowry "Suitor" 229
3   Lillian C. Freudmann, *Antisemitism in the New Testament* (Maryland etc; University Press of America, 1994), 265
4   *Antisemitism* 264

approvingly the view of Roy Eckhardt that 8:44-47 can be called "the road to Auschwitz".[5] She herself writes about these verses,

> Passages like the one above make antisemitism respectable and encourage aggression against Jews. With 'inspiration' like this, pious churchgoers have considered it acceptable at a minimum, and perhaps even their Christian duty, to join in massive attacks upon Jews. Unfortunately, John's virulence is not limited to this citation nor is it mitigated by any offsetting expression of kindness or friendship for Jews.[6]

This is sobering indeed for Christians who *do* regard John's Gospel as 'inspired'. But Freudmann's attack (and many others like it) must be taken seriously. For John's language has certainly prompted or at least fuelled attacks on Jews. Just to take two examples:

(1) In 386 or 387 AD John Chrysostom delivered a series of eight sermons 'Against the Jews' in Antioch, which Robert Wilken calls "the most vituperative and vindictive attack on the Jews from Christian antiquity".[7] Chrysostom was worried by the popularity of the synagogue amongst Christians, many of whom participated the Jewish festivals. His response was to denounce the Jews as demon-possessed idolaters plagued by every sin and vice. Although he never specifically develops the charge that they are descended from the devil, he comes close. It is the devil who attracts people to the synagogue.[8] "They are fighting against God's command, and it is the devil who leads them in their revels and dance."[9] In *Disc.* 8:8:4-6 he quotes "He was a murderer from the beginning" from John 8:44, and comments, "If the devil is a murderer, it is clear that the demons who serve him are murderers too". This connects with his very frequent accusation of murder against the Jews for the cruci-fixion of Christ.

(2) In 1543 Martin Luther published his infamous treatise 'On the Jews and Their Lies',[10] in which "You are of your father the devil"

---

5   *Antisemitism* 267

6   *Antisemitism* 267

7   R.L. Wilken, *Judaism and the Early Christian Mind* (New Haven & London: Yale University Press, 1971), 19

8   *Disc.* 1:4:6, 2:3:4

9   *Disc.* 4:7:4, trans. P.W. Harkins, *Saint John Chrysostom: Discourses Against Judaizing Christians* (Washington, D.C.: Catholic University of America Press, 1979), 92

10   To be found in Franklin Sherman (ed.), *Luther's Works, Vol 47* (Philadel-phia: Fortress Press, 1971), 121-306 (trans. Martin H. Bertram)

is quoted in the introduction as one of the presuppositions on which the work rests.[11] He calls synagogues "nothing but a den of devils", and urges Christians to exercise "a sharp mercy" by setting fire to synagogues and schools, destroying Jewish homes, confiscating all their sacred books, prohibiting all teaching, forbidding all travel, impounding all their money and imposing forced labour on them — until they become Christians.[12] These proposals have a horribly prophetic ring. Martin Bertram comments, "it remained for a later century to refine and systematize them and apply them on a massive scale".[13]

At the time, Luther's outbursts were not taken seriously. But not surprisingly, post-Holocaust Christian theology has felt very uncomfortable about this aspect of Christian history and its apparent roots in the New Testament itself. Some have called for a radical re-writing of Christianity as a consequence. For instance, Rosemary Ruether traces the roots of antisemitism back to "the theological dispute between Christianity and Judaism over the messiahship of Jesus",[14] and insists that "there is no way to rid Christianity of its anti-Judaism, which constantly takes social expression in anti-Semitism, without grappling finally with its christological hermeneutic itself".[15] This means a root-and-branch revision of Christian tradition which starts by rejecting the 'high' christology of the Fourth Gospel. Such a relaying of foundations would be hard for many Christians to contemplate. Is there an alternative?

One alternative is offered to us by Clark Williamson and Ronald Allen. They suggest that the hatred towards the Jews evinced in passages like John 8:44 is inconsistent with the overall johannine theology of love, so that it can be ejected like a cuckoo from the nest. Preachers may turn their backs on it with a clear conscience, for *John himself* would reject it, if he applied his own message consistently.[16] Superficially attractive though it is, this approach leaves us with uncomfortable theological and historical problems.

Theologically, Freudmann's shaft about 'inspiration' is telling. We

---

11 *Op. cit.* 141
12 *Op. cit.* 172, 268-272
13 *Op. cit.* 136
14 Ruether *Fratricide* 28
15 *Fratricide* 116
16 C. Williamson & R. Allen, *Interpreting Difficult Texts: Anti-Judaism and Christian Preaching* (London; SCM, 1989): e.g. referring to the anti-Judaism implicit in the Good Shepherd discourse, they argue that Christian preaching should act upon the logic of John 3:16 (God's love for the *world*), and reject the anti-Judaism of such passages. "Anything less involves John in an open self-contradiction" (92).

cannot help feeling that, of all people, the evangelist himself should have been able to judge what was or was not consistent with his Good News. If his anti-Judaism is fundamentally *unChristian*, then we are faced with a theological mine-field which we must cross without the help of our sacred literature to show us the way. For we must surely agree with Ruether that, unless appearances are mistaken, John's message and status as an apostle of the church are undermined, if they are paired with a basic hostility towards Jews.

Unless appearances are mistaken ... Could they be? If all we had were the texts of the New Testament and their reception by the church and its theological tradition, then we would be hard put to it to resist the charge that our sacred literature demonises unbelieving Jews and thus prompts the persecution of them. But theology has an older sister, whom she has frequently tried to disown, but who stubbornly maintains the right to check the unruly behaviour of her younger sibling.

Her name is *history*. In this case she insistently poses the question *whether John has been gravely misused by these later antisemitic appropriations of his language*. Theology replies that it does not matter if he has, for the language is there and has its effect, irrespective of its original intent or setting. In any case, how can you accuse someone of satanic ancestry without hostility? History replies that the world is a strange place, and that we cannot simply disregard original intent or setting. After all, 'authority' in Christianity has always been person-shaped: ascribed not to *texts*, but to *people*, whether apostles or Christ himself.

This book accepts and rests upon this argument from theology's older sister. It starts from the presupposition that, if it is possible to rescue the Fourth Gospel as *word of God* for the church today, then it will be through patient investigation of it *in its own terms*, allowing it to speak with its own true voice. But we do *not* presuppose in advance that this approach will guarantee vindication from the grave charges advanced by Freudmann and others. We would incur the wrath of the older sister for such an assumption. She will allow us hope, but no more.

In fact the prospects are not auspicious. At the moment historical scholarship is widely committed to a sharply anti-Jewish interpretation of the Fourth Gospel. For according to the dominant consensus on its historical situation and occasion, *its anti-Judaism is in fact central to its message*. J. Louis Martyn has carried the day with his epoch-making reconstruction of the background to the Gospel,[17] according to which it reflects a situation in which a substantial, possibly total, breach has occurred between a Jewish Christian community and its parent synagogue. This breach has been marked by some kind of expulsion of the Christians from the synagogue, and this traumatic state of affairs has had marked social consequences for the Christian group. In this situation the Gospel form has been employed in order to 'write up' the history of the group as the history of Jesus, so that the breach may been seen as a re-living of his experience. Such a literary effort also enabled the community to lay claim to the Scriptures and to their Jewish heritage generally.

On this understanding, *the hostility towards the Jews in John is not an unfortunate 'blip' on a Gospel whose basic impulses are love and universalism, but is deeply constitutive of it, so that it becomes very difficult to defuse a basic anti-Judaism at the heart of the Gospel.*

Attempts have of course been made. Elizabeth Johnson recognises frankly that John "drips with vitriol toward the Jews", but argues that, because this attitude was prompted by particular historical reasons (the expulsion from the synagogue), it cannot therefore be used to justify later antisemitism.[18] Its very historical particularity divorces it from its later appropriation. But this argument has little force, for, whether we like it or not, the Gospel inevitably set an example for later generations.

Others — for instance, James Dunn — have sought to tone down the effect of the anti-Jewish polemic by suggesting that "the Jews" are merely a rhetorical symbol for the hostility of *the world* towards God.[19] But, even if the Fourth Gospel treats them symbolically in this way (which is quite likely), the 'Martyn hypothesis' requires us to recognise that "the Jews" in mind are yet the flesh-and-blood people who expelled the johannine community and who have thus provoked the hostility directed at them by the text before us — as indeed Dunn recognises. "You are of your father the devil" is a *personal address.*

A further option is offered by recent narrative-critical approaches to the Gospel, following the lead of Alan Culpepper's *Anatomy of the Fourth Gospel* (1983). This approach can certainly rescue it as word of God, for it turns its back on the troubling historical questions of background and ethos, and emphasises its quality just as *text.* As Culpepper puts it, within this approach "we are no more concerned with the historical Jews than with the historical Jesus".[20]

17 Martyn *History & Theology*
18 Johnson "Jews" 115
19 Dunn *Partings* 159

Comments like this have unleashed, within New Testament scholar-ship, an argument equivalent to that between the two sisters outlined above, and this argument continues still.

So, even if our interest focuses on 8:31-59, it cannot rest there. We find ourselves led straight into wider questions concerning the background and purpose of the Fourth Gospel, and thus into this argument between 'historical' and 'literary' approaches to the text. To date (to my mind), there has been no truly successful integration of the new 'literary' approach with the older historical approach represented by Martyn.

But hope is not dead. In this study I propose and employ a method which attempts just such an integration. From the 'narrative' side, I have drawn on the impulses of 'reader response' criticism so as to focus upon the *reading experience* the text provides, rather than seek to reconstruct the purposes of the originating author or commu-nity; but – historically – I have focused my study on a *first-century* reading experience, rather than a later or a contemporary one. I have employed the highly useful concept of the 'implied reader', but have given this reader historical features, rather than purely literary ones. And in the pursuance of this *historical* interest (the analysis of the first-century reading experience), I have employed some of the fruits of recent narrative criticism, particularly its study of plot, irony, symbolism, and conversation. The justification of this method is attempted *en route.*

This study thus has a three-fold aim:

(1) *John and "the Jews":* The interest in 8:31-59 and the issue of "the Jews" acts as a motivation for the whole study, which reaches a climax in the long chapter 7 on 8:31-59. But the exegesis of 8:31-59 depends completely on the preceding material, in which

(2) the *method of interpretation* outlined above is proposed and defended in debate with recent scholarship (chapters 1, 4), and

(3) the method is applied in broad terms to the Fourth Gospel, and *a proposal is made about its function* within the setting of late first-century Judaism (chapters 2, 3). In these chapters I argue for the unpopular view that the Gospel would have functioned evangel-istically — that is, that it would have been heard by many Jews as an appeal, directed at them, to believe in Jesus as Messiah. The exegetical chapters 5, 6 and 7 build on this foundation and serve to exemplify the application of the method, and to vindicate (I believe) this proposal about the Gospel's function.

---

20   Culpepper *Anatomy* 125

This is an unlikely proposal to defend! The polemic against "the Jews" in the Gospel, and in 8:31-59 in particular, has frequently been used as an argument *against* the view that the Gospel was intended to convert Jews to Christ. How can you convince people by vilifying them? I shall argue, however, that this is a misunderstanding of the way in which the Gospel would have functioned among many Jews in the late first century. And in this project the recent 'narrative' techniques, mentioned above, are of great assistance. Employing them, I seek to enter the confused world of late first-century Judaism, to share its trauma and its crisis of identity in the wake of the destruction of the Temple, and to 'hear' the Gospel with ears sensitised to the agonies and longings felt by so many Jews at that time. The reasons for approaching the Gospel in this way are discussed in chapters 2-3.

Readers who want to concentrate on the precise issue of "the Jews" can bypass the more technical discussions of johannine scholarship and interpretative method and theory in chapters 1 and 4, and read just the broader 'background' chapters (2 and 3) and the application of the method to the text in chapters 5-7. But my hope is that this study will contribute not just to our understanding of the thorny issue of 'the Jews in John', but also to the vigorous contemporary debate about exegetical method. And that is where our focus first falls, in the chapter which follows.

1

Arguments about Method
in the Interpretation of the Fourth Gospel

Reviewing the literature on the the Fourth Gospel published between 1980 and 1984, Jürgen Becker in 1986 used the title "Argument about Method" to summarise the period, and proceeded to outline no fewer than twelve "impulses" in johannine studies in that period, many of them distinguishable by method, rather than by content.[1] The same methodological variety, and focus of interest, has continued to the present, as we shall see. One of the most significant recent monographs, Mark Stibbe's *John as Storyteller*, is primarily occupied with questions of method — and is in fact the first major attempt to settle the argument and to integrate different methods with each other[2].

In this chapter we will first review and engage with the main methodological impulses in contemporary study of John (1.1), then discuss the validity of the use of *inference from the text* in the reconstruction of its setting and function (1.2), and finally make a preliminary statement of the method employed in this study (1.3).

1.1 Method in recent studies of the Fourth Gospel

Becker's twelve "impulses" may be reduced to five distinct approaches or interpretative methods. They are not, of course, mutually exclusive, and individual scholars often employ insights drawn from several in the course of a single study. However, the work of any particular scholar may usually be classified under one of the following categories.

---

1   Becker "Methoden"
2   An earlier attempt was made by Takashi Onuki in 1984 ("Analyse"). But since he began by announcing the inadequacy of the historical-critical method, his attempt cannot be deemed successful.

1.1.1 The synchronic, literary, 'text-as-unity' approach

Pride of place must be given here to Alan Culpepper, whose *Anatomy of the Fourth Gospel* (1983) ushered in a new era in the study of John by prompting an intense new interest in its literary features. This is not to say that such interest had previously been lacking. But Culpepper gave it a new impetus by employing ideas drawn from modern literary criticism, especially the work of Seymour Chatman, Gérard Genette and Wayne Booth.[3] He thus mediated to johannine scholarship terms and ideas of foreign-sounding intrigue, such as 'implied author' and 'implied reader', 'implicit and explicit commentary', 'narrator' and 'narratee', 'focalisation', 'plot', and 'characterisation'. The publication of *Anatomy of the Fourth Gospel* has given rise to a flood of literature employing and extending the approach.[4]

Culpepper starts with an assumption of the unity of the text, which for him implies a rejection of the traditional methods of source- and redaction-criticism. "Dissection and stratification have no place in the study of the gospel and may distort and confuse one's view of the text".[5] Rather than use the text as a "window" onto something else (its pre-history, or the history of the community behind it, or the history of Jesus), the text should be treated as a "mirror", with "meaning" located between the reader and the text:

> Meaning is produced in the experience of reading the text as a whole and making the mental moves the text calls for its reader to make, quite apart from questions concerning its sources and origin.[6]

Many scholars are not ready for such a radical marginalisation of the traditional questions of historical scholarship. John Ashton, for instance, while applauding the treatment of the wedding at Cana by Jeffrey Lloyd Staley, one of the scholars writing in the wake of Culpepper ("a brilliant piece of exegesis that powerfully vindicates the

---

3   Chatman, *Discourse*; G. Genette, *Narrative Discourse. An Essay in Method* (Ithaca; Cornell University Press, 1980); W. Booth, *The Rhetoric of Fiction* (Chicago; University of Chicago Press, 1961)

4   The main monographs employing this new literary criticism in the wake of Culpepper include: Duke *Irony* (1985); O'Day *Revelation* (1986); Staley *Kiss* (1988); Okure *Mission* (1988); and Stibbe *Storyteller* (1992). None, of course, slavishly reproduce his method. Boers *Mountain* (1988) illustrates another aspect of this new approach, linguistic rather than literary, applying the semiotic theory of A.J. Greimas to the interpretation of John 4.

5   *Anatomy* 5

6   *Anatomy* 4

use of the new methods"[7]), nonetheless fails to give this new approach any space at all in his review of recent scholarship, and makes no use of "the new methods" in his own exegesis. His reason is clear: they are

> vitiated by a neglect of any diachronic perspective, so necessary if one is to make any real progress in the study of a many-layered text like the Fourth Gospel.[8]

Ashton's attitude is surprising in the light of his own insistence, in interaction with Bultmann, on *the text of the Gospel* as the *locus* of revelation. He criticises Bultmann for being "too anxious to discard the narrative husk of the Gospel in order to get at the kernel of revelation inside",[9] and concludes his entire book with the words, "The matter of the Gospel, its true content, is indistinguishable from its form: the medium is the message".[10] One might have thought that this would make him more open to literary approaches alongside his own strongly source-critical approach.

The reason lies in the fact that the narrative method turns its back diachronic questions wholesale. Culpepper, for instance, shows as little interest in the *historical origins* of the Fourth Gospel as he does in its *literary sources*. However the two need not be lumped together in this way. As Stibbe shows, it is perfectly possible to combine a synchronic emphasis on the final form of the Gospel text, with a diachronic interest in its origins, both literary and historical. This combination is attempted not just by some of the subsequent studies, but also before Culpepper by no less a scholar than C.H. Dodd, whose *Interpretation* combines within one volume both a wide-ranging investigation of the background to John, and a chapter-by-chapter survey of the argument of the text as it stands. This latter section is built on the

---

7   Ashton *Understanding* 114 n. 1

8   Ashton *ibid*. The term "diachronic" means "across a period of time", and thus points to a study of the *development* of the Gospel, focusing either on the *historical causes* or the *literary processes* which created it. In contrast the word "synchronic" means "at a point in time" and thus refers to an approach or study which ignores background questions and simply focuses on the text as we have it.

9   *Understanding* 552

10   *Understanding* 553. We may connect these closing words with his earlier discussion of genre, in which he moves away from the term "history" as a way of classifying the evangelist's purpose, in favour of "story": "In the Fourth Gospel *story* and interpretation are inseparably locked together" (427, his emph.).

provisional working hypothesis that the present order is not fortuitous, but deliberately designed by somebody — even if he were only a scribe doing his best.

He suggests that it is

the duty of an interpreter at least to see what can be done with the document as it has come down to us before attempting to improve upon it.[11]

Similarly Marinus de Jonge in 1977 argued that the Gospel should be regarded as

a new literary entity, which has to be studied on its own, because it functioned as a whole among people who did *not* take its prehistory into account.[12]

De Jonge points us in a helpful direction. His approach allows a synthesis, because *it views the Fourth Gospel as a unity and seeks to hear its voice in the situation in which it first spoke in this form.* This is an historical question, which concerns the *function* of the Gospel in its present narrative shape. In chapter 4 we will ask (a) whether we can regard such an historical approach as *indispensable,* and (b) whether there is any compelling reason for giving priority to the way in which the Gospel spoke to its *first* readers, as opposed to every other generation of readers who have appreciated it without taking its prehistory into account.

Anticipating our conclusions there, the approach adopted in this study is to endorse the new literary criticism and to seek to make use of its insights, focusing on the text of John in its final form; but at the same time to resist the myopic tendencies of Culpepper's use of the method and to seek to hear the 'dynamics' of the text within its original historical context. In 1.1.5 below I shall review some other recent contributions which employ this broad approach.

---

11   *Interpretation* 290. Ashton *Understanding* 79-81 criticises Dodd trenchantly for underestimating the evidence for dislocation in the text, and for the question-begging use of the word "improve". And it may indeed be asked to what extent Dodd is really open to finding evidence which would undermine this presumption of unity. But it must also be recognised that dislocation of the text of the Fourth Gospel is not a fact to be recognised (as Ashton implies) but an exegetical judgment to be reached: and Dodd holds that the evidence is not as compelling as Ashton maintains.

12   De Jonge *Jesus* 198 (his emph.)

1.1.2 The diachronic historical-critical approach

This is the approach most typical of the last 150 years of New Testament scholarship — and thus far there is little *rapprochement* between it and the new 'narrative' approach we have just reviewed. Whereas the new method is essentially synchronic, and resists treating the text as a 'window', this diachronic approach emphasises precisely the 'window' quality of the text and underlines the extent to which the understanding of its final form depends upon awareness of its development to that state.

The study of the pre-history of the Gospel has two elements, as we have seen — literary and historical. The *literary* element received epoch-making attention from Rudolph Bultmann, who actually based his commentary on a text restored by him to an earlier order.[13] At the root of his approach lay three conjectured sources behind the Gospel, a passion narrative, a discourse-source, and a "signs-source".[14] The first two have failed to win general agreement as discreet literary sources, but the "Sign-source" is now quite widely accepted. The work of R.T. Fortna has been particularly significant in the further development of this aspect of Bultmann's work. He conjectures an early edition of the Gospel in which the sign-source was expanded with a passion narrative to form a "Signs Gospel".[15] However, R.E. Brown dispenses with the sign-source in his detailed reconstruction of the composition of the Gospel,[16] and several scholars express scepticism about the possibility of reconstructing the sources of the Gospel from the Gospel itself.[17]

The *historical* element of the Gospel's pre-history, however, received scant attention from Bultmann. Ashton suggests that, because of his theological existentialism, "the situation in which the message was first proclaimed had ... no importance for Bultmann".[18] But this lack has been amply supplied by subsequent scholarship, most particularly through and following the publication of J.L. Martyn's *History and Theology in the Fourth Gospel* in 1968.

---

13   Bultmann argued (e.g. 10f) that a redactor had radically re-ordered the Gospel, and had also contributed several new sections to it. In the course of his reconstruction 8:12-59, the focus of our interest, is split into no fewer than ten fragments and dispersed among the material in chs. 5-12.

14   E.g. Bultmann 6-7

15   Fortna *Gospel of Signs*; also *Predecessor*. Cf also von Wahlde *Earliest Version*.

16   Brown 1:xxxiv-xxxix

17   E.g. de Jonge *Jesus* 198; Hengel *Question* 89-92; Carson 41f; Stibbe *Storyteller* 83f.

18   Ashton *Understanding* 101f; cf also Wengst *Gemeinde* 32

Martyn's book, revised and enlarged in 1979 and supported by subsequent articles,[19] created a revolution in johannine scholarship. Ashton is undoubtedly right to judge it "probably the most important single work on the Gospel since Bultmann's commentary".[20] Although some aspects of Martyn's theory have not commanded wide agreement, the list of those who have accepted its basic perspectives reads like a *vade mecum* of leading names in contemporary johannine studies.[21] Any study which seeks to illumine the historical background of the Fourth Gospel (as this one does) must engage with Martyn.

His revolution consisted in a new way of reading the Gospel, especially the narrative portions, which enabled scholars to fill in yawning gaps in their knowledge of the circumstances surrounding the composition of the Gospel. Hoskyns had complained,

> It is ... extremely difficult to gain from the Gospel any direct information concerning its original readers, and for this reason it is hard to come by the key to its historical understanding.[22]

But with the publication of Martyn's work the key was provided. He argued that the Gospel presents a "two-level drama", in which events in the life of Jesus are "a witness to Jesus' powerful presence in actual events experienced by the johannine church".[23] Thus the actors in the gospel stories are taken as representative of figures in the environment of the community in which the Gospel was written: Jesus is a Jewish Christian preacher and healer, a leader of the johannine church; the Sanhedrin is the "Gerousia", the local Jewish council in John's "city"; the Pharisees are the "Jamnia loyalists", keen to enforce the decrees emerging from the new rabbinic academy at (?nearby) Jamnia (or Yavneh); "the Jews" are the "rank-and-file Jews" of the local synagogue; Nicodemus represents secret Jewish

---

19   The three main articles are collected in his *The Gospel of John in Christian History: Essays for Interpreters* (New York, etc; Paulist Press, 1978).

20   *Understanding* 107

21   It includes Meeks, Gräßer, Aune, De Jonge, Brown, Barrett, Schnackenburg, Pancaro, Nicol, Kysar, Bartholomew, Townsend, Neyrey, Rensberger, Painter, Beasley-Murray, Culpepper, Smith, Wengst, Dunn, Rebell, Wiefel, Gryglewicz, Freyne, Thyen, Onuki, Koenig, Ellis, Fortna, Whitacre, Schenke, Segovia, Yee, Karris and most recently Ashton, Stibbe, de Boer and Koester. Dissidents include Robinson, Woll, Hengel, Carson and now also Thyen (who has changed his view) and Pryor.

22   Hoskyns 50

23   *History & Theology2* 30

believers who have not separated themselves from the synagogue to join the johannine church; the lame man and the blind man are Jews who were healed by a Christian, using the power of Jesus (with different results in each case: one believed in Jesus, and was expelled from the synagogue, while the other turned traitor); and supremely, the expulsion from the synagogue, mentioned in 9:22, 12:42 and 16:2, actually refers to the action taken against Jewish Christians by the Yavneh academy in the introduction of the *birkat ha-minim*, the 'curse on the heretics', which Martyn dates early in the period between 85 and 115 AD.

Whereas previously the Gospel had largely been interpreted within a broad history of *ideas* (see 1.1.3 below), suddenly its history became local and particular. The belief that the Gospel reflects the circumstances of the time of writing was not in itself new. Oscar Cullmann, for instance, had presented an interpretation of John which laid emphasis on the interaction between the two 'levels', the time of writing and the time of Jesus' ministry.[24] And Beasley-Murray points out that Hoskyns had already expressed the theory on which Martyn based his reconstruction.[25] The newness consisted in the *particularity* of the situation proposed, and in the vigour with which he carried through what amounted to an allegorisation of the narratives. His approach has proved enormously attractive and fruitful, for three reasons:

• (1) It appeals because of its 'fit'. Ashton suggests that Martyn's case

> carries conviction because of the wealth of illumination it sheds upon the Gospel itself and the satisfactory way it accounts for one of its most puzzling features: why is the Gospel at once so Jewish and yet so anti-Jewish?[26]

This is an argument from *results* — a legitimate argument, but difficult to handle. It needs to be well supported by other arguments, to save the scholarly mind from being swept away by enthusiasm. There are other theories which can explain the Gospel's "love-hate" relationship to Judaism[27] just as successfully — for instance, the

---

24   In *Early Christian Worship* (London; SCM, 1953: first published in French in 1951)

25   Beasley-Murray *Themes* 14f; Hoskyns 362. According to Jocz "Juden" 134f, the view that the conditions and circumstances of the later church are read back into the life of Jesus in the Fourth Gospel is as old as Holtzmann.

26   Ashton *Understanding* 109

27   Thyen uses this expression: he calls it one of the "unsolved riddles" of the

proposal made in this book.[28]

• (2) Martyn's theory partly drew upon, but also massively contributed to, the new interest in sociological interpretations of the New Testament (see 1.1.4 below). This approach emphasises the social function of texts, the role they play within a network of human relationships. Martyn enabled this approach to be applied enthusiastically to the Fourth Gospel. He himself does not discuss the precise function of the Gospel, but paints such a clear picture of the situation reflected by it that others have been able to build upon his work in this respect.

• (3) His work has also enabled a strengthening of traditional source- and redaction-criticism in the study of John. On the basis of Martyn's theory it is possible to reconstruct the history of the johannine community, which can then be integrated with the literary history of the Gospel material.

Martyn himself contributed to this process with his 1977 essay "Glimpses into the History of the Johannine Community", in which he suggested that the community, and the Gospel, passed through three stages of development: (i) an early period in which it was Torah-observant, integrated with the synagogue, and a 'signs gospel' was composed for evangelistic purposes; (ii) a middle period in which a 'higher' christology developed (reflected in passages like 5:19ff) and the community was expelled by the introduction of the *birkat ha-minim*; and (iii) a late period in which the community consolidated itself and drew boundaries sharply against Christian Jews who wanted to retain dual loyalty, *and who are attacked in 8:31-59*. Christians who stay in the synagogue are guilty of murdering Jesus.

A similar picture, but considerably elaborated, was presented by R.E. Brown in 1979, and by J.H. Neyrey in 1988, both of whom express their debt to Martyn.[29] The source-critical work of Robert

---

Fourth Gospel ("Heil" 163).

28   The danger of the argument from results is illustrated, I believe, by R.T. Fortna's work on the hypothetical "Signs Gospel". He calls it "a hypothesis whose vindication is not finally based on probabilities or argument about criteria but on its usefulness in coming to terms with this elusive and insistent Gospel", and rates his own confidence in the hypothesis at seven on a one-to-ten scale (*Predecessor*, xii). An hypothesis which rests so wholly on its "usefulness", and which so consciously sets aside "criteria", can never warrant such confidence, I believe.

29   Brown *Community* 17, 174; Neyrey *Revolt* 3. Another significant figure here is Georg Richter, whose reconstruction of the history of the johannine community and literature bears some similarity to Martyn's, most notably in the movement from a 'low' to a 'high' christology, but Richter posited *conflict* between

Fortna is considerably weakened by the fact that, though he finds Martyn's reconstruction "highly persuasive",[30] he does not seek this integration between historical and literary (i.e. source-critical) approaches.

However there are five respects in which the 'Martyn hypothesis' needs to be challenged, four of them relating to method. All four will concern us later, so adumbration will suffice here:

(1) Martyn's use of the *birkat ha-minim* will concern us in chapter 3. Many scholars now accept that his interpretation of 9:22 as a direct allusion to the *birkat ha-minim* cannot be sustained, for a variety of reasons.

(2) His treatment of the narratives employs allegorisation without the necessary form-critical justification.

(3) His reconstruction of the story of the community from the Gospel rests on a methodologically uncontrolled use of *inference*.

(4) His use both of the johannine text and of the available background information is highly selective.

(5) Finally, as mentioned above, he does not engage seriously with the issue of *function*.

We will return to the last four points later in this chapter. Alongside these criticisms, however, must be set a strong affirmation of Martyn's historicising impulse. His work brought a much-needed breath of fresh air into a tradition in which the 'historical location' of the Fourth Gospel was generally understood to mean its location just in the history of *ideas* or of *texts*.

1.1.3. The 'world of ideas' approach

It is interesting to compare Martyn's *History & Theology* with Dodd's essay "Behind a Johannine Dialogue", the English translation of which was also published in 1968.[31] Dodd discusses the *Sitz im Leben* of John 8:31-58, but for him this means seeking its *Sitz* in relation to earlier *traditions*, Pauline and synoptic. For Dodd, as indeed for pre-Martyn scholarship generally, this was essentially what 'history' meant in this context. And there is much to be affirmed in this approach. As Robert Kysar puts it,

One's understanding of a text depends in every case upon the establishment of a context of thought out of which the text has been

each stage. See Mattill "Richter".

30   *Predecessor* 224

31   In his *More New Testament Studies* (Manchester: Manchester University Press, 1968), 41-57. It was originally published in French in *RHPR* 1 (1957), 5-17.

written.

This is the opening sentence of his chapter entitled "The Intellectual Milieu of the Evangelist".[32] In the context of a discussion of method we need not devote much space to a review of the proposed answers to this question. Suffice it to say that the situation today is much the same as it was when Kysar published his review in 1975. He noted that defining John's context of thought "remains a thorny problem", with numerous alternatives suggested, but discerned a general consensus that it should be located in "a Palestinian, Old Testament, Jewish setting".[33] Now as then, however, there is no agreement about which particular form of Judaism provides the Gospel's intellectual home, and now as then there is a continuing reluctance to abandon influences from outside Judaism altogether.

Amongst recent studies John Painter's *Quest* illustrates the complexity of the problem: on the one hand he emphasises the Qumran literature as providing the intellectual climate of the Fourth Gospel, but on the other he argues that the dualism both at Qumran and in John owed much to pagan Gnosticism.[34] Again, on the one hand he argues that the 'quest' stories in John 1-4 draw upon a tradition illustrable from Graeco-Roman biographies and rhetorical texts,[35] but on the other that (for instance) the particular 'quest' story in John 4 draws upon an Old Testament literary type, that of the 'betrothal type-scene' set at a well.[36]

Some recent literary studies have described connections between the Fourth Gospel and Graeco-Roman literature,[37] but at the same time many others have interpreted it chiefly against an Old Testament and Jewish background.[38] In this study I stand in the latter

---

32   Kysar *Evangelist* 102-146

33   *Evangelist* 144

34   *Quest* 29-39

35   *Quest* 132-5

36   *Quest* 165f. This suggestion was apparently first made by Robert Alter in his *The Art of Biblical Narrative* (London & Sydney; George Allen & Unwin, 1981) 51-62, and has been widely accepted: cf also Staley *Kiss* 96-103, Eslinger "Wooing" 169, Rebell *Gemeinde* 189, Kermode "John" 451 and (partly) Polhill "John 1-4" 455.

37   Most notably Stibbe *Storyteller*, who argues that John draws on 'tragic' patterns attestable in Greek tragedy, and points particularly to Euripides' *Bacchae*; Kemper "Gestalt" makes a similar point but directs the comparison to the tragedies of Seneca.

38   Perhaps the most notable here are Dunn "John"; Brooke "Law"; Carson "OT"; Coetzee "EGO EIMI"; Evans "Servant"; Hengel "OT"; Bühner *Gesandte*; Thyen "Johannes 10", Thomas "Judaism" and the string of articles by Manns in *SBFLA* — all drawing in different ways on OT or Jewish sources to illumine the

stream, but seek to integrate it with an historicising approach in the Martyn tradition.

1.1.4 The Sociological and Sociolinguistic Approach

Wayne Meeks was the first scholar consciously to seek to apply insights from sociology to the study of the Fourth Gospel. Building upon the work of Martyn, and upon that of the sociologists Peter Berger and Thomas Luckmann, he explored in his famous essay "The Man From Heaven in Johannine Sectarianism" (1972) the role which the 'ascent-descent' language of John might have played for a community experiencing alienation and hostility. Following this impetus, at least five monographs since 1980 have sought to apply sociological theory to the understanding of the Fourth Gospel.[39]

The main positive fruit has been a reinforced emphasis on *the function of the Gospel within the life of the johannine community*. The existence of a Gospel 'community' is presupposed by these sociological approaches. However the emphasis on function has a wider methodological basis than just social science. It derives ultimately from the linguist Ferdinand de Saussure and his understanding of linguistic meaning as 'conventional'. Influenced by him, and by the later Wittgenstein and the 'Speech Act' theory of J.L Austin,[40] linguists have generally moved away from a 'referential' understanding of language — according to which language 'describes' the world in an objective way — and towards a 'functional' understanding, which stresses the way in which language interacts with its context (both literary and social) and expresses a meaning particular to each context. This outlook is becoming well embedded in biblical studies.[41]

In this respect Meeks' approach had been anticipated by Herbert Leroy's influential book on the use of "riddles" in John.[42] Leroy argued that the johannine misunderstandings had a social function, expressing and reinforcing the distinction between the 'in'-group which grasps the heavenly, spiritual meaning of Jesus' words, and the outsiders who do not. Leroy offered a full form-critical study of

---

Fourth Gospel.

39   Woll *Conflict;* Onuki *Gemeinde;* Rebell *Gemeinde;* Neyrey *Revolt;* and now Stibbe *Storyteller.* All of them draw upon different sociologists and different aspects of sociological theory (though Onuki and Rebell share with Meeks the use of the sociology of knowledge, drawn from Peter Berger). Cf also Bassler "Nicodemus", Domeris "Community" and Malina's important essay "Sociolinguistic Perspective".

40   Saussure, *Linguistics;* Austin, *Words*

41   Cf Cotterell & Turner *Linguistics,* Louw "Semiotic"

42   *Rätsel und Missverständnis* (1968)

the misunderstandings, in that he argued (a) that the 'riddle' was a literary device of a distinct type, and (b) — more importantly — that this 'form' played a distinct and definite role in the life of the church, a role which it was developed to fulfil. The weakness of Leroy's study was that he attempted to infer the social situation of the johannine community from this single feature of the text, and thus (a) did not seek a function for the *whole* Gospel, and (b) did not sufficiently allow the meaning of the 'riddles' he studied to be shaped by their co-text. In fact, of the studies published to date, only Onuki's *Gemeinde und Welt* attempts to use sociological theory to describe the social function of the Gospel as a whole.

The new sociological impetus, therefore, builds upon concerns as old as form-criticism, already strengthened by input from linguistics. But David Rensberger makes an important distinction between a "social" and a "sociological" analysis: the former simply attempts to describe "social realities behind the text", while the latter seeks to apply theoretical models to these descriptions.[43] Like him, I shall attempt simply the former (which might well provide the raw material for the latter). But our focus on 8:31-59 inevitably means that we cannot attempt a functional analysis of the whole Gospel.

1.1.5 The historical-contextual approach

We conclude this survey by glancing at the work of four scholars whose method is distinguished by its synchronic focus on the historical situation of the final text. In this respect their work comes close to the approach for which I argue, although none of them seek to make use also of narrative-critical insights.

Becker devotes two substantial sections in his review to Wengst and Dunn, whose work for our purposes can be considered together.[44] Klaus Wengst's *Bedrängte Gemeinde* (1981) relies heavily on the 'Martyn hypothesis' and the *birkat ha-minim* in painting a picture of a Christian community in alienation from Judaism and yet in daily contact with it. Becker, a champion of the source-critical approach, regards Wengst's thesis as undermined by his lack of diachronic interest in the text. However we may surely reply on Wengst's behalf (as above), that the historical situation and function of the final form of the text is a legitimate focus of study — allowing, of course, that light may be shed on it by anything that may be discovered about the pre-history of the text, and *vice versa*.

The importance of *finding the right background* is highlighted by

---

43   Rensberger *Community* 30
44   Becker "Methoden" 45-48 (Dunn), 51-56 (Wengst)

comparing Wengst with Dunn's important 1982 essay "Let John be John". He too focuses on the synchronic situation of the final text, and criticises as equally anachronistic both the interpretation of the Fourth Gospel in the light of later Nicene orthodoxy or Gnostic heterodoxy, and an overriding emphasis on the investigation of previous traditions. Study of the 'pre-' and 'post-' history of the johannine material is important, he grants, but both must take second place to "attempting to understand the finished product of the Fourth Gospel in its own terms, within its own context".[45] This is close to Wengst: but when the method is 'cashed' Dunn makes little use of the *birkat ha-minim*, and seeks to illumine the setting and 'voice' of the Gospel against the background of late first century apocalyptic, mystical and 'wisdom' traditions. The difference between his *results* and those of Wengst, obtained by the use of an almost identical *method*, highlights the need for as much rigour as possible in the delineation of the background against which the Gospel should be read.

Teresa Okure and David Rensberger both also attempt a synchronic description of the function of the Fourth Gospel.[46] We will consider their work in more detail in the next section, because they raise the issue of the relative balance of internal and external evidence in reconstructing the 'voice' of the text. Okure proceeds primarily by inferring the situation of the johannine community from within the Gospel; Rensberger, on the other hand, attempts to illumine it with broad reference to contemporary politics. Both are stimulating and important, but again their results are so different that the issue of method is highlighted. By what methods, and with what certainty, can the text of the Gospel be used as a source of inferences about the situation and needs addressed by it?

1.2 The use of inference as a heuristic device

We have now completed our survey of the five main products on offer in the marketplace of interpretative methods. Four of the five employ inference as a central feature of their procedure: that is, they infer the text's background or setting by making connections between the text and entities outside it — literary parallels, historical events, social movements, religious traditions. In principle this is wholly unobjectionable, for the Gospel certainly did not arise in a

---

45   Dunn "John" 317
46   Okure *Mission*; Rensberger *Community*

vacuum. But we clearly need methodological controls to enable us to employ inference with more certainty than simply inspired guess-work!

Because of our interest in "the Jews" and thus in the social and religious setting of the Gospel, we will focus our thoughts around scholars working in this area.

1.2.1 The method in action

Wayne Meeks describes a methodological movement which begins with a literary analysis of the text (in his case, focusing on the 'ascent-descent' language in John), and then proceeds to infer the social function of the text for the community which produced it:

> In the following pages an attempt is made to discern the function which the motif 'ascent and descent' serves, *first*, within the literary structure of the Fourth Gospel, *then, by analogy*, within the structure of the Johannine community and its relationships to its environment.[47]

The bulk of his article is taken up with the first half of this programme, in which he examines the main 'ascent-descent' passages in the Gospel. The second half of the programme is introduced with the question, "What functions did this particular system of metaphors have for the group that developed it?".[48] He answers that

> *The book functions for its readers in precisely the same way that the epiphany of its hero functions within its narratives and dialogues.*[49]

We have no independent information about the johannine group, "nevertheless, the structural characteristics of the literature permit certain deductions".[50] The use of the word "deductions" is interesting, for what Meeks actually describes is a process of *inference*. The difference between deduction and inference is profound, and its blurring here attests a positivist confidence in the power of the process — visible also in his statement of the "deductions":

> There can be no question, as Louis Martyn has shown, that the actual trauma of the Johannine community's separation from the synagogue and its continuing hostile relationships with the synagogue

---

47 "Man From Heaven" 50, my emph.
48 "Man From Heaven" 68
49 "Man From Heaven" 69, his emph.
50 "Man From Heaven" 69

come clearly to expression [*in the hostility between Jesus and the Jews in the Gospel*].[51]

We may infer the nature of the relationship between the johannine community and the synagogue from the way in which the 'hero' of the Fourth Gospel relates to 'the Jews': countering rejection with a private language which they could not have understood. Meeks further infers that

> coming to faith in Jesus is for the Johannine group a change in social location. Mere belief without joining the Johannine community, without making the decisive break with "the world", particularly the world of Judaism, is a diabolic "lie".[52]

So the Gospel functioned as "an etiology of the Johannine group". It "provided a symbolic universe which gave religious legitimacy, a theodicy, to the group's actual isolation from the larger society".[53]

As we noted above, in making this inferential movement from text to group Meeks relies explicitly on the sociology of knowledge proposed by Peter Berger and Thomas Luckmann in *The Social Construction of Reality* (1967). The work of these sociologists, especially that of Berger, has been increasingly influential in johannine studies in the past twenty years, and Meeks was one of the first to draw on it.[54] He cites their description of the way in which a text like the Fourth Gospel can lead to a change of world for the one who accepts its ideology. 'World' means the symbolic universe in which one lives, and by which one gives meaning to existence. The 'closed' nature of the johannine language creates such a self-contained 'world' for all who believe it:

> The language patterns we have been describing have the effect, for the insider who accepts them, of demolishing the logic of the world, particularly the world of Judaism, and progressively emphasising the sectarian consciousness.[55]

The result is a strong reinforcement, from sociological theory, of the process begun by Martyn whereby the story of the johannine Jesus is decoded as the history of the johannine community.

---

51   "Man From Heaven" 69
52   "Man From Heaven" 69
53   "Man From Heaven" 69-70
54   Cf Woll *Conflict* 120; Onuki "Analyse" 200-203; Rebell *Gemeinde* 15
55   "Man From Heaven" 71

This inferential method is strongly endorsed by Stibbe. Like Meeks, he argues that the paucity of external evidence relating to the johannine community leaves us with no alternative.[56] He cites, to illustrate what would be desirable for John (but which he feels is sadly impossible), the work of Leslie Hotson on Shakespeare's *Twelfth Night:* by utilising contemporary sources Hotson was able to show the particular reference of the play to the circumstances of its first production before the court of Elizabeth I.[57] "It is obvious that Hotson's method is always going to be more rigorous and plausible than Martyn's", because contemporary sources are so much more abundant. Hotson starts with the text, moves to the contemporary evidence, and then back to the text "to highlight the social significance of its language for the first audience".[58]

Failing this, Stibbe argues that the next best thing is to follow the method adopted by Meeks and Malina, who "begin with a literary analysis, then employ categories of explanation from the sociology of knowledge in an attempt to appreciate the social function of Johannine language".[59]

The picture of the johannine community which has been painted by this process has come to be regarded almost as part of the primary *data* of the Gospel. For instance, Martin de Boer writes that the history of the community is

> imbedded, [sic] or encoded, within the text itself and any imaginative reconstruction of this history must find its impetus and its foundation and *certainly its confirmation* in the evidence provided by that text.[60]

For de Boer, historical criticism may provide *"further* confirmation outside of the text",[61] but the primary evidence comes from within it.

We may summarise the procedure as follows. We (a) formulate an hypothesis concerning the social function of the text, based on internal evidence; then (b) search for external evidence which may confirm it; and finally (c) refine and elaborate the hypothesis in the

---

56 *Storyteller* 65
57 L. Hotson, *The First Night of Twelfth Night* (London; Rupert Hart-Davis, 1954)
58 *Storyteller* 65
59 *Storyteller* 65
60 "Narrative Criticism" 43, my emph.
61 "Narrative Criticism" 43 n. 39, his emph.

light of a proposed 'fit' between internal and external evidence. However it is easy to be unaware of the weaknesses and dangers in this procedure. The following sections outline these, and evaluate its application to the Fourth Gospel.

1.2.2 The pitfalls of 'mirror-reading'

The reconstructions of the history of the johannine community and of the development of the johannine literature provided (e.g.) by Martyn, Brown and Richter represent a critical *tour de force* in each case. But their work depends to a large extent on what some Pauline scholars have dubbed 'mirror-reading' of the text. This not entirely appropriate expression is used to describe precisely this process of inferring the situation of the text from its *data*.[62] But mirror-reading is fraught with the possibility of error, as John Barclay has shown.[63] He highlights the dangers of *undue selectivity* (fastening upon features of the text which actually give a false impression of relating to a particular background[64]), of *over-interpretation* (simply making too much of perhaps quite innocent texts), and — particularly relevant to the Fourth Gospel — of *mishandling polemics* (assuming that the opponents attacked actually match the charges made against them).[65]

Barclay sets up some careful criteria to guide the process of 'mirror-reading', including *tone* (statements made with particular force may relate to particular needs), *frequency* (a motif is likely to be repeated if it is relevant to the situation addressed), *unfamiliarity* (an unusual idea or expression may be prompted by the situation) and *historical plausibility* (the last stage – external evidence is brought in as a control).[66]

Barclay himself notes the relevance of his discussion to johannine polemic,[67] and we will find all these criteria playing a role in our own reconstruction of the situation behind the Fourth Gospel. The criticisms he makes of particular Pauline scholars for uncontrolled use of 'mirror-reading' could also be made, I believe, of Martyn, Brown and Richter. All three have failed to give due weight to the

---

62   E.g. Lyons *Pauline Autobiography* 75ff, esp. 96-105

63   Barclay "Mirror-Reading". Cautions are also expressed by Klaus Berger ("Methode"), but he does not discuss either the method or the pitfalls as clearly as Barclay.

64   For Barclay the sheer variety of 'mirror-readings' of Galatians makes this point: "Mirror-Reading" 79.

65   "Mirror-Reading" 79-81

66   "Mirror-Reading" 84f

67   "Mirror-Reading" 73

emphasis in the Fourth Gospel on the Temple and its rituals (the criterion of *frequency*), to the appearance of some unusual political expressions like "freedom" (8:32f: the criterion of *unfamiliarity*) and to the broader evidence about the conditions in Judaism in the period after the destruction of the Temple (the criterion of *historical plausibility*). Above all, they have not used much of the available background historical information, because of an *a priori* restriction of their interest to the particular concerns of the johannine community and its history.

1.2.3 The partial use of evidence

This inferential process depends upon the creative, intuitive construction of connections between intra- and extra-textual features which are not obviously connected already. This means that the partial use of evidence is a pitfall always at hand.

Martyn illustrates this pitfall very clearly. He makes no attempt to consider the *whole* text of the Fourth Gospel, and his engagement with Jewish sources is also highly selective. A revealing statement in the *Preface* to *History and Theology* makes plain his partial approach to both, as well as the creative power of the inferential process:

> Several remarkable points of correspondence between certain passages in the Fourth Gospel and data from Jewish sources gradually pressed their special claim on me.[68]

As far as the Fourth Gospel is concerned, he starts his reconstruction with an examination of John 9, which he treats without reference to ch. 8. He does not consider the possibility that the mere presence of ch. 8 may have quite a radical effect on the interpretation of ch. 9. (I will argue below that it does.) He further highlights the word ἀποσυνάγωγος ("expelled from the synagogue") as a significant feature of the text, although the text itself does not 'mark' it linguistically, apart from its three-fold occurrence. It receives significance simply because of the connection forged with the *birkat ha-minim*.

As far as the Jewish sources are concerned, it is remarkable that, although he wants to give the Gospel its *Sitz im Leben* in a controversy with the synagogue, Martyn attempts no overview of Judaism in the post-70 period, does not engage at all with the issues surrounding the destruction of the Temple and its aftermath, and leaves many contemporary Jewish sources untouched. A glance at his Index

---

68 *History & Theology1* xii

reveals only four references to Josephus, one to Philo, four to the Qumran documents, and none at all to any of the contemporary apocalypses. He includes sections discussing the various types of synagogue ban, especially the *birkat ha-minim* (43f, 50-62), the rabbinic understanding of Jesus as a "deceiver" (78-81), some aspects of contemporary messianism (106-111), and the Son of Man in 1 Enoch (138f). This does not amount to substantial coverage!

The response to paucity of evidence cannot be to ignore such evidence as we have. Our knowledge of first-century Judaism has grown considerably in recent years, alongside the appreciation that this is the proper milieu in which to set the Fourth Gospel. The precise circumstances of its composition are not accessible through external evidence, but the *overall* circumstances — that is, evidence concerning its wider cultural and historical setting — are much more accessible than contemporary writing on the setting of the Fourth Gospel would lead one to suspect.

The perspective of a ancient social historian with a particular interest in the New Testament period is telling: Edwin Judge responded to Bruce Malina's essay "Sociolinguistic Perspective" with the criticism,

> The trouble with the paper we have discussed is that it seems to have solved everything in one last blow, too quickly ... The great problem of the New Testament people, it seems to me, is that they incestuously concentrate all their time on their few texts, when there is a magnificent array of contextual material all around their texts, increasing rapidly every year. Much of this material is very relevant to New Testament studies, but the relevance of it cannot be divined simply by looking at this bit or that bit.[69]

This is a timely challenge. The only recent attempt to relate a theory about the Fourth Gospel to this wider political and social background is Rensberger's *Community*. But his survey of the evidence is barely more than one page long,[70] and is then brought into relationship only with the trial narrative in 18:1-19:16. Stibbe regards Rensberger's method as having "much to commend it", and as contributing "an important insight" into the political background to the Fourth Gospel. But he rejects the method, on the ground that it depends upon a "questionable" evaluation of the characterisation of Pilate.[71]

---

69   Judge "Response" 51
70   *Community* 88-89

However, the analysis of Pilate which Rensberger proposes is incidental to the value of the method he employs. Even if his judgment about the characterisation of Pilate is wrong, his attempt to illumine John's narrative against the background of the political realities of the late first century has a validity in its own right, and points towards a wider application of the same approach: one which will give closer attention to *all* the available evidence, political, cultural and religious, and then attempt to read the *whole* gospel in the light of it.

Paradoxically, it is precisely the *historical illumination* provided by Martyn which makes his reconstruction so appealing. The reconstruction has now lost its heart (the connection with the *birkat ha-minim*), but it hangs onto life nonetheless. Stibbe, for instance, affirms the Martyn view,[72] but then recognises that the connection between John 9:22 and the *birkat ha-minim* cannot stand. So in the end his verdict is simply is that *"in general terms* [John] reflects a severe controversy with Judaism".[73]

It would be wrong to give the impression either that Martyn alone employs creative inference in this way, or that the procedure is wholly to be avoided. On the contrary, it is *indispensable*, and all good scholars engaged in historical criticism employ it. We may point, for instance, to Teresa Okure's work on 'mission' themes,[74] to Stephen Smalley's inference of a polemical setting for the christology of the Fourth Gospel,[75] to Bruce Woll's theory about the role within the johannine community of "charismatic leaders who considered themselves on a par with Jesus or even superior to him", and who were in sharp competition with each other,[76] and to David Aune's similar theory about the charismatic endowment of the whole johannine community.[77] Some of the same criticisms may be directed at these scholars. Woll, for instance, has rightly been criticised for

71 *Storyteller* 149

72 *Storyteller* 56-58

73 *Storyteller* 61, my emphasis

74 Okure *Mission*. She honestly recognises that, simply on the basis of the text, it is very difficult to infer the precise social setting in which the language may have functioned (*Mission* 230-35), and finds external evidence in the Epistles of John. An approach to the Gospel from the Epistles is the distinguishing feature also of Hengel's *Johannine Question*.

75 Smalley, "Community"; for him the external evidence is provided by the Apocalypse, which he uses in much the same way as Okure uses the Epistles.

76 Woll *Conflict* 91: his external connection is found in pneumatic Corinthian Christianity.

77 Aune *Setting* 45-135, esp. 89-102: his external evidence is drawn from a wide consideration of realised eschatology in the New Testament.

building a theory out of just one section of the gospel, which he treats in isolation from the rest.[78]

The antidote to such partiality is at least an *attempt* to approach both poles holistically. The time is ripe for a reassessment of the question, utilising far more information about contemporary Judaism. The present study attempts to take a step in this direction, and to set up a properly controlled dialectical discussion between the Gospel and its whole background.

1.2.4 The uncontrolled use of allegory

The inferential method, as applied to the Fourth Gospel, has tended to rely upon an uncontrolled use of 'allegory' as a genre classification. Stibbe recognises the difficulties this causes:

> One of the problems with Johannine redaction criticism is that it tends to allegorize details of the gospel into incidents from the community's reconstructed history.[79]

And so he calls for the redaction criticism of John to move away from "the hypothetical reconstructions of Martyn and Brown" in the direction of "more sociological approaches".[80] Martyn's reconstruction caught the imagination of the scholarly world because of its compelling consistency and vigour, but few have laid bare the form-critical assumptions that underlie his and Brown's treatment of the johannine narrative. Quite apart from its "rather arbitrary and subjective" nature,[81] the treatment of the stories (especially in John 5 and 9) as allegories needs to be justified on form-critical grounds. Martyn recognises the need for such a form-critical undergirding of his theory,[82] and suggests that the 'two-level drama' originated in apocalyptic dualism. But he himself then lists three far-reaching differences between apocalyptic dualism and John's technique,[83] and offers no form-critical support for John's radical translation of the dualism into a different genre. It is somehow regarded as self-evident that the johannine community could naturally express its own history as the history of Jesus.[84]

---

78   Becker "Methoden" 43
79   *Storyteller* 148
80   *Storyteller* 61
81   Stibbe *Storyteller* 148
82   "John did not create the literary form of the two-level drama" (*History & Theology2* 135).
83   *History & Theology2* 136f

Ashton complains about the lack of form-critical studies on John, mentioning only Dodd's *Historical Tradition* and Leroy's *Rätsel*.[85] But he himself accepts (for instance) Martyn's "strong reading of the allegories in 10:1-18",[86] without apparently recognising that such a classification cannot be made in the absence of the kind of form-critical study that Leroy has undertaken for John's 'riddles'.

In fact there seems to be no literary precedent for this kind of allegorical narrative. The closest contemporary parallel might be the vision of the woman mourning for her dead son in *4 Ezra* 9:38ff. She turns out to be an allegorical representation of Zion. I will argue below that this passage suggests fruitful lines of interpretation in John 9. But there are great differences between this allegory, with its simple one-for-one correspondence between the woman and Zion and its explicit interpretation, and the complex, multi-figure, uninterpreted allegories which Martyn and his successors find in John's narrative.

Literary precedent may be lacking, but Ashton at least seeks to give this allegorical approach a methodological foundation. He follows Leroy in arguing that John 2:19-22 is a particularly important 'riddle' whose purpose is "to alert the readers of the Gospel as early as possible to the way in which they have to interpret the subsequent revelations".[87] 2:19-22, he suggests, reveals a contrast between the time of Jesus' ministry and that of the church, with true understanding of the former only available later to those who believe. Jesus' first hearers could not have understood his remark as a comment about his own body, and so there are two levels of meaning, the plain and the esoteric, relating to two periods, that of the ministry and that of the church. Ashton thus concludes that 2:19-22 confirms the rightness of Martyn's 'two-level drama' approach to the Gospel.[88]

However the observation that expressions of double meaning pervade John is not a sufficient basis for the allegorical treatment of the narratives. There is plenty of literary precedent for the small-

---

84 Brown *Community* takes the allegorising process further than Martyn, by treating the chronology of the narrative as itself an allegory, so that the Gospel actually gives a stage-by-stage history of the johannine community, from the earliest converts among the followers of John the Baptist (1-3), through the entry of some anti-Temple Samaritans (4), to the development of a 'high' christology (5) with the inevitable ensuing conflict with Judaism (7-10).

85 *Understanding* 109f, 163
86 *Understanding* 173
87 *Understanding* 414
88 *Understanding* 412-420

scale tropes John employs, but not for the wholesale allegorisation of a narrative which purports to be history. In any case, we will argue below (a) that the 'plain' meaning of Jesus' saying in 2:19 — referring to the Temple — is still a vital part of its contemporary (i.e. post-resurrection) meaning; and (b) that the 'esoteric' meaning is made available to non-believers precisely by this candid, up-front proclamation. The distinction between the time of Jesus' ministry and that of the church is indeed basic to the use and understanding of the expressions of double meaning in John, as Carson has shown.[89] But this observation only takes one small step towards the form-critical vindication which Martyn's allegorisation requires.

It does not seem that the move to a "more sociological" approach, for which Stibbe calls, will deliver us from this allegorisation. One of the latest full-scale sociological studies of the Fourth Gospel, Jerome Neyrey's *An Ideology of Revolt* (1988), is thoroughly Martynesque in its treatment of the narrative: he depends upon "clues" to the history of the johannine community which are "encoded in the Gospel's narrative" in order to furnish himself with the raw material on which to exercise his sociological theory.[90]

1.2.5 *The inappropriate appeal to Berger and Luckmann*

Our final criticism of the inferential method, as applied to the Fourth Gospel, concerns the appeal made in particular by Meeks to Berger and Luckmann's sociology of knowledge. I believe that their theory has been misapplied. Meeks uses it to support his inferences about the social location of the johannine community, by pointing to the way in which the language of the Fourth Gospel seems (to him) to reinforce the private mores and ethos of an alienated group who seek to assert their identity against the dominant (Jewish) culture. But Berger and Luckmann specifically deny that inferences of this sort can be made, because of the sheer *varieties* of relationship which may exist between a wider society and particular groupings within it.

Basic to Berger and Luckmann's theory is the view that

> socialization always takes place in the context of a particular social structure. Not only its contents but also its measure of 'success' have social-structural conditions and social-structural consequences. In other words, the micro-sociological or social-psychological analysis of phenomena of internalization must always have as its background

---

89   Carson "Misunderstandings"
90   Neyrey *Revolt* 148f

a macro-sociological understanding of their structural aspects.[91]

In a footnote at this point they comment:

> Our argument implies the necessity of a macro-sociological back-ground for analyses of internalization, that is, of an understanding of the *social structure* within which internalization occurs. American social psychology today is greatly weakened by the fact that such a background is widely lacking.[92]

'Internalisation' is the process "by which the objectivated social world is retrojected into consciousness in the course of socializa-tion"[93] — in other words, it is the process whereby the norms and values of a society are learned by individuals within it. Berger and Luckmann emphasise the complexity of this process. For instance, they comment on the variety of ways in which a 'sectarian' mentality — such as is frequently proposed for the johannine community — may be internalised. The underlying ideological conflict may arise between two cultures encountering one another for the first time (125f), or between a deviant sub-society and a monopolistic surroun-ding culture (139-142), or between various sub-societies in a basically pluralist culture (142-145). The vital conclusion is that *observers cannot infer the social 'location' of any particular group merely from a study of its mentality.*

In fact, deduction from the general to the particular, rather than inference in the other direction, is a "necessity", according to Berger and Luckmann, if understanding of the particular is to be soundly based. As they put it, there must be "a macro-sociological back-ground for analyses of internalization". Their comment above about American social psychology could be written of the johannine community: 'the study of the social psychology of the community is greatly weakened by the fact that the macro-sociological background is widely lacking' — in fact, almost totally so. There must at least be some *attempt* to move from the background to the text, even if success cannot be guaranteed.

---

91   Berger & Luckmann *Construction* 183
92   *Construction* 232 n. 32, their emph.
93   *Construction* 78f

1.3 The method employed in this study

So there is an urgent need for a method which holds together the new literary approaches with historical criticism, and which resists the prevailing passion for insecure inferences from the text. The need is widely recognised. For instance, J.A. Du Rand argues, in his essay applying narrative criteria to John 9-10, that

> The historical information on the possible socio-cultural setting of the Johannine community (although hypothetical) should be linked up with the text-immanent analyses. ... The pragmatic dimension ... makes use of the syntactic and semantic analyses and describes the meaning to be materialised in the relation between narrator and audience.[94]

— but unfortunately he takes no steps towards achieving this goal. Similarly Stibbe criticises Culpepper for proposing a narrative criticism which ignores historical questions,[95] and writes about his own work,

> It is my aim to introduce a form of narrative criticism which does full justice to John as a first-century narrative by taking into account historical questions concerning sources and community.[96]

This study involves a further attempt to achieve this goal. This section will outline the interpretative method with which we will work, and then after its initial application in chapters 2 and 3 we will return to the issue in chapter 4, to discuss the *theory* on which the method rests. Stibbe rightly recognises that a study of *sources* is a central feature of any historical approach, but I do not tackle it on the ground that the historical setting and function of the final form of the text represents a self-contained and legitimate study of quite sufficient proportions!

We seek to adopt a holistic approach which moves as much as possible in the direction Berger and Luckmann prescribe, from the general to the particular. The method may be visualised as a movement inward through a series of concentric circles, from *context* to *co-text*, and finally to the *text* on which our interest focuses.[97] For

---

94   Du Rand "Narratological" 96
95   *Storyteller* 67
96   *Storyteller* 12
97   For this helpful distinction (context = total social setting; co-text =

this reason, the exegesis of 8:31-59 is not undertaken until the final chapter, when its "pragmatic dimension", its voice within the context in which it functioned, may be clearly heard. The method may be formulated in relation to the internal and external poles discussed above:

- (1) The first stage is to seek, within the text, indications of its social setting (by 'mirror-reading'). In order to do this, however, we cannot rely simply on narrative or literary criteria. An analysis based on these will succeed in isolating features which have a *designed, literary* prominence. But it will not spot features which depend for their prominence on a quiet allusion to some extra-textual feature, or background fact, or Old Testament text. And since such allusions, especially ironic ones, seem to be part of the johannine stock-in-trade, we need *appropriate external indicators* to supplement literary analysis in the hunt for those features of the text which point to its social function.

James Dunn illustrates this method in his important 1983 essay, "Let John be John". He first takes a broad "preliminary 'fix' on John",[98] setting it in the general context of Jewish-Christian dispute over the messiahship of Jesus in the last decades of the first century. This involves seeking "points of sensitivity" within the text, that is, "the points at which an effort is evidently being made to clarify some confusion or to counter opposing views".[99]

Barclay would rightly urge caution over the word "evidently" here. On what will we rest our conviction that we have encountered 'evidence'? How rigorously will we check our intuitions? Martyn latched onto one piece of background — the *birkat ha-minim* — and made a connection to John. Dunn rightly broadens the background against which he takes his "preliminary fix". But increasingly we will be pressed outside the text to examine that background — which leads us to stage two:

- (2) Now we move outside the text, guided by our preliminary awareness of where the concerns of the Gospel seem to lie, to look at the broad scene in which it seems to be at home. A holistic approach to the text needs to be matched by a holistic approach to the background information, and not one which rushes to select the items which seem most relevant at first glance.

- (3) Finally we return to the text, to re-read it against the background now more fully delineated. As Dunn puts it, we "'spiral in'

surrounding text), see Cotterell & Turner *Linguistics* 39.
98   Dunn "John" 317
99   Dunn "John" 318

to gain a closer look at the Fourth Gospel within its historical context".[100] Hopefully, now, more "points of sensitivity" will appear,
and the text as *address* will be properly heard.

This movement from the text outwards, and then inwards again,
offers us the best hope for a realistic 'hearing' of its message within
its social setting. This shapes the arrangement of the chapters which
follow:

• (1) Chapter 2: we first seek the "points of sensitivity" signalled
within the text itself, bearing the broad external context in mind; and
then

• (2) Chapter 3: we proceed outward to the background 'scene',
bearing the whole text in mind while studying all the available information which might have relevance. Thus a dialectical relationship is
established between text and background, a relationship which
hopefully will enable us to identify in broad terms the 'voice' of the
text in its social and historical setting. Then:

• (3) Chapters 5-7: we return to the text to refine and develop our
appreciation of its force, first looking broadly at John 6-12 (chapters
5-6), then focusing finally on 8:31-59 (chapter 7). Ideally, the approach should be applied to the whole Gospel, but our interest in
8:31-59 and the issue of "the Jews" creates our focus in chapters 5-7.

Such a method at least it offers more hope of success than a
method which makes no effort to escape from partiality. We proceed
on the presupposition that the Gospel is a bigger phenomenon than
merely the words that compose it; and this is nowhere clearer than in
relation to its anti-Judaism. The fact of its anti-Judaism summons us
behind the immediate words of the text and throws us headlong into
the world of late first-century Jews and Christians. What were the
factors constraining their relationships in this period? How does the
Gospel engage with them? These questions carry us forward.

---

100 Dunn "John" 317

Searching for 'Points of Sensitivity'
in the Fourth Gospel

As we saw in the previous chapter, the expression "points of sensitivity" is used by James Dunn to describe those features of the Gospel which seem to engage with issues or needs in its environment. Dunn identifies several of these,[1] but his list can be considerably amplified, and needs to be supplemented by tighter control over the method by which these 'points of sensitivity' are identified. This is what we attempt in this chapter. And our broad-brush approach to the issue of John's anti-Judaism will be justified as we observe that "the Jews" (whatever this expression means!) clearly emerge as one of these 'sensitive' issues.

Like the patterns in the children's puzzles which only appear when coloured glasses are used, so the text reveals its 'points of sensitivity' when it is viewed through the lens, or against the background, of first-century Judaism — the broad setting within which contemporary scholarship is content to locate the Fourth Gospel. There is now a wide consensus, heralded by J.A.T Robinson in 1959,[2] that this is its natural 'home'. Scholars like Günter Reim, Frédéric Manns and J.C. Thomas have even sought to show that John's narrative interlocks with specific rabbinic traditions, so that knowledge of the latter is essential for a clear understanding of the former. Such work will be amply illustrated below.

But what is the *quality* of this engagement with Judaism? Because of the prominence of passages where "the Jews" appear as enemies of Jesus, many scholars (as we have seen) infer that it is fundamentally *conflict*. However, we should be cautious about making this inference. Edwin Judge made this point at the colloquy in 1985

---

1   He lists: the repeated contrast with John the Baptist, the battles over the law and the Sabbath, the *krisis* facing the wavering crowd in the middle chapters, and the development in the disciples' faith to the climax in 20:28 ("John" 318). He emphasises the christological focus of all these points.

2   Robinson "New Look" 98f

which discussed Bruce Malina's attempt to infer the social location of the johannine community from the polemic against the Jews:

> There is no reason why the community is one that is being kicked out of the synagogue at all. The fact that the Gospel deals with Jesus' conflicts with the Jews may arise because that is what happened to Jesus. You may well be using that to instruct people who are having some other kind of conflict problem.[3]

Rephrased, we may say with Judge that the narrative of the Gospel cannot be presumed to be a mirror of its setting. Such a presumption restricts the functional possibilities of the text, and is unaware of the dangers of mirror-reading discussed in the last chapter. The presentation of Jesus' conflict with "the Jews" may have a wider purpose than merely to speak to a parallel conflict in the experience of the readers — and I shall argue that it does.

So we institute our search for John's 'points of sensitivity'. We identify and discuss seven in this chapter: The Temple and the Festivals (2.1), the law (2.2), revelation and apocalyptic (2.3), Judea and "the Jews" (2.4), the creation of faith (2.5), the signs (2.6), and some aspects of johannine language and argumentation (2.7).

2.1 The Temple and the Festivals

Viewed against the background of late first-century Judaism, this feature of the narrative is immediately thrown into relief. One of the most pointed differences between John and the synoptics is the emphasis in the latter on the Temple and the Jerusalem festivals. Not only is the cleansing of the Temple given a prominent position at the head of the narrative, but the festivals are closely woven into the structure of the Gospel. This has been noted by many scholars. Brown, for instance, underlines

> the importance given to the theme of Jesus' replacement of Jewish institutions like ritual purification, the Temple, and worship in Jerusalem (chs. ii-iv) and of Jewish feasts like the Sabbath, Passover, Tabernacles and Dedication (chs. v-x).[4]

Brown naturally asks, "Why this emphasis in John?" and finds the answer in the need for a Christian apologetic to counter Jewish

---

3   Judge "Response" 48. The paper under discussion was Malina "Socio-linguistic".

4   Brown 1:lxx. Cf also Yee *Feasts* 27

unbelief and to reinforce the distinction between the synagogue and the Christian community.[5] Recently Gale Yee has refined this general view: the treatment of the feasts is *defensive Christian self-assertion* against the synagogue, from which the Christian community has been expelled:

> The johannine Jesus ... nullified and replaced all the Jewish liturgical institutions that the community lost in its divorce from the synagogue.[6]

This view requires a symbolic decoding of John's narrative: Jesus' replacement of the *Temple* institutions makes sense of separation from the *synagogue*. This is especially problematical for Brown, who wants to argue that John is directed at *diaspora* Jewish Christians still loyal to the synagogue. His argument thus depends upon the assumption that the Jerusalem feasts were still of crucial importance for diaspora Jews — an assumption recently (and rightly) questioned by Neusner.[7] But even if, with Yee, we locate the centre of johannine interest closer to Jerusalem, it is still worth asking *whether the loss of the synagogue is the vital motivating factor, or the loss of the Temple itself*.

Yee is the only recent scholar to explore to any extent the relationship between the johannine emphasis on the Temple and its worship, and the destruction of the Temple and the cessation of that worship in 70 AD.[8] The extent to which the relevance of these events has been ignored is quite remarkable. Neyrey, for instance, is able to write a 250-page monograph on the social setting and function of John's christology without once mentioning the destruction of the Temple.[9] Others — like Brown — pass over it with a bare reference.[10]

The reasons for this extraordinary neglect seem to be several. We could suggest the continuing influence of Bultmann's neglect of

5   Brown 1:lxx-lxxv

6   Yee *Feasts* 25f

7   Neusner "Destruction" 86: even before 70 AD, "for large numbers of ordinary Jews outside of Palestine, as well as substantial numbers within, the temple was a remote and, if holy, unimportant place. For them, piety was fully expressed through synagogue worship".

8   However see now P.W.L. Walker's treatment of John in *The Holy City. New Testament Perspectives on Jerusalem* (Grand Rapids; Eerdmans, 1996)

9   Neyrey *Revolt*. Similarly, so far as I can see, Woll *Conflict* and Whitacre *Polemic* — even though the focus of their work is John's historical setting and function.

10   Brown 1:lxxiv; cf Rensberger *Community* 88f

historical questions,[11] the concentration on the limited history of the johannine community at the expense of an interest in the wider environment of the Gospel,[12] the influence of the new ahistorical literary approaches, and the all-absorbing attention which has been given to the application of various sociological methods to John.[13]

Whatever the reasons, the fact remains that no full-scale work has yet explored the thesis which seems to arise most naturally from the johannine concentration on the Temple and its worship — namely, that the 'point of sensitivity' here signalled is, *directly*, the trauma resulting from the destruction of the Temple and the cessation of its worship.

This de-historicising of John may be illustrated from the treatments of the reference to the destruction of the Temple in 2:19. Undoubtedly, in the post-70 situation, Jesus' words "Destroy this temple, and in three days I will rebuild it" — and indeed the whole episode of the 'cleansing' of the Temple — rang with nuances and connotations fed by the readers' situation. But commentators generally bypass this.

Schnackenburg's treatment is fuller than most, but typical in its features. He interprets the narrative 'internally', that is, just with reference to the relationships between the various actors within the story. He speculates that the sellers of doves complained to the Temple authorities about Jesus' action; he refers "zeal for your house will destroy me" (2:17) forward to the passion; he explores the christological meaning of the "enigmatic saying" in 2:19, "which cannot but remain obscure" to the Jews: "Jesus means only his body, which he will 'raise up' again in three days, if the Jews 'demolish' it", so the Jews' limited reference of Jesus' words to the building in which they stand is a misunderstanding; then he discusses the

---

11   See above, 1.1.2

12   Martyn *Essays* 6 illustrates this: summarising his view of the three stages of history in the johannine community, he remarks that "The Early Period presumably began before the Jewish revolt and lasted until some point in the eighties ... We see here a *group of Christian Jews* living in a stream of relatively untroubled theological and social continuity within the synagogue" (his emph.). Only tunnel-vision resulting from an exclusive interest in the history of this Christian group could explain the blending-out of the trauma of 70 AD here. No Jewish group, Christian or not, experienced the period straddling that date as one of "untroubled theological and social continuity".

13   This is certainly the case with Neyrey: his *Revolt* is a sustained attempt to utilise Mary Douglas' group/grid model of sociological analysis to explain the history of the johannine community. But the 'history' he discovers is entirely constructed out of the theory, and does not engage with any real-time events in the history of the period, nor with any other texts.

replacement theme in 2:21, and adds a long note on the relationship to the synoptic traditions.[14]

Conspicuous by its absence is any interest in the *function* of this story in the post-70 situation, when "destroy this temple" has become a horrible reality — even though this is the period in which Schnackenburg dates the Gospel.[15] Indeed, so poignant and power-ful would this story be for those who had faced the trauma of the Jewish war, that this is in itself an argument for setting the Gospel in that situation. We could well find the reason for the prominence given to this story, and then to the festivals, in the evangelist's desire to address this trauma. Several features of the story support this:

(1) The saying about *destruction and reconstruction* in 2:19 works with deep irony against this background. Formally the imperative "tear down this temple" has a conditional force,[16] but Barrett notes an ironic overtone on the pattern of "Come to Bethel and transgress" (Amos 4:4).[17] Because of the widespread view that the destruction of the Temple was a judgment upon corruption within it (see the next point), readers would have felt the ironic force of this imperative. Schnackenburg tries to play down the reference to the physical Temple, but Bultmann, Barrett and Brown all rightly insist that this reference is primary.[18] In a situation in which despair and hope jostled with many different proposed solutions (as we shall see in the next chapter), the offer of *rebuilding* has a powerful emotive effect. And readers are immediately admitted into the privileged position which irony confers: while the Jews in the text try in vain to interpret Jesus' enigmatic offer, the evangelist signals to the readers that this saying concerns his resurrection (2:21f).

(2) The concern with *addressing corruption in the Temple* would also have rung ironic bells with such readers. The view that the destruction of the Temple had resulted from corruption within it was widespread: we find it in Josephus, in contemporary apocal-yptic, and amongst the *tannaim* — and of course this would have been the view of the heirs of the Qumran sectarians.[19] Many must

---

14 Schnackenburg 1:347-353 (quotations from 349, 350)

15 1:100-104

16 Schnackenburg 1:350 n. 27; Brown 1:115

17 Barrett 199; also Bultmann 125

18 As Whitacre notes (*Polemic* 28), there is a strongly positive attitude to the Temple here: "it is God's house and Jesus is zealous for it".

19 Josephus *War* 5:412; *Apoc. Abr.* 25:1-6, 27:7; 2 *Bar.* 10:18; 4 *Bar.* 1:1,8, 4:7f; *t. Menah.* 13:22 — etc. The understanding of the nature of the corruption differs in each case, but the diagnosis of the cause of the disaster is the same. Cf Neusner *Yohanan2* 11f. We examine this more closely in the next chapter.

have felt the zeal to which 2:17 refers, and wished that someone had been able to cleanse the Temple of its impurities before it was too late. But readers would be aware that the precise corruption on which Jesus focuses, the use of the outer court as a market before Passover, had continued unchecked right up to the destruction. If any readers found themselves wishing that Jesus' action had been welcomed, rather than suspiciously rejected (2:18), then the narrative is leading them into sympathy with Jesus' cause.

(3) The *exploded myth of permanence and invincibility* is a further factor. The response of "the Jews" in 2:20 is full of pathos, from a post-70 perspective: "it has taken 46 years to build this Temple" expresses not just dismissive contempt at the thought that they should ever contemplate demolishing it, but also a 'pathetic' sense of the Temple's invincibility. And yet — the Temple was demolished, and they were responsible! Readers might have been reminded of the other Jesus who repeatedly prophesied the imminent doom of Temple and city before the war, and who was likewise ignored and rejected.[20]

Leroy and Ashton are right, I believe, to suggest that this passage is programmatic for the rest of the Gospel.[21] But whereas they relate it to the 'misunderstandings', suggesting that this passage lays the foundation for the two levels on which the Gospel operates, the approach that I am proposing would make this passage programmatic for the later treatment of the festivals: just as the Temple has been replaced by "the temple of his body" (2:21), so also the worship of the Temple has been superseded by faith in the Christ.

Read within a post-70 situation, there would be no difficulty for any reader, Jew or Christian, in comprehending the claim made for Jesus in 2:21f: his resurrection constitutes a rebuilding of the destroyed temple. The Jews did not misunderstand, when they thought that he was referring to the physical temple in Jerusalem: they simply could not grasp how he could make such a claim. Neither could the disciples, until Jesus' resurrection took place and then 'the penny dropped', and they realised how Jesus' zeal for the Temple had borne positive fruit.[22] Thus the reader is invited by this

---

20   Josephus *War* 6:300-309; cf Horsley & Hanson *Bandits* 173f. The rejection implicit in 2:18 is drawn out by Hahn "Prozess" 70. Whitacre *Polemic* 28 makes it just a mild questioning, but it must be more.

21   Leroy *Rätsel* 145-7, Ashton *Understanding* 414-416

22   It seems best to understand "the Scripture" in 2:22 (contra Barrett 201; Carson 183) as a reference to Ps. 69:10 quoted in 2:17: so (hesitantly) Schnackenburg 1:353; Beasley-Murray 41; Sanders 120.

passage on a voyage of discovery. *How* Jesus' resurrection can constitute a rebuilding of the Temple is not specified: but the reader is made aware that the disciples (the "we" of 1:14) have forged a bridge of understanding between his Temple saying and his resurrection, and that they believe Jesus to be the answer to the agonising problem of the post-70 period: how can we re-shape our lives without the Temple?

The two further references to the destruction of the Temple take on powerful ironic overtones when read against this background:

(1) The words of the Sanhedrin and of Caiaphas in 11:47-50 have long been recognised as one of the supreme examples of johannine irony. In fact three ironies may be distinguished here:

• (a) Paul Duke points out how the Sanhedrin "neatly forecast the future in triplicate" in 11:48, even though they are immediately accused by Caiaphas of knowing nothing at all.[23] They know all too much about what will happen! But

• (b) post-70 readers are only too aware that the action they and Caiaphas propose in order to prevent the disaster totally failed in its purpose. An irony attaches to their impotence while they take steps to shape events their way.

• (c) But did they fail completely? In a final twist the evangelist explains that the murder they plan *will* achieve the salvation of "the people", and indeed also of "the place" (τόπος, 11:48 — an expression for the Temple), whose restoration is implicit in the idea of regathering the nation from exile (11:52).[24]

(2) There is a similar combination of tragic irony and hope in 4:21. The irony of "neither on this mountain nor in Jerusalem" is heart-wrenching, when this text is read in a post-70 setting. The fate that befell the schismatic Samaritan temple at the hands of John Hyrkanus[25] has now befallen Jerusalem at the hands of the Romans! "You will not worship on that mountain" had been the Jewish charge against the Samaritans for centuries. Jesus quotes this charge, augments it with its horrifying complement — "nor in Jerusalem!" — but then transforms it into a positive statement of the purpose of God and what he *seeks* (4:23).

So in all three passages we find the same combination of irony and hope. In chs. 2 and 11 it is the *tragic* irony of authority-figures

---

23   Duke *Irony* 87

24   The doublet of 11:48, ὁ τόπος καὶ τὸ ἔθνος, is picked up in 11:51-2, ἔθνος in 51 and τόπος in 52. Against the background of OT prophetic expectation, especially Ezekiel, the gathering of the nation εἰς ἕν connotes the restoration of the "place" where they gather.

25   Josephus *Ant.* 13:256

confidently exercising their power, unaware of the shaky ground on which they stand; in ch. 4 it is a *dramatic* irony, a secret communication between author and readers by which the latter become aware of the real significance of Jesus' words. But in all three the irony is not hopeless or cynical — far from it. The trauma is add ressed with hope.[26]

These reflections illustrate our method. When internal literary prominence is linked to prominent external events, a clear 'point of sensitivity' is revealed. And so we pursue our aim of illuminating the text by reference to its *reception* in its 'home' environment.[27] As the discussion develops we will consider whether the text seems to engage more fittingly with the concerns of Christian, or of Jewish, readers.

2.2 The law and 'midrashic discussion'

Since the massive work of Pancaro (*Law*, 1975) all doubt about the importance of the law for John has been dispelled. It seems now to be recognised on all sides that his interest in the law is not merely apologetic, a convenient means of presenting the real subject, Jesus. Rather, the issue of the legitimacy of the law in relation to Christ is itself a crucial concern.[28] The number of formal quotations from the Old Testament is not large, but they are supplemented by a very large number of allusions. For instance, we will find particularly important for 8:31-59 the insight of George Brooke, that chs. 7-10 engage with the decalogue in a quiet but fairly systematic way;[29] and we will find the 'false prophet' passages in Deut 13 and 18 to be an unspoken but determining presence. Further examples could be

26 Recent scholarship contains some fine discussions of the various types of irony as background to their use in John: especially MacRae "Irony", Culpepper *Anatomy* 165-180, Duke *Irony* 18-27 and O'Day *Revelation* 11-32. None of them, however, refer to ironic treatment of the destruction of the Temple.

27 We thus formally leave open whether the Gospel was actually written before or after the Jewish war, although the latter would seem more appropriate. Two recent scholars have actually used 2:18-22 to argue for a *pre-70* date for the Gospel: Robinson *Redating* 277 and Kemper "Gestalt" 248. Robinson assumes that the time-reference in 2:20 must apply outside the narrative, as well as within it — a totally unwarranted and highly misleading assumption. Kemper asserts that the story of the cleansing of the Temple would be "worthless — indeed laughable" if the readers knew the Temple had been destroyed: but why? He does not allow for the powerful presence of irony.

28 See esp. Pancaro *Law* 501

29 Brooke "Law"

multiplied.

John's engagement with the law undoubtedly signals a 'point of sensitivity' for him, as it did for Paul. It is important, however, to set this observation in its proper cultural and religious context. For Paul, the issue of the law arose in the context of his Gentile mission, and therefore focused around the Jewish institutions most relevant to that context, in particular circumcision. For John, *the Jerusalem festivals* play an analogous role within his theology to that of circumcision within Paul's: here too the question is, 'participation or not?', as we shall see, and Jesus is presented as the fulfiller and superseder in both cases.

Pancaro gives prominence to the issue of Sabbath-observance in his analysis of the law in John, but hardly touches on the festivals. This reflects a skewed understanding of the cultural context within which the lifestyle of 'the law' was set, at any rate within John's circle of concern. It arises, I believe, because Pancaro is inclined — along with many others — to treat John's use of the Old Testament purely as an example of literary and theological dependence, rather than as something arising within and reflecting a living religious context.

Something of that religious context has been uncovered by those who have observed the 'Jewish' style of the argumentation at many points in the Fourth Gospel. In this Peder Borgen has led the field, particularly with his study of the use of the Old Testament in John 6, which (he suggests) conforms to rabbinic exegetical technique.[30] He has been ably supported by many others, for instance by the targumist Roger Le Déaut, who finds seven points at which John engages specifically with ideas typically found in the Targums.[31] Others have pointed to numerous possible parallels with rabbinic thought, some of them more likely than others. Thyen describes the Fourth Gospel as "full of subliminal allusions to specifically Jewish traditions, and of motifs adapted from the Targums and midrash".[32]

Martyn points out how the engagement with midrashic techniques is not just seen in the use of the Old Testament in John. He uses the phrase "midrashic discussion" to describe what Nicodemus, the

---

30 P. Borgen, "Observations on the Midrashic Character of John 6", *ZNW* 54 (1963), 232-240

31 Le Déaut "Targumic": in this survey of the whole New Testament the Fourth Gospel occupies the longest section (265-283). We shall have occasion to note some of his points later.

32 Thyen "Heil" 174. We return to this quotation below.

Galilean crowd and the Pharisees seek to initiate in 3:4, 6:30f, and
7:52, 8:13, 9:28f respectively.[33] It was a style of argumentation
typical of the rabbinic schools of the first century, in which a point of
interpretation or religious practice would form a centre of debate
between master and pupils. Martyn suggests that there is an
ambivalent attitude to such "midrashic discussion" in John: on the
one hand there are clear examples of it, as Borgen has shown, but on
the other the whole atmosphere and tone of the Gospel seems
different. "John allows Jesus paradoxically to employ a form of midrashic discussion in order to terminate all midrashic discussion!"[34]
The questions of Nicodemus, the crowd and the Pharisees are met,
not with midrashic justification of the claims just made, but with
proclamation.

This ambivalence is explicitly signalled within the text, at 7:14f.
On the one hand, Jesus does what all scribes do: he goes to the
Temple and "teaches", and "the Jews" recognise that his teaching is
competent (γράμματα οἶδεν, "he knows letters" — i.e. he is clearly a
γραμματεύς, a scribe). But at the same time he is μὴ μεμαθηκώς,
"unlearned", which is best taken to mean that he has not followed
the standard route to learning: "How is it that this man who has
never been a disciple in the rabbinic schools can carry on a learned
disputation?".[35] So, while Jesus may be given a social label,
"scribe", he is clearly unique: "no one ever spoke like this man!"
(7:46).

We shall return to the style of Jesus' teaching in 2.7 below. The
point to be made here is that the dialogues of the Gospel, including
that in ch. 8, are a kind of *parody* of the "midrashic discussion" with
which many first-century Jews would have been familiar. This is a
genre judgment which seems to me to fit the evidence better than the
view that the dialogues of John illustrate the adaptability of the
continuing Platonic dialogue tradition,[36] or that they are dramatic
devices drawing on the traditions of Greek drama,[37] or that they are
dramatised trials,[38] or simply that they are vivid ways of compelling choice, like the parables in the synoptics.[39]

---

33   Martyn *History & Theology*2 121, 131-3

34   Martyn *History & Theology*2 128

35   Barrett's paraphrase (317): so also Bornhäuser *Missionsschrift* 50f; Manns
"Réponse" 73; Duke *Irony* 72; Lindars 287

36   So Dodd "Dialogue" 63-65

37   So Kemper "Gestalt", Schenke "Szene", Bartholomew *Sermon-Drama* (with
reference just to 8:31-59)

38   So Neyrey "Process" (specifically on chs. 7-8); Harvey *Trial*; Trites *Witness*
(though we will suggest below in 6.2 that there is *some* truth in this view).

Thus the johannine dialogues, and their use of the Old Testament, would be both familiar and unfamiliar to Jewish readers. We shall return to this issue of genre in chapter 6, where we will attempt to define more precisely the element of unfamiliarity.

2.3 Revelation and the Open Heaven

Our search for 'points of sensitivity' within the text leads us to the emphasis on *Jesus as Revealer*, and to the promise of revelation to his disciples. Rudolph Bultmann made this aspect of John's christology its central feature, and argued that it showed the Gospel's Gnostic background. In the emphasis on revelation he built upon the work of the Swedish scholar Hugo Odeberg; but Odeberg had interpreted it against the background of the *Jewish* 'merkabah' mystical tradition,[40] and this line of interpretation has been re-explored in the context of the modern interest in John's Jewish origins.

Wayne Meeks was one of the first to re-awaken interest,[41] with his influential study of Moses traditions in John, *The Prophet-King* (1967). He argued that the contemporary understanding of Moses as one who *journeyed to heaven*, there to receive heavenly revelations, had influenced John's christology, and that a polemic against contemporary claims to have made such journeys is found in 1:18, 3:11-13, and 5:37.[42]

David Aune followed suit in his study of realised eschatology in the New Testament. But whereas Meeks was cautious about whether heavenly ascents and revelation were open to Jesus' disciples as well to him,[43] Aune's explanation of the realised eschatology of John was that the johannine church enjoyed a "recurring actualization of his future Parousia" in the visions and 'heavenly journeys' which were a feature of their worship.[44] This picture of the johannine

---

39   So Hooker "Secret" 49f; Rebell *Gemeinde* 78 (he uses insights from didactic theory to support this view of the dialogues)

40   Odeberg's 'commentary' was published in 1929. See especially 94ff. He argued that the *exclusive* emphasis on Jesus as Revealer ("no one has ascended into heaven but he who descended ...", 3:13) indicated a contemporary polemic against other sources of apocalyptic revelation. The 'merkabah' (= 'chariot') tradition used meditation on the chariot vision of Ezekiel 1 as the means of further visionary experiences.

41   — although according to Jocz "Juden" 132f Jewish scholars had long been alive to this feature of John.

42   Meeks *Prophet-King* 295-301; cf also "Man From Heaven" 52f

43   "Man From Heaven" 68

44   E.g. Aune *Setting* 99-101 (quotation 101)

church as a charismatic community is also basic to Woll's interpretation of the first farewell discourse.[45] More recently Dunn has taken up this approach and emphasised the importance of apocalyptic and 'merkabah' mysticism for the interpretation of John.[46]

In the light of all this work we can make the following assertions with reasonable certainty:

(1) The presentation of Jesus as the Revealer draws not just on prophetic and Wisdom traditions but also on apocalyptic and 'heavenly journey' traditions, especially those associated with the patriarchs. The importance of this for the interpretation of the Nicodemus episode[47] and verses like 1:51, 8:38 and 8:56 has been widely recognised.

(2) The insistence on the Son of Man as the *sole* Revealer of heavenly things (1:18, 3:13, 3:31-36, 14:6) is a polemic against such claims made by others.

(3) The promise of continuing revelation to the church, especially through the 'Paraclete' (1:51, 14:26, 16:12-15), should be interpreted against the same background (whether the promised revelatory experiences are conceived as modelled on those of Jesus or not).

2.4 Judea and "the Jews"

We now reach and tackle a topic central to our concern. The adjective Ἰουδαῖος ("Jew" or "Jewish") is used 71 times in the Fourth Gospel, the vast majority of these (68) in the plural referring to "the Jews" as a group. This statistic alone would be sufficient to identify this as a 'point of sensitivity', although it has proved remarkably difficult to understand what is signalled by it.

---

45   Woll *Conflict*

46   Dunn "John" 322-325

47   This interpretation of the Nicodemus episode is by far the best. Nicodemus does not represent Jewish Christians stuck in the synagogue, nor does he represent Jews stuck in the night of ignorance and unbelief (highly popular options in the allegorising tradition), but he is a realistic figure, the Pharisee who longs for heavenly knowledge, and who comes at night because that is the time when the *merkabah* may be expounded: so Bornhäuser *Missionsschrift* 26f, 29; Schlatter 85; cf Bultmann 133 n. 5. It is surprising that Meeks does not take this view, for he follows Odeberg in the view that the ascent-descent language in 3:13 must be construed as a polemic against the claims of apocalyptists within Judaism.

This interpretation is confirmed (a) by the tradition of "night" as the time for visionary experiences in, for example, 4 Ezra 3:14 ("you loved him [Abraham] and to him only you revealed the end of the times, secretly by night"), 6:12, 10:58f, 13:1, 2 Baruch 36:1, and (b) by the rabbinic reticence about discussing the *merkabah* openly.

This is partly because it is so difficult for modern readers to 'hear' John's language with first-century ears, and thus opinions about the meaning of "the Jews" vary greatly. All too often a careful historical 'hearing' is jammed by a sense of horror at John's apparent anti-semitism. So, for instance, Richard Lowry dismisses all attempts to discover the nuanced meaning of the term:

> Let one cite every extenuation one can think of ... the fact remains that, no matter what John 'means', what it says is 'the Jews'.[48]

This is an obstinate 'hearing' which will only listen on one channel and refuses to tune in to the wavelengths of the text itself. But even when scholars work hard to be open and fair to John, the distracting effect of historical antisemitism is still discernible. It works as an implicit motivation underlying various attempts to limit the semantic range of "the Jews". So, for instance, Urban von Wahlde, who argues that the term means "the Jewish authorities", writes, "If the term refers only to authorities, it hardly provides evidence that the gospel is an attack on the attitudes of all Jews".[49] Similarly Malcolm Lowe, who argues that οἱ Ἰουδαῖοι should be translated "the Judeans", comments that the usual translation "has provided ... a constant excuse for antisemitism whose further exis-tence cannot be permitted."[50]

A vital pre-requisite for hearing the text in its own right is linguistic clarity. Ashton rightly discerns, in the sheer variety of proposals for the 'meaning' of the expression, a failure to distinguish between its *sense* and its *reference*.[51] The importance of this vital distinction is illustrated by the following quotation from Jouette Bassler:

> [*"The Jews" is used in a variety of ways in John, but]* a characteristically johannine usage emerges in which the term loses its nationalistic meaning and comes to designate unreceptivity — even hostility — toward Jesus. Already [by chapter 3] the term has acquired these negative connotations.[52]

Here the words "usage", "meaning", "designate" and "connota-

---

48   Lowry "Suitor" 229f
49   von Wahlde "Jews" 33
50   Lowe "ΙΟΥΔΑΙΟΙ" 130
51   Ashton "Identity" 57-59
52   Bassler "Nicodemus" 636f

tions" jostle each other as if referring interchangeably to one phenomenon, with the implication that the expression can only have *one*
such 'thing'. So if it 'designates' hostility, it must lose its other
'meaning'. But this is linguistically naive. The *sense* of a term may be
defined as its 'hub' or 'heart' meaning, its 'denotation' which it is
likely to retain across a range of usages within a language-group. To
its *sense* various *references* may be attached, according to usage.
"England batted first" involves the basic *sense* (the country), allied
to two *references* (the people of the country, and the cricket team);
and of course such a statement may be coloured by a range of
affective or connotative meanings, involving images of empire,
straight bats, and stiff upper lips.[53] To ask after the 'meaning' of
"the Jews" in John is extraordinarily complex, but to define the
question as precisely as possible is a good start:

(1) What is the 'hub' *sense*?
(2) What further *references* are present?
(3) What further important *connotations* are discernible?

The discussion has been bedevilled by a failure to make these
distinctions.[54]

With these preliminaries we will now survey the various explanations canvassed for the 'meaning' of "the Jews" in John.

2.4.1 The Jews as 'Judeans'

Ashton actually employs the distinction between sense and reference in his 1985 article: the *sense*, he suggests, is "the Judeans" and
the *reference* is "representatives of unbelief".[55] But he does not

---

53   The complexities of 'meaning' are well illustrated and summarised by
Geoffrey Leech, who analyses no fewer than seven different "ingredients" which
may be present: *Semantics: the Study of Meaning* (Harmondsworth; Penguin, 1981),
9-23.

54   The literature is peppered with linguistically naive judgments like the
following from John Koenig (*Dialogue* 129): "The phrase 'the Jews' becomes a
shibboleth which usually *means nothing other than* 'unbelievers' and 'enemies of
God'" (my emph.). Cf also Hoskyns 173: "Throughout his Gospel the Evangelist ...
uses the phrase 'the Jews' to *denote* the national rejection of the Christ and especially
His rejection by the Jewish authorities" (my emph.); and Nickelsburg "Wisdom" 83:
"In the Fourth Gospel, the term "the Jews" is a *veritable synonym* for those who do
not believe in him and who are, therefore, lost" (my emph.).

55   "Identity" 53, 59f. He draws on Lowe for the former, and Bultmann for the
latter. He uses "sense" interchangeably with "connotation" (cf 53 with 59). Others
who understand "the Jews" to mean "the Judeans" include Fortna "Locale"; Meeks
"Breaking Away" 96 (cf "Jew" 182); Thyen "Heil" 179f; and Geyser "Israel" 14f.
Dodd *Tradition* 242 n. 2 allows that the "geographical meaning" may be "present"
even when the word is used with another "meaning".

make the distinction with sufficient rigour. There are clearly instances not included in this 'sense', most notably 6:41, 12:11 and 18:20: there are Galilean Ἰουδαῖοι (6:41), Ἰουδαῖοι who believe (12:11), and the Temple is described as the place where "all the Ἰουδαῖοι gather" (18:20), most naturally connoting the pilgrim festivals which brought many from the diaspora. In any case, the term has a fundamental religious significance which is not represented by "the Judeans" as a definition of its primary sense.[56]

Some scholars have sought to reinforce and refine this view by arguing that "Galilee is the land of acceptance, refuge, and belief in Jesus, while Judea is the land of rejection, hostility, and disbelief".[57] It is certainly generally true that the johannine Jesus finds more acceptance outside Judea than in it. But there is sufficient unbelief in Galilee (6:36) and faith in Judea (11:45) to make it impossible that "Galilean" and "Judean" should be understood as tags meaning "believer" and "unbeliever" respectively.

2.4.2 The Jews as representatives of unbelief

They are "representatives of unbelief (and thereby ... of the unbelieving 'world' in general)".[58] With Bultmann's influence, this view has proved highly influential.[59] This too, at first sight, takes the sting out of the hostility towards the Jews: it can be interpreted as hostility towards unbelief and 'worldliness', wherever encountered. Thus Fortna is able finally to argue that John

> does not set Jew and Gentile against each other ... He is not finally concerned with Judaism itself as a historical phenomenon alongside Christianity, so much as with the human condition.[60]

---

56   So Wengst *Gemeinde* 39f, arguing against Lowe. Ashton now accepts this point (*Understanding* 134), and has changed his view.

57   Bassler "Galileans" 250. So also Fortna "Locale", Meeks "Breaking Away" 96f

58   Bultmann 86, cf *Theology* 2:5

59   In addition to Bultmann and Ashton, also Lona *Johannes 8* 337; Ibuki *Wahrheit* 99, 112; Gräßer "Polemik" 89; Dahl "History" 135; Culpepper *Anatomy* 129; Rensberger *Community* 27; Hahn "Prozeß" 79; Wengst *Gemeinde* 37-39; Fortna "Locale" 92-95; Baumbach "Gemeinde" 123; Trites *Witness* 79; Onuki *Gemeinde* 34-37; Cook "Jews" 267; Knight "Antisemitism" 85f; Leibig "Jews" 215f.

For some scholars the idea is slightly reduced: rather than 'representatives of the world / unbelief', the Jews just stand for 'opponents of Jesus, enemies of God': so e.g. Dodd *Tradition* 242 n. 2; Dahl "History" 128; Rensberger *Community* 27, 34 n. 64; Schenke "Szene" 176; Koenig *Dialogue* 129; Bassler "Nicodemus" 636f.

60   Fortna "Locale" 94f

But even if "the Jews" are symbols of something else, we must still ask, "which Jews?". A derived symbolic *reference* feeds on a primary *sense*, as Rosemary Ruether has acutely seen in objecting that this symbolic interpretation of "the Jews" does not absolve the fourth evangelist of anti-Judaism, as some of its proponents had hoped: the term still 'refers' to flesh and blood.[61]

But which flesh and blood? The literature offers several answers to this:

2.4.3 'The Jews' as an indefinite description

Several scholars suggest that it is a catch-all expression, not specifying any particular group, but reducing the varied groups of the synoptics to one all-embracing term. This view naturally goes with the 'representative' interpretation, as is clear from Fortna's expression of it:

> The phrase *hoi Ioudaioi* obliterates virtually all distinctions within first century Palestinian society by speaking of the Jews in an external, monolithic way. Gone are the rich and poor, sinners and righteous, Sadducees, Herodians, Zealots, scribes, elders, tax-collectors, prostitutes. John's phrase gives the impression of a stereo-type.[62]

It is true that many of these terms are not used in John. But to suggest that he obliterates social distinctions is a gross overstate-ment. We may think of the deliberate contrast between Nicodemus and the Samaritan woman, or of the sharp, instinctive hostility between the blind man and the Pharisees in ch. 9, or of the Pharisees' dismissive attitude towards "this crowd" (7:49). "The Jews" is simply the most prominent within a colourful range of social desig-nations which appear throughout the Gospel: priests and Levites, Pharisees, Israel, disciples, rulers, the world, Samaritans, Galileans, royal official, the sick, the crowd, inhabitants of Jerusalem, high priests and Pharisees, servants, sinners, bandits, Romans, the people, the High Priest, the Greeks, his own, the soldiers.[63] All these

---

61   Ruether *Fratricide* 116

62   Fortna "Locale" 90; so also Culpepper *Anatomy* 128f; Rebell *Gemeinde* 100f; Wengst *Gemeinde* 37f; Gräßer "Polemik" 76, "Teufelssöhne" 161 n. 15; Pancaro *Law* 293ff; Wittenberger "Judenpolemik" 322; Whitacre *Polemic* 20; Bassler "Galileans" 243f; Leibig "Jews" 215

63   These are given in approximately the order in which they make their first appearance. In addition there are metaphors with social content — sheep, the vine — and "scribes" as a social designation is connoted in 7:15. Other groups, like the disciples of John the Baptist, may be addressed by the narrative. And groups would

expressions interlock and overlap as components in a wide social environment which is by no means flattened or undifferentiated. The challenge to scholarship is to determine *what precise semantic range attaches to "the Jews" within this environment.* Granted this differentiation within the narrative, it seems *a priori* unlikely that "the Jews" covers a wide, catch-all range.[64]

2.4.4 The Jews as the Jewish authorities

Not a few scholars limit the semantic range by referring it to the authorities.[65] The chief argument for this is the alternation between "the Jews" and "the Pharisees" in some important passages (e.g. 9:13-22, 11:47 cf 18:14, 9:22 cf 12:42), for the Pharisees are portrayed as an authoritative group, sometimes bracketed with "the high priests" (7:32, 45; 11:47; 12:42).

But this argument too skates on thin linguistic ice. The fact that two terms are used in parallel with each other hardly indicates that they cover an identical, or even overlapping, semantic range. To take an illustration at random: *The Independent* for 7 May 1992 (front page) reported a leading politician's desire for a Government "which will be gentler, more concerned with constructing consensus, more committed to building a nation". Here there is a certain semantic overlap between "consensus" and "a nation", but not much. Yet the argument we are considering would require us to conclude that the one term 'means' the other.

Our problem is historical. It is familiarity with English which preserves the reader from drawing false conclusions about the meaning of "consensus" and "a nation". We already know what they mean, and bring that knowledge *to* the text, rather than seeking to derive it *from* the text. But we do not know the precise semantic range of "the Jews", and need to make deductions from its use. We need to be careful.

In fact there is plenty of evidence to question "the Jewish authorities, hostile to Jesus" as the reference of οἱ Ἰουδαῖοι. Von

also be connoted as representative attitudes are expressed by characters within the narrative: a prime candidate for this (as we shall see) is 8:33.

64   Ashton *Understanding* 136 argues against this view on the ground that "it overlooks the peculiarly Jewish character of the evangelist's own ideas". He himself is clearly Jewish, so "the Jews" must be less than "the Jewish nation as a whole".

65   So Dodd *Tradition* 242 n. 2; Brown 1:lxxi, *Community* 41; Beasley-Murray lxxxix, *Themes* 10; von Wahlde "Jews" 41f; Crossan "Anti-Semitism" 199; Baumbach "Gemeinde" 124; Leistner *Antijudaismus* 143; Dunn "John" 318f, *Partings* 156-9 (with qualifications); Baumbach "Gemeinde" 124; and Painter *Quest* 101, 249

Wahlde, one of the chief exponents of this view, in fact studies less than half of the references, setting aside those he calls "neutral", and concentrating on "the typically johannine use", where "the Jews" are Jesus' enemies.[66] This prior distinction is loaded with the conclusion he wants to reach. Many of these "neutral" uses are actually positive, showing "Jews" who are well-disposed towards Jesus, even believers in him — most notably the references in ch. 11, and the "Jews who had believed in him" of 8:31 (whom von Wahlde declares to be a redactor's insertion.[67]) And some of these also clearly refer to 'ordinary' Jews: in 12:9-11 a specific distinction is made between "the Jews" and the Jerusalem authorities.

In the light of this variety, we are again pressed back to the question, what is the primary *sense* of this term?

One of the attractions of the "authorities" interpretation is that it fits neatly with the 'Martyn hypothesis' about the Gospel's origin. The disappearance of the Sadducees and the elevation of the Pharisees to the ruling elite in John is held to reflect the post-70 situation in which the Pharisees formed the academy at Yavneh around which Judaism slowly reconstituted itself.[68] There may well be some truth in this, although (a) the Sadducees are certainly present in the johannine narrative, even if unnamed, and (b) it is by no means certain that the position accorded to the Pharisees could *only* be true in the post-70 situation, as some have argued.[69] But an emphasis on the *hearing* of the Gospel in the post-70 situation would suggest that the leading role ascribed to the Pharisees might resonate with readers' experience, especially in Palestine.

2.4.5 The Jews as ambivalent, divided figures

The idea that features of the presentation of "the Jews" might reflect the evangelist's / readers' situation is prominent here too. Not a few scholars have emphasised the ambivalence both *towards* and *among* "the Jews" in the Fourth Gospel. Positive and negative atti-

---

66   Von Wahlde "Jews" 46
67   Von Wahlde "Jews" 50f
68   So e.g. Wengst *Gemeinde* 41, 48f; Nicol *Semeia* 144f; Vouga *Cadre* 66; Smith "Life Setting" 435f; Rebell *Gemeinde* 102; Koenig *Dialogue* 127f; Onuki *Gemeinde* 29f — and of course Martyn himself, *History & Theology2* 84f
69   So Martyn, Vouga, Koenig, Onuki. On the other hand Leistner *Antijudaismus* 142 and Gryglewicz "Pharisäer" 145 argue that the association of the Pharisees with the high priests (John 7:32 etc) was perfectly possible for the time of Jesus. There are two instances of the combination in Josephus (*Vita* 21, *War* 2:411). In this connection Bornhäuser *Missionsschrift* 145 points to the role of the Pharisees in the deposition of John Hyrkanus.

tudes and statements sit side by side. Thyen underlines the positive as a counter-balance to the prevailing negative, starting from 4:22, which he regards as constitutive for the whole Gospel. Against this background, he argues that what underlies the "desperate hostility" of the anti-Jewish passages is "disappointed love": the evangelist and his circle cannot imagine the promised oneness of the flock being achieved without Israel.[70] At the same time "the Jews" themselves are divided in their attitude towards Jesus — a division particularly emphasised in John 7-10, as we shall see.[71]

Ashton disputes Thyen's description of John's attitude to the Jews as a "love-hate" one — "whereas in fact there is no love and little sympathy, only hostility tinged with fear".[72] But this seems a grudging judgment about a Gospel in which the Jews are described as the ἴδιοι ("his own") of the Word (1:11),[73] in which the final climactic title accorded to him is "King of the Jews" (19:19 — creating an *inclusio* with 1:49), in which "the Jews" are the comforters of Mary and Martha and then the believing witnesses of the resurrection of Lazarus (11:45), and in which salvation is said to come from them (4:22).

The 'Martyn hypothesis', of course, emphasises the negative references. But we need an understanding of the Gospel which does justice also to the positive. It is tempting to suggest that passages like 7:12-13, 7:40-43 and especially 12:11, which describe both acceptance *and* rejection by "the Jews", reflect at the very least what the evangelist *wanted* to be true in his situation, possibly what actually *was* true. It is interesting that, although he emphasised the breach created by the *birkat ha-minim*, Martyn argued that "Yet the Conversation Continues" between church and synagogue.[74]

But to observe that "the Jews" are shown in both good and bad light is (from a linguistic perspective) to explore the *connotations* of the word, not its *sense* or *reference*. What components of meaning actually give body to this term? This brings us to the last (and best)

---

70 Thyen "Heil" 177. The German phrases are "verzweifelte Schärfe" and "enttäuschte Liebe".

71 Others who point to this dividedness both towards and among the Jews include Vouga *Cadre* 70f; Rebell *Gemeinde* 100f; Onuki "Analyse" 190; Wiefel "Scheidung" 220-224; Painter *Quest* 101; Culpepper "Jews" 280; Gryglewicz "Pharisäer" 150-152; Hahn "Juden"; Hickling "Judaism"; Townsend "Jews" 79-81; Wengst *Gemeinde* 45-47. Some of these — Hickling, Townsend — find in this ambivalence evidence of different sources or stages of development behind the text.

72 Ashton *Understanding* 131, quoting Thyen "Heil" 163

73 For a convincing defence of this view, cf Pryor "1:11".

74 This is one of his chapter-titles (*History & Theology2* 90-100).

option:

2.4.6 The Jews as 'the religious of Judea'

I believe that the most convincing proposal is essentially that now defended by Ashton in his *Understanding*, abandoning his previous commitment to the 'Jews as Judeans' view. This suggestion was first proposed in modern times by Wilhelm Lütgert in 1914, then reinforced by Karl Bornhäuser in 1928.[75] Bultmann speaks warmly of Lütgert's view and unites it with his own.[76] In 1953 Jacob Jocz affirmed it and maintained that it was the view of a majority of *Jewish* scholars at that time.[77] More recently it has been supported, with different nuances, by Blank, Reim, Meeks and Freyne.[78]

The view, in essence, is that "the Jews" with whom Jesus clashes are a *party within Judaism*, the supremely religious, those whom Bornhäuser calls the "Torafanatiker" ("fanatics for the law"),[79] Blank "die Jerusalemer Kultgemeinde" ("the Temple-party in Jerusalem") and Morton Smith the "Yahweh-alone party":[80] they are the sticklers for the law, essentially the *Pharisees* in the period before 70, who sought to maintain Temple purity in the home, and the *sages of Yavneh* and their followers in the period after 70, who dropped the title "Pharisees" and sought to reinforce the same piety, as the authentic form of Judaism but now deprived of the Temple cult.[81]

The evidence for this may be summarised as follows:

(1) The dispute in John is clearly a *religious* one, centering on the proper observance of the law and of the festivals. Even within the Gospel "the Jews" are distinguished from others who are technically Jewish, for instance in 7:13 where the Tabernacles crowd does not speak openly about Jesus "for fear of the Jews". This seems to match the distinction between the Pharisees, on the one hand, who are the guardians of orthopraxy and "disciples of Moses" (9:28), and "the crowd" on the other, who have been "deceived" into believing something Scripturally impossible (7:47-52).

---

75   Lütgert "Juden"; Bornhäuser *Missionsschrift* 19-22, 140f

76   Bultmann 87 n. 2

77   Jocz "Juden" 139

78   Blank *Krisis* 246-251; Reim *Hintergrund* 142f; Meeks "Jew" 182; Freyne "Vilifying" 123

79   Bornhäuser *Missionsschrift* 141

80   Smith *Parties* 82-98 argues that a distinction between an exclusivist Yahweh-cult, based in Jerusalem, and a syncretistic Yahweh-cult, found in many forms in the diaspora, typifies the whole period from the Assyrian deportation of the northern kingdom in the 8th century BC to the establishment of rabbinic Judaism in post-New Testament times.

81   For this understanding of the development, cf Neusner "Destruction" 89-93

(2) This distinction also fits what we know of Judaism in the period. To anticipate the conclusion of chapter 3 it seems clear that first century Judaism was highly diverse, and that the rabbinic orthodoxy which eventually came to represent authentic Judaism was only one of several forms in which Jewish faith found expression. Diaspora Jews generally would have recognised the intense, Torah- and Temple-centred piety of Judean Pharisaism as something distinct within this overall spectrum. This is not to say that such piety was not found in the diaspora: Paul came of a diaspora Pharisee family (Phil 3:5). But wherever such piety was found, it was special and distinct, and especially associated with Judea.

(3) This view also fits the evidence for the basic 'sense' of Ἰουδαῖος. Josephus uses it equally in a geographical or a religious sense, to mean either "Judean" or "Jew" — the latter applicable to any of Jewish descent, whether in Judea or the diaspora. Scholars have long recognised that οἱ Ἰουδαῖοι was the name used among Gentiles, or by Jews in contact with Gentiles, while "Israel" was an internal self-designation especially among Palestinian Jews.[82]

J. Plescia offers a reflection which supports the contention that that this double force of Ἰουδαῖος — both geographical and religious — was a permanent feature of its currency in the wider world. From a background in Roman jurisprudence he suggests that the reason why the Jews were allowed to observe their *religio* not just in Judea but throughout the Empire was because theirs "was the *religio* of a recognised political unit". Correspondingly, as soon as Christianity became distinct from Judaism it "became a *religio* without a political basis, hence a *superstitio* under political suspicion".[83]

However, though it could be used to mean 'the religion of Judea' wherever practised, there is some evidence that Ἰουδαῖος also connoted the *special* religious commitment associated with Judean Jewry in particular. Ashton summarises evidence from Josephus to this effect.[84] It may also be seen in inter-testamental usage: Bornhäuser cites Daniel 1:3-8 and Susanna 56f to illustrate this point.[85] The latter is particularly interesting, in that (a) the lecherous elders are said to have behaved ὡς Σιδῶνος καὶ οὐχ ὡς Ἰουδα (56 — "as if they belonged to Sidon and not to Judea"), and (b) a distinction is made between "the daughters of *Israel*" who in the past gave in to their advances, and the "daughter of *Judea*" who has now resisted

---

82   Kuhn *TDNT* 3:360f; Painter "Christ" 359; Ashton *Understanding* 153
83   Plescia "Persecution" 123
84   *Understanding* 153f
85   *Missionsschrift* 19-21

them (57).

In 1 Thess 2:14-16 Paul clearly uses Ἰουδαῖοι to mean "the especially religious in Judea". And in an interesting passage in his *Dialogue,* Justin lists some of the Jewish sects known to him, and remarks that, although they all claim to be Ἰουδαίους καὶ τέκνα Ἀβραάμ ("Jews and children of Abraham"), yet they deserve the name "Jew" as little as Christians who deny the resurrection deserve to be called "Christian". This passage attests both the *general* usage, referring broadly to all who identify with 'the religion of Judea', and the *particular,* applied to the ὀρθογνώμονες ("orthodox") as distinct from the adherents of "sects".[86]

Along these lines Robert Murray has suggested that there were basically two meanings of "Jewish" in the late second-temple period: (1) Jewish "in the proper sense, that is, accepting the Jerusalem establishment's terms of reference", and (2) as denoting all those who were out of fellowship with the Jerusalem establishment.[87] The linguistic terminology here is loose but the distinction may be helpful.

2.4.7 Conclusion

So all in all it seems right to offer the following socio-semantic analysis of Ἰουδαῖοι in John, following the three questions with which we began this section:

(1) The *primary sense* of the term denotes those who identify themselves as Jews and adhere to the religion of Judea, whether living in Judea or not.

(2a) In an important *derived reference* the term frequently designates adherents of the particularly strict, Torah- and Temple-centred religion found especially (but not exclusively) in Judea and Jerusalem. In this sense it is not a synonym for Φαρισαῖοι ("Pharisees"). Rather, the Φαρισαῖοι form the core and leading group within the Ἰουδαῖοι.[88] The prominent use of the expression "Pharisees" in John does not reflect contemporary usage, but the influence of historical tradition: for the Yavneh sages seem to have avoided this title. But readers would naturally have twinned the narrative's "Pharisees" and "Jews" with their post-70 heirs, namely the Yavneh sages and the movement they led. And thus the message of Jesus is brought into dialogue with those intensely religious Judean Jews who reasserted Torah as their response to the loss of the

---

86 Justin *Dial.* 80:4-5
87 Murray "Disaffected" 265
88 So Lütgert "Juden" 149, Bornhäuser *Missionsschrift* 23, 140f

Temple.

(2b) There also seems to be a *derived metaphorical reference* in which "the Jews" stand for "the world". This is signalled in the Prologue, in the parallel between "the world" and "his own" in 1:10f; it is then developed in 3:16-21, where the Nicodemus dialogue leads into a statement about the universal relevance of the gift of the Son, even though he is rejected by "people" who love darkness more than light (3:19) — although we have only been introduced so far to *Jews* rejecting Jesus.[89] Several scholars have pointed out the way in which "the world" seems to take the place of "the Jews" in the farewell discourses.[90] I believe that this representative function of "the Jews" has been greatly overplayed by Bultmann and his heirs, but it is clearly there.

(3) Within the narrative it falls to the lot of these Ἰουδαῖοι to be the prime movers against Jesus, and so the word acquires a pejorative *connotation* as the narrative proceeds. This is particularly clear in the passion narrative. However this connotation never supplants the word's basic sense (it never comes to *mean* "unbelievers"), and only in the later stages of the narrative are examples found in which Ἰουδαῖοι clearly contributes a pejorative force *to* its co-text, rather than merely deriving it *from* it (e.g. 19:7, 38).[91]

The precise force of the word needs to be judged on each occurrence, but I believe that this analysis enables us to 'hear' the expression with first-century ears. Most interestingly, it turns out that "the Jews" are those who would have been most directly affected by the destruction of the Temple, and also those most concerned with the law and 'midrashic discussion': so the 'points of sensitivity' we have identified begin to shape themselves into a coherent picture.

2.5 20:31 and the question of purpose

In our search for 'points of sensitivity' within the text we have not yet touched on what might be considered the obvious starting-point, namely the statement of purpose in 20:30f. Whatever their meaning,

---

89   Suggit "Nicodemus" 94 sees Nicodemus as representative of mankind, and not just of the Jews.

90   E.g. Onuki *Gemeinde* 34-37

91   Leistner *Antijudaismus* 143-5 rightly urges that the extent of the johannine polemic against "the Jews" should not be over-estimated. Also Carson "Purpose" 648

these two verses must signal something of vital import to the evangelist and of great significance for the reading experience. At this point, if not before, readers realise what response is expected of them. In the next three sections we will consider three points which all relate to the purpose (or rather, the *function*) of the Gospel: the force of *the twinned purpose-clauses* in 20:31 (2.5), the role of *the signs* whose importance is underlined in 20:30 (2.6), and *the johannine language and style of argumentation* (2.7).

20:30f is one of only two occasions on which the narrator directly addresses the narratee. On the other occasion, 19:35, the address also relates to the purpose of writing, ἵνα καὶ ὑμεῖς πιστεύ[σ]ητε ("so that you too may believe"). Both in 20:31 and in 19:35 we encounter a textual uncertainty about the tense of the verb — so that, formally, the purpose of the Gospel could either be to prolong an already existing faith (present tense), or to prompt an as yet non-existent faith (aorist).

But in fact this distinction probably lays too much weight on the respective force of the present and aorist subjective. That there is a distinction is amply illustrated by 10:38, ἵνα γνῶτε καὶ γινώσκητε ("so that you may know (aorist) and know (present)"). But in 6:29, as Carson notes, the present subjunctive (ἵνα πιστεύητε, "so that you may believe") is used to cover both *initial* and *continuing* faith.[92]

The above points are made by many commentators, but surprisingly few remark on the relevance of the relationship between the two purpose-clauses for the interpretation of this verse. Generally speaking, the second is assumed to add nothing to the first beyond a mention of the *result* of faith — life. However a good case can be made, I believe, for the distinction proposed by Martin Warner:

> Not all who 'believe' in his name have 'life' in his name, but there is an internal relation between a certain sort of belief and a certain form of 'life'.[93]

As we shall see, the Gospel has sensitised us to the possibility that faith may not lead to life. Scholars (including Warner) have tended to point to "sorts" or "stages" of faith in John, and to use expressions like "full faith" to describe the final stage which John wishes his readers to reach.[94] But in an important, yet finally wrong-headed essay Yu Ibuki has challenged this view.[95] He argues that 2:23-25

---

92   Carson "Purpose" 640. The text is uncertain in 6:29 also! But there the better reading seems clearly to be present subjunctive.

93   Warner "Persuasion" 154

94   E.g. Brown 1:530f; Schnackenburg 1:570f; Culpepper "Theology" 426f

makes it clear from the start that *all faith may be inadequate,* particularly faith which is a response to the signs.[96] Following this start, we must suspect all faith, and ask in each case whether it is genuine or not:

> There are fundamentally no different kinds of faith, but either faith or unbelief — each fully expressed. John nowhere indicates a progression of stages of faith.[97]

Ibuki is so committed to a Bultmannian rejection of all *legitimation* for faith, and of every hint that faith may be a human work, that he ends up almost denying the possibility of *genuine* faith. He certainly denies the possibility of ever being *sure* that faith is genuine.[98] But this is to take a good idea much too far. 20:31 contains an assurance that true faith may be a conscious experience. However, Ibuki is probably right to reject the idea of 'stages of faith' as a description of John's presentation. What we find, rather, is that faith is *consistently associated with other things by which it must be supplemented if it is to lead to life.* Faith *on its own* carries no automatic promise of life at all.

So Nicodemus, for instance, representing the group of believers referred to in 2:23-25,[99] is told that he must be born again if he is to see the kingdom (3:3). It is very easy to read 3:14-16 through Pauline spectacles, and thus to miss the distinctive johannine understanding of faith there. Nicodemus and his contemporaries, for all their faith that Jesus is "from God" (3:2), are accused of not believing his testimony (3:11-12).[100] Against this background, 3:14-16 functions as a *warning,* as much as a promise. Believers must "exalt the Son of Man", so that their faith in him may issue in eternal life (14f: it seems right to give ὑψωθῆναι ("lift up") in 14 the same double meaning as in 8:28). This 'exaltation' is then described in 16a: rather than acknowledge him just as a "teacher from God", he must be seen as God's μονογενής ("one and only son") given by him to the world,

---

95   Ibuki "Viele"

96   "Viele" 133f

97   "Viele" 142f, following Louise Schottroff

98   In this he goes much further than Bultmann, who certainly allows for stages of faith, and allows it to be "true" — if incomplete — at every stage (e.g. 207f: he traces three stages in the faith of the royal official).

99   So Meeks "Man From Heaven" 55. Nicodemus is introduced as ἄνθρωπος ("a man", 3:1) in continuity with the ἄνθρωπος of 2:25.

100   For the basic semantic equivalence of "believing" and "receiving", see Schnackenburg 1:563f.

and only *such* believers will not perish but have eternal life. *Implicit in 16b is the possibility that believers may "perish".*

This does not mean that Nicodemus' faith is viewed negatively. On the contrary, "the one who believes in him is not condemned" (3:18a) — that is, faith in Jesus does not constitute a sin, while failure to believe in him most certainly does (18b). Nicodemus falls into the category of those who come to the light, and who thus reveal the basically 'toward-God' orientation of their lives (3:21). But this does not (yet) mean the possession of eternal life![101]

The faith that means eternal life is faith that takes the step Nicodemus has not yet taken — it "hears my word and believes him who sent me" (5:24). Implicit in the faith of 5:24 is a *discipleship* which is prepared to run the gauntlet of the opposition which Jesus' word has just provoked (5:17f). So, in its narrative context, it is more than just intellectual assent.[102]

Faith *even of the fullest kind* is immediately put to the test. Peter's confession in 6:69 means a commitment to discipleship in contrast to those who leave Jesus at that point, and is immediately challenged with the prediction that one of the twelve will betray Jesus (6:70). Martha's confession in 11:27 is immediately tested before Lazarus' tomb: will she act on her faith and have the stone removed? Her hesitation in 11:39 is countered by Jesus' "Did I not say to you that *if you believe* you will see the glory of God?" (11:40). She has already believed, as her confession shows; but the confession alone is not enough. In fact, the faith expressed in her confession is more a *potential* than a *goal*, for she still faces the challenge to "believe" and open the tomb.[103]

This distinction between faith and discipleship is vital for the exegesis of 8:31ff, as we shall see. The believing Jews of 8:31 face the same challenge as Martha, to turn their faith into discipleship (8:32).

---

101 So Godet 2:76f ("Every truly upright man rejoices to come into close contact with Christ the living embodiment of holiness"); contra Bultmann 158-60, Haenchen 205. That Nicodemus is still in mind in 3:21 is confirmed by the observation made by e.g. Rebell *Gemeinde* 145, that 3:21 forms a clear *inclusio* with the beginning of the dialogue in 3:2.

102 I believe that Schnackenburg is right in his contention that the *essence* of johannine faith is "rational assent" (1:562). But rational assent alone is never enough.

103 Schnackenburg underlines the *testing* of faith as an important feature of John's presentation (1:572). However he relates the testing of faith to its progression through various stages to "the full Messianic and Christological confession" which is "real faith" (571), without drawing out this distinction between faith and *discipleship*, which seems to be much more important for John than that between the various levels of conviction about Jesus.

And *this is precisely the distinction expressed so succinctly in the two purpose-clauses of 20:31.* The repetition of πιστεύοντες ("believing") in the second expresses the sequence. To believe "that Jesus is the Christ ..." is only the first step; that those who believe should "have life" is a second step, closely linked to the first, but not taken by all, as the Jews of 8:31ff so clearly illustrate. This 'potential' quality about all faith in John is signalled in the Prologue, where those who believe are given "power to become" children of God (1:12): the status is not conferred automatically or immediately on all believers.

If faith is just a starting-point, then *the view that 20:31 expresses an evangelistic aim for the Gospel is strengthened.* If the Gospel were aimed simply at reinforcing the faith of a Christian community, we would expect the substance just of the second purpose-clause to be expressed here — which is what we find in the parallel statement of purpose in 1 John 5:13.[104] In the light of the rest of the Gospel, we can with some confidence make the following statements, related in turn to the two purpose-clauses:

(1) The Gospel is aimed at those who have not yet reached the conviction expressed by Martha (11:27) or Thomas (20:28). These could be people like Nicodemus and the Jews of 2:23-25, who conclude from the signs that Jesus is "a teacher from God", or the Jews of 7:12 and 7:40f, who are divided and confused. Or they could be people with a negative evaluation of Jesus. For all such, the aim of the Gospel is to create the conviction that "Jesus is the Christ, the Son of God".

(2) Because mere intellectual conviction is not life-giving, the Gospel seeks to move all believers, whatever their conviction, to the kind of discipleship which will give life. The nature of this discipleship has become clear in the course of the Gospel, most particularly in the farewell discourses, where *union with the Christ* is set at the heart of it. "Because I live, you will live also ... you in me, I in you" (14:19f) — but this union with Jesus means that his disciples must expect to be treated like him, facing hatred and persecution (esp. 15:18-16:4).

We will find that this conclusion is of very considerable significance for our study, although at first sight it causes difficulties for the interpretation of 8:31-59. For, as we noted in the Introduction, the apparent hostility towards "the Jews" in this passage is frequently adduced as evidence to counter the view that the Fourth Gospel was a missionary tract for Jews.[105] We will face this difficulty in due

---

104 "I have written these things to you, so that you may know that you have eternal life, you who believe in the name of the Son of God."

course. For the moment we note simply that this appears to be the most natural interpretation of the Gospel's own summary of its purpose.[106]

2.6 The role of the signs

We do not need the statement in 20:30f to suggest to us that the signs are a 'point of sensitivity'. A structural study of the Gospel quickly reveals their pivotal importance. So 20:30f, when it comes, gives the signs a status equivalent to their prominence in the narrative.

But *why* is such emphasis laid on them? Here we have an example of designed literary prominence which does not seem related, at first glance, to any obvious external factors. However a way forward would be to continue the discussion of the last section, and to ask after the *evidential value* of the signs as contributory to the persuasive power of the Gospel. Can we envisage the signs making the christological claim of the Gospel more credible to Jewish readers? This discussion will be important as background to our study of 8:31-59.

20:30f certainly ascribes evidential value to the signs. But several scholars have argued that these verses reflect the theology of the "Signs Gospel", rather than that of the Gospel in its final form. This is argued (a) because the phrase "many other signs" (30) does not seem to relate to the immediate context, (b) because the ταῦτα ("these") of 20:31a refers most naturally to the signs just mentioned, rather than to the content of the whole Gospel, and (c) because there are places in the Gospel where faith based on signs seems to be regarded as inadequate (2:23-25, 4:48), and furthermore places where

---

105 So e.g. Nicol *Semeia* 143; Ashton *Understanding* 105; Painter *Quest* 103

106 That the Gospel has a missionary purpose is held by Bornhäuser *Missionsschrift*, Moule "Intention" 103f, Robinson "Destination", Dodd *Interpretation* 9, Van Unnik "Purpose", Freed "Converts", Trites *Witness* 78, Carson "Purpose", and Wind "Destination" 48. Apart from Dodd, most of these scholars maintain that the Gospel was directed at Jews (Freed: also at Samaritans; Trites does not specify). Others ascribe an evangelistic intent either to parts of the Gospel (Reim — ch 9; Painter — ch 5) or to some of the proposed earlier forms of the Gospel material (Fortna, Nicol, Smith), while others yet again allow that it may have had a dual purpose, evangelism and the strengthening of believers (Brown, Thyen, Beasley-Murray, Rebell, Domeris).

But the majority interpret 20:31 as applying just to Christians: as Vouga puts it, in an expression much quoted by others (but no less obscure for its popularity), John's purpose is "to make believers become Christians" (*Cadre* 35).

signs are presented as insufficient to create faith (6:26, 11:47, 12:37).

The third point is the most important, and the most germane to our purpose. This discrepancy has been taken to indicate that the evangelist wanted to dissuade his community from over-dependence on the miraculous, a dependence which had been fostered in earlier stages of their history by the use of a written collection of signs as an evangelistic tool. In the more nuanced theology of the final Gospel, it is argued, faith based just on the *word* of Jesus is commended.[107]

However this view may be challenged. Why should the evangelist give such prominence to the signs, if he is fundamentally uneasy about dependence on them? Becker offers the highly unlikely theory that he emphasised the signs in order deliberately to create an *obstacle* to faith — so that, if faith managed to overcome dependence on the signs and rest solely on the word of Jesus, it would be all the stronger.[108] But the text seems much more straightforward than this, and the time is ripe, I believe, for a reassessment of the texts which are held to express opposition to signs-faith.

In 6:26 (cf 6:36) and in 12:37 the culpability of unbelievers is highlighted by the fact that so many signs have been performed before them. They *should* have believed when they saw the signs, but did not. Here the evidential value of the signs is not questioned — far from it. 2:11 gives the 'natural' progression: in the provision of the wine "Jesus manifested his glory, and his disciples believed in him".[109] In the first century world, both Jewish and Gentile, miraculous happenings were assumed to be manifestations of divine power. Within Judaism this is illustrated by the examples of Honi the Circle-Drawer and Hanina ben Dosa, the latter in all likelihood a contemporary of Jesus. In their cases, there was no difficulty in recognising the power they exercised: "their supernatural powers were attributed to their immediate relation to God".[110] Against this background, some of the johannine texts relating to Jesus' signs take

---

107 This is basically the view of Martyn, Becker, Fortna, Nicol and D.M. Smith — with the variations mentioned below.

108 Becker, "Wunder"

109 Barrett 193 points out how 2:11 anticipates 20:30f.

110 G. Vermes, *Jesus the Jew* (London; Collins, 1973), 79. Vermes describes these two figures on pp 69-80. For the Gentile world, see H.C. Kee, *Medicine, Miracle and Magic in New Testament Times* (Cambridge; CUP, 1986), especially pp 88-94 where he compares John and Plutarch. He summarises: "Whether in a Jewish sectarian setting or in a shrine of a Hellenistic god, miracle is portrayed in the epoch of our study as a response to human petitions and human need. The divine is directly disclosed in human experience ..." (93).

on an almost indignant quality: "If this man were not from God, he could do nothing!" (9:33).

Hanina ben Dosa was regarded by later Rabbis as the last of the "men of deed".[111] The Rabbis developed a suspicion of the evidential value of the miraculous, as is strikingly illustrated by the story of the excommunication of R. Eliezer ben Hyrkanus. The testimony of both miraculous signs and a *bath qol* in support of Eliezer was rejected by his fellow-Rabbis.[112] W.D. Davies has no doubt "that part of the reason for the emphatic rejection of these two media of revelation [miracles and the *bath qol*] was the weight placed upon them in Christianity."[113] It seems likely that the beginnings of this suspicion are traceable behind the Fourth Gospel: both miracles and a *bath qol* appear in John 12 (28-30, 37), where both are described as rejected by "the Jews".

In the face of this *new* suspicion, so unusual in the ancient world, the response of the Fourth Gospel is to reaffirm the evidential value of the signs. In 10:38 and 14:11 Jesus points first "the Jews" and then his disciples *away* from his word *to* the evidence of his "works": "believe me, that I am in the Father, and the Father in me: or else, believe because of the works themselves" (14:11) — the reverse of that which we are led to expect. 10:38 expresses their evidential force with a "so that", as in 20:30f. And in 15:24 — very strikingly — the wilful rejection of the evidence of Jesus' "works" is treated as the supreme and ultimate sin.

4:48 seems out of place within this overall affirmation of the signs. With his "unless you see signs and wonders, you will not believe", Jesus appears to criticise the royal official — and all like him — for the dependence of their faith on the signs. Brown's judgment is typical of many: "Such a statement reflects the johannine distrust of the marvelous element in the miracle". Brown is prepared to allow that "such inadequate believers have taken one step on the road to salvation", but only a very preliminary one.[114] Bultmann goes further:

> For the Evangelist the very appearance of Jesus means that men are faced with the challenge to believe in him as the Revealer; and for him it is a misunderstanding if 'faith' expects from Jesus a miraculous liberation from physical distress.[115]

---

111 *m. Sot.* 9:15, quoted by Vermes *op, cit.* 79. He supports the view that "deed" in this context refers to miracle. Cf also Vermes "Hanina" 187f.

112 *b. B. Mes.* 59a

113 Davies *Setting* 285

114 Brown 1:528

Bultmann feels that the story pictures the movement of the man from false faith to "faith proper" in v. 53 — but Ibuki denies even this. He maintains that the whole thrust of the story is to attack signs-faith, so that the faith of the "royal official" in v. 53 is "the faith which is criticised".[116] One wonders why Jesus performed the miracle at all!

I believe that 4:48 has been misunderstood. Both Bultmann and Ibuki note that it seems out of place:

> [It] makes no sense after v. 47, since the βασιλικός ["royal official"] has in no way asked for a miracle as a proof of Jesus' authority. On the contrary his request proves his faith, and so his reply (v. 49) can only be to repeat his request, which makes it hard to see why this should now persuade Jesus to change his mind.[117]

But the saying fits beautifully if it is heard as expressing *Jesus'* reason for *acceding* to the man's request, rather than *the man's* reason for *asking*. Jesus' motivation in responding positively to the man's request is different from his in making it. Whereas the goal for the father is his son's health, Jesus has a greater goal in view: "signs and wonders" are intended to produce *faith.*

The father is thus set a test. He has to take on board Jesus' goal as well as his own. Twice he asks Jesus to "come down" (47, 49), but instead he has to leave alone, taking just a word of Jesus with him. As with Martha and the opening of Lazarus' tomb, the faith he already has is immediately stretched, and he risks the life of his son by leaving without the healer. "The man believed ..." (50): this shows that *Jesus'* goal is being achieved, as well as the man's, and in 4:53 we see Jesus' purpose amply vindicated.[118]

Far from playing down the role of the signs in creating faith, therefore, this story could hardly emphasise it more. Bultmann's and Ibuki's approach depends on v. 48 being ultimately *untrue:* But within the theology of the Fourth Gospel it is not untrue. Signs are indeed an essential prerequisite for true faith — and this is precisely what 20:30f expresses as the strategy for the whole Gospel, and the reason for the prominence of the signs within its structure. What the

---

115 Bultmann 207

116 Ibuki "Viele" 155

117 Bultmann 205

118 The only other scholar — so far as I am aware — who does not find a denigration of signs-faith in 4:48 is Thompson *Humanity* 73.

intratextual characters *saw*, the readers may now *hear*, as a result of the *writing*, the truth of which rests on the *testimony* of those who saw (1:14, 2:11, 19:35, 21:24).

Nicol argued that the signs-source was compiled as a missionary tract for Jews. D. Moody Smith rightly criticised this view on the ground that miracle-stories alone "could scarcely set aside the objections or questions raised by the fact of Jesus' crucifixion",[119] and so supported Fortna in his view that the "Signs Gospel" was a combination of a signs-collection and a passion narrative, with the latter added precisely in order to show, using Old Testament *testimonia* (proof-texts), "that the death of Jesus took place according to God's will".[120]

But we might similarly criticise Smith on the ground that miracle-stories alone, without accompanying interpretation, would not convince Jews that Jesus was the Messiah. Nobody apparently concluded that Hanina ben Dosa was the Messiah, solely on the ground of his miraculous powers: simply that he lived close to God. John Painter has pointed out how essential is the interpretation of the sign in John 5, and argues that the story *and its accompanying dialogue* were originally used to persuade Jews that Jesus was the Christ.[121] Apart from the dialogue, the 'word' of the sign remains mute and unclear: so the interpretation avoids the other things on which Jews might have fastened (such as the interesting question about the legal status of the land over which the bed was carried: public or private?), and focuses on the unity between Jesus and his Father. The same point could be made about each sign.

The effect of this argument is progressively to extend the range of the material which has to be included before we arrive at a document which would suffice to convince Jews that "Jesus is the Christ, the Son of God". Craig Evans enthusiastically endorses Smith's argument about the necessity of a passion narrative, and uses it as the basis of a study of the Old Testament quotations in the second half of the Gospel He convincingly argues that John's purpose was

> to prove ... that the disgrace of the crucifixion, a controversial item in any dialogue with Jews, was Jesus' very purpose and work, and indeed, was his hour of glorification.[122]

119 Smith "Setting" 86
120 Smith "Setting" 88
121 Painter "John 5"
122 Evans "Servant" 228.

Evans seems to forget that Smith actually made this point about the *Signs Gospel*, not about the Gospel we now have. Yet what is to stop us from following Evans' lead, and widening the circle until 20:30f describes the purpose of the whole present Gospel — to convince Jews that Jesus is the Christ?

Actually, of course, our project is less than this: I want to leave aside speculations about *purpose*, and simply argue that the Gospel in its present form would have *functioned* in this way.

In view of the integration of signs and discourses in the Gospel, "these" in 20:31a is best understood as referring ambiguously both to the signs and to the broad content of the Gospel.[123] We see this integration also in ch. 8, where the signs are not explicitly mentioned, and yet they pervade the discussion. The witness of the Father on Jesus' behalf (8:18) has previously been related to the "works" which the Father has granted him to perform (5:36f). Similarly the saying in 5:19, "the Son can do nothing from himself, but only what he sees the Father doing", which connotes the miracle just performed, is picked up in 8:28, with the "work" interpreted as Jesus' *speech:* "I do nothing from myself, but I speak the things that the Father has taught me". The faith of "the Jews" in 8:30 is hardly explicable except in the overall narrative context, in which Jesus' *word* has been integrated with his *work*. The man who performs unique works (9:32) also utters unique speech (7:46).[124]

But again, if this is correct, we are faced with the question: how does 8:31-59 fit coherently into an evangelistic strategy embracing the whole Gospel? Or is the strategy incoherent? This question must wait its time, but some preliminary orientation may be gained by considering the final topic in our search for 'points of sensitivity':

2.7 Language and style of argumentation

In this section we pick up two of the features of the Gospel identified by Dunn as 'points of sensitivity'. The *controversial style* is one of the most obvious features of the presentation of Jesus' public ministry. As the hostility grows, so the exchanges become more intense. Jesus responds to the first sign of murderous opposition (5:18) with a defiant speech in which he claims to act and speak for God, adducing witness to 'prove' his claim, and tells his learned

---

123 So Brown 2:1056

124 Bornhäuser *Missionsschrift* 16-19 has no doubt: the signs in John are the authenticating signs of the Messiah. So also Thompson *Humanity* 53-86.

opponents, for whom Torah is a way of life, that they do not have God's word in them (5:38). This foreshadows John 7-8, where we do not have a monologue from Jesus but debating exchanges involving the expression of conflicting opinions and doubt about Jesus, as well as the growing rejection which climaxes with the attempt to stone him in 8:59.

How should we interpret this feature of the Gospel? Once again, the need for the *right interpretative background* is the most pressing. Interaction with scholarly discussion will one again help us chart our course.

Numerous scholars maintain that the Gospel's argumentative style is inconsistent with an evangelistic purpose. We may discern three interlocking lines of thought:

(1) Some suggest that the johannine use of *misunderstanding and irony* requires a Christian readership. The leading voice here is that of Francois Vouga.[125] His argument is that irony functions by engaging the reader's sympathies for one side or other of a debate in which the pretensions and misunderstandings of one side are being shown up. In the case of John, the *a priori* sympathies of the reader must be on Jesus' side, for else *Jesus* would be shown up as the object of ridicule. The Gospel must therefore be aimed at Christians, who are invited to enjoy a sense of superior insight over against "the Jews". This view of irony strongly shapes Vouga's approach to ch. 8, which "is nothing but a long misunderstanding".[126]

(2) Discernible also in Vouga's treatment is another line of thought, which owes its origin to Bultmann. The johannine use of irony and misunderstanding (between which Vouga scarcely distinguishes) "derives from christology":[127] it is a writing style appropriate in connection with a figure who is not "of this world", who cannot therefore be grasped by human language and thought-forms, but may only apprehended when all human certainties are abandoned. This abandonment, Vouga suggests, is the challenge laid before "the Jews" in 8:31ff.

The legacy of Bultmann is clear here. The world takes offence at Jesus because

> the Revealer appears as a man whose claim to be the Son of God is one which he cannot, indeed, must not, prove to the world. For the Revelation is judgment upon the world ... [So] the world inevitably

---

125 Vouga *Cadre* 34f; cf Rebell *Gemeinde* 129; Wengst *Gemeinde* 34-36
126 *Cadre* 33
127 *Cadre* 35

misunderstands the words and deeds of the Revealer, or they remain a riddle for it (10:6; 16:25, 29), even though Jesus has said everything openly all along (18:20).[128]

So the argumentation in the Fourth Gospel *must* run within its own, closed circle, presupposing the point at issue (that Jesus is the Son of God). If Jesus at any point appears to found his claim on an external authority — such as the Old Testament — then the use of such an argument must be regarded as satirical, and not genuine.[129]

We find the continuing legacy of this viewpoint in the work, for example, of Blank (the Old Testament can speak only to Christians),[130] Dahl (John makes no attempt to convince Jews of Jesus' messiahship),[131] Lona (there is a complete breakdown of the linguistic 'code' between Jesus and "the Jews"),[132] and Rebell (the reader must become trapped in a "logical cul-de-sac" before he can be reborn into the truth).[133]

(3) The view that John's argumentation runs within a closed Christian circle has recently been reinforced by sociological and historical considerations foreign to Bultmann's approach. The work of Herbert Leroy was pioneering here: he emphasised the "Sondersprache" ("special language") of the johannine community, which he found particularly expressed in the eleven 'riddles' upon which he focused his study (four of them in 8:31-59). These riddles involved the investing of ordinary language with special, technical meanings

---

128 Bultmann *Theology* 2:46

129 Bultmann for instance comments on Jesus' appeal to the law about two witnesses in 8:17f that it is "not an argument at all but an expression of scorn ... God's revelation does not have to answer for itself before men ... for otherwise the rule about two witnesses would have to be applied, and *that is sheerly absurd*" (Bultmann 282, my emph.). But maybe the *petitio principii* here is Bultmann's, not John's!

   Whitacre *Polemic* 36 makes the same point about 8:17f. Jesus' argument "only makes sense to one who appreciates Jesus' identity".

130 Blank *Krisis* 210f

131 Dahl "History" 130; so also Martyn *History & Theology2* e.g. 123: the issue of Jesus' messiahship may not be a matter of "midrashic discussion"; and cf the extraordinary view of Wengst *Gemeinde* 101: John actually *accepts* the Jewish objections to Jesus' messiahship with which he interacts, and makes no attempt to counter them, because his conviction about Jesus stands aloof and alone. Wengst does not consider why the evangelist should include sharply expressed objections to Jesus' messiahship when he has no concern to reply to them.

132 Lona *Johannes 8* e.g. 393

133 Rebell *Gemeinde* 163 (German: "logische Auswegslosigkeit"); cf 83, 112, 162. He argues "that johannine thought-processes move in a closed circle of understanding, which does not open itself up for outsiders" (112).

comprehensible only within the circle of the initiated, such as Jesus' talk about "departing" which is given a secret, Christian reference ("return to heaven").

This served to reinforce the social distinctness of the johannine community over against the synagogue, because "the Jews" fail completely to hear the deeper meaning, and so are "thoroughly defamed, and made to appear as 'the idiots'". The johannine reader, on the other hand, discovers "his own superiority over the Jews", because he sees the meaning they have missed.[134] This is essentially the view also of Meeks in his "Man From Heaven" (although he focuses on different aspects of johannine language), and more recently of Bruce Malina.[135]

Reviewing these three lines of interpretation in recent study, it is interesting to note how frequently either Nicodemus or "the Jews" of John 8 are used to illustrate one aspect or another of this overall approach. In these instances particularly, it is held, the fundamental dualism of the Fourth Gospel comes to expression, with "the Jews" unable to understand Jesus because they are "from below", while Jesus is "from above" (8:23). For Meeks, the Nicodemus dialogue is

> a virtual *parody* of a revelation discourse. What is 'revealed' is that Jesus is *incomprehensible*, even to 'the teacher of Israel' ... within the context of Jewish piety. ... The reader without special prior information would be as puzzled as Nicodemus.[136]

In a pattern familiar in later Gnosticism, "the Jews" are *demonised* as the counterpoint to this Christian self-reinforcement.[137]

This new emphasis on the function of the text is welcome and vital. However *there are fundamental misconceptions in these lines of thought.* To a large extent the justification of this assertion will have to await our later exegetical chapters, where I shall argue (a) that the Gospel does indeed seek to justify Jesus' messiahship within con-temporary Jewish terms, (b) that its contentions about Jesus would have been perfectly comprehensible within late first century Judaism, and (c) that the use of irony and polemic is part of an

---

134 E.g. Leroy *Rätsel* 62

135 Malina "Sociolinguistic" argues that johannine language is essentially "anti-language", because the johannine community is an "antisocial group", that is, "a collectivity that is set up within a larger society as a conscious alternative to it" (11). This social opposition is expressed by partially "relexicalising" the language of the wider society (12).

136 Meeks "Man From Heaven" 57, his emph.

137 "Man From Heaven" 67f

effective strategy to persuade *outsiders*. Our growth in knowledge of Judaism in this period seriously undermines the view that John employs a private language comprehensible only within closed Christian circles.

However three general points may be made in advance of the exegesis:

(1) The extent of John's indebtedness to Jewish traditions becomes ever clearer, as we noted above. Meeks is one of those who, in the last twenty-five years, have most significantly advanced our knowledge in this respect. He seeks to argue that John turns Jewish arguments against the Jews — that, in fact, "the Fourth Gospel is most anti-Jewish just at the points it is most Jewish".[138] However the fascinating — and, for this viewpoint, disturbing — observation is that the Fourth Gospel is most Jewish just at the points it is most *Christian*. It is not just the polemic which is informed by engagement with Torah, wisdom and apocalyptic texts and themes, but also the positive presentation of "the Christ", from the Prologue onward.

Thyen comments on

> the manner in which [the Fourth Gospel] is full of subliminal allusions to specifically Jewish traditions, and of motifs adapted from the Targums and midrash, all of which would be comprehensible only to 'insiders'. This makes me think that only a group of Christian Jews could possibly have been the first recipients and bearers of the Gospel.[139]

But once one admits that it is the *Judaism* of the readers, rather than their *Christianity*, which makes the Gospel comprehensible to them, then (a) the 'special Christian language' view has lost its rationale,[140] and (b) we must reckon seriously with the possibility that the "insiders" whom such language addresses are simply "Jews", and not specifically "Christian Jews". Although Thyen maintains that the final form of the Gospel is not evangelistic, he argues that much of the material was developed in a mission context, in which the *content* of Christian faith had to be explained to Jews in a way that would really communicate, and not immediately create rejection before a true hearing was given. Engaging with Bultmann, he suggests that the repetition of the mere *fact* of Jesus' existence may have been enough for internal consumption, but not for external

---

138 Meeks "Jew" 172 — an aphorism quoted by many.
139 Thyen "Heil" 174, my trans.
140 Thyen "Johannes 10" 121 rejects it.

persuasion — and this latter intention provides the interpretative key to much of the Gospel material.[141] In the light of 20:30f, we may ask, Why not to all of it?

(2) Many of these scholars (though not Bultmann) rightly emphasise the necessity of interpreting the Gospel at the level of *hearing*. Lona in particular, one of the first to seek to apply modern linguistic theory to the interpretation of John, distinguishes between two levels on which communication takes place in John 8 — the "intratextual level" (on which Jesus and "the Jews" communicate with each other — or fail to do so), and the "extratextual level" (on which readers interact with the text in their situation).[142]

Unfortunately Lona then devotes hardly any attention to the investigation of the second level. Even if we were to grant his central thesis — that language itself collapses in the dialogue in John 8 — we could not then justify a simple inference from the "intratextual level" to the situation of the readers. It could conceivably be the author's intention to *prevent* precisely such a breakdown of language in the hearers' situation. The text must indeed be interpreted at the point of *hearing*, but the dynamic of its interaction with its first hearers cannot safely be inferred from within the text, but must be reconstructed from outside the text as much as possible.

(3) It is simply wrong to argue that the johannine irony requires a Christian readership. We have already suggested ways in which features of the text could have worked with powerful ironic force on any Jewish reader in the post-70 situation. We will take this process further below, and propose, with Gail O'Day (though our arguments are very different from hers), that John's irony is a literary device intended to *draw the reader into the experience of revelation*.[143] O'Day's is a literary study which leaves historical questions aside and does not seek to identify "the reader" on whom the irony will work. This omission weakens her presentation. Her case about the way irony functions would be strengthened by a fusion of literary with historical impulses, of the kind we are attempting.

---

141 "Heil" 168
142 Lona *Johannes 8* 387
143 O'Day *Revelation* 93-96

2.8 Conclusion

This chapter has attempted to discover within the text itself the 'points of sensitivity' which glow with a quiet light, fuelled by the situation it addresses. We have tried to keep in mind, in general terms, the setting in which most scholars place the Fourth Gospel, Judaism of the late first century. Employing the notion of *hearing* as a hermeneutical key, we have found evidence to suggest that John would have been heard to address the situation faced after the destruction of the Temple in 70 AD, particularly in Judea where the loss of the Temple and its worship were felt most keenly. On this basis we have tentatively suggested that the statement of purpose in 20:30f should be interpreted as giving the Gospel an evangelistic intent, addressed to "Jews", in order to persuade them that Jesus is the Christ who can meet the particular needs of Israel, facing that total loss.

In what follows we proceed to the next stage in our method, moving now outside the text to look more closely at Judaism in this period, and to discover in what precise ways John might be heard to address it. Our findings will form the basis of our exegesis in chapters 5-7 below.

3

The world outside the text: Jews and Judaism after the destruction of the Temple

We now move outside the Gospel to survey the world into which it was written, that of late first-century Judaism. Building on the conclusion of the last chapter — that the Fourth Gospel shows *prima facie* internal indications of addressing the pressing needs of Judaism in the aftermath of the destruction of the Temple — the aim of this chapter is to clarify the points of reference which enabled the text to be heard as *Gospel* in that world. While it is vital to avoid the trap of selectivity,[1] yet we will focus our survey around responses to the destruction of the Temple, which in any case was an 'issue' as prominent in Jewish life in that period as it seems to be within the narrative structure of John.

This is the point at which features of the text not marked with *literary* prominence might assume *semiotic* prominence when read against this background. Louis Martyn 'discovered' ἀποσυνάγωγος ("thrown out of the synagogue") in this way: the word is not marked within the text (see 9:22, 12:42, 16:2), but it gained prominence as he related it to his understanding of the *birkat ha-minim* ('curse on the heretics') introduced into synagogue prayers towards the end of the first century. We will argue against this particular case, but will suggest that the procedure holds good for other features of the Gospel. For instance, the 'theodicy' question raised in John 9, the gnomic use of "freedom" in 8:32, the employment of 'prophet' categories in connection with Jesus, the use of "house" in 8:35 and 14:2, and the references to the devil in connection both with "the Jews" and with Judas (6:70, 8:44, 13:27), all gain semiotic significance when 'heard' in the setting we are proposing.[2] These things take their place alongside the features of the narrative already marked with literary prominence, enabling the Gospel to be *Good News* in the

1   See the criticism of Martyn and others in chapter 1 (esp. 1.2.3).
2   We are concerned with broad background in this chapter, so some of these detailed suggestions will be explored in the later exegetical chapters.

environment of late first-century Judaism.

In this chapter we are able to draw on considerable advances in knowledge made in the last twenty-five years. It used to be maintained that the Pharisaic party, under the leadership first of Yohanan ben Zakkai and then of Gamaliel II, reshaped Judaism through the new academy at Yavneh, and enabled it to come to terms with the loss of the Temple remarkably quickly.[3] But now it is widely recognised that the situation was much more complex and slow-moving. The diversity which had characterised Judaism in the pre-70 period continued to do so after the war, and that it was not until after the Bar Kokba revolt in 132-5 AD that 'rabbinic orthodoxy' became established as the dominant and authentic voice of Judaism.

This change in perspective is due supremely to the work of Jacob Neusner, who argues (for instance) that even though Pharisaism was ultimately "the sole significant force to emerge from the catastrophe of 70", yet its influence in the period 70-135 was "almost certainly ... negligible": "the very fact of the war of 132-5 suggests that others, not Pharisees, held predominance in the life of the Jewish people".[4]

The erosion of the older view has two consequences for the study of our period:

(1) Evidence derived from later rabbinic sources cannot be presumed to reflect conditions widely experienced, nor can the Rabbis be presumed to have wielded the kind of authority they exercised 100 years later. It is no longer possible, for instance, to argue with Wengst that Christians experienced total social ostracism when they were expelled from the synagogue, just on the basis of the rabbinic instructions not to have dealings with *minim* (heretics).[5] Even if these instructions are authentic, and even if the *minim* in mind were really Jewish Christians, at the very most this evidence shows that *some* Rabbis thought that this *ought* to happen, not that it actually did. The very fact that they gave such instructions could be taken to imply that it was *not* happening, and that (in their view) there was

3   See for instance Isaiah Gafni "The Historical Background", *Stone* 27-31.
4   Neusner "Destruction" 93
5   Wengst *Gemeinde* 59: he refers to *t. Hul.* 2:20 (which forbids selling to *minim*, having any business or educational relationships with them, and going to them for healing: cf *b. Abod. Zar.* 27b), *t. Sabb.* 13:5 (Rabbi Tarfon's famous saying about fleeing rather into the house of an idolater than the house of a *min* — "for idolaters do not know God and deny him, but these [*minim*] know him and deny him"), and the encouragement in *t. B. Mes.* 2:33 actually to push *minim* into ditches (rather than just leaving them there, the treatment prescribed for other law-breakers). So also Gryglewicz "Pharisäer" 156f

all too much social contact with Christians. The case that Martyn makes about the *birkat ha-minim* suffers the same fate, as we shall see.

(2) Alongside the rabbinic literature must be set the wide range of other writings which give evidence for our period. Many scholars who seek to illumine the New Testament against a 'Jewish' background still turn before all else to the rabbis for illumination, and John is no exception. This is an honourable tradition, looking to Strack and Billerbeck, to Odeberg, Schlatter and F.-M. Braun, kept alive in the present by Reim, Manns and the Jewish scholar E.E. Urbach.

But in the early period with which we are concerned, the rabbis represented only one stream of tradition. Neusner criticises Urbach for handling the sages as an enclosed corpus, and for not seeking to set them within their historical context, using the wider range of literature available particularly from the first century, when rabbinic Judaism came to birth in the aftermath of the war.[6] We could make the same criticism of many of the attempts to illumine the Jewish background to John. But not of all: Ashton makes use of the *Apocalypse of Abraham* and the *Testament of Moses*,[7] and it is to be hoped that the republication of many of the first- and second-century apocalypses and other writings in Charlesworth's *Old Testament Pseudepigrapha* will facilitate an ever wider use of these priceless sources of evidence.

They need to be handled, not so much in relation to individual points of contact with John — although this is important and fascinating — as in order to draw a wider picture of the problems facing Jews after the destruction of the Temple, and the range of responses made. What follows is necessarily speculative, because we have no idea whether, in sum, our evidence enables anything like a comprehensive picture of Judaism in this period. But at the least it is clear that many varying viewpoints were held, from the ethical universalism of the *Testament of Abraham* which does not even mention covenant or Torah, to the intense nationalism of the fifth book of *Sibylline Oracles* — both quite possibly written contemporaneously in Egypt.[8]

---

6   Neusner "Formation" 100-108, reviewing Urbach *Sages*

7   Ashton *Understanding* 142-5 (*Apoc. Abr.*), 443-478 (*Test. Mos.*). He argues that the former illumines the use of the divine name in 8:58, and the latter the relationship between Jesus and the Paraclete in the farewell discourse.

8   These are the views of the two editors in *OTP*: respectively E.P. Sanders (1:874f) and J.J. Collins (1:390).

We will survey the material under three headings: the trauma, explanations, and responses.

3.1 The trauma of the destruction of Jerusalem

The trauma experienced in and through the war of 66-73 AD consisted by no means just in the dreadful physical suffering and displacement. The event called into question Israel's status as the chosen and protected people of God, and thus provoked "a profound and far-reaching crisis in their inner and spiritual existence".[9] In addition, as several have pointed out, the Temple provided a point of cohesion and unity for the many diverse groups in Judaism, so that its destruction precipitated a social crisis also.[10] The profundity of the crisis may be imagined from some of the expressions of confidence in the invincibility of Jerusalem which predate the disaster. For instance, looking ahead to the eschatological tribulation, *Sib. Or. 3* proclaims that

> the sons of the great God will all live peacefully around the Temple, rejoicing in these things which the Creator, just judge and sole ruler, will give. For he alone will shield them, standing by them magnificently as if he had a wall of blazing fire round about. They will be free from war in towns and country. No hand of evil war, but rather the Immortal himself and the hand of the Holy One will be fighting for them. Then all the islands and cities will say, 'How much the Immortal loves those men! for everything fights on their side and helps them, heaven, divinely driven sun and moon'.[11]

Then follows a moving vision of peace throughout the earth, centering on the worship of the Temple in Jerusalem.[12] The 'conceit' that the heavenly powers will fight for Israel — a motif drawn from Judges 5:20 — is found also in the *Biblical Antiquities* of Pseudo-Philo, where Balaam, the archetypal enemy of Israel, says,

> It is easier to take away the foundations and the topmost part of the earth and to extinguish the light of the sun and to darken the light of the moon than for anyone to uproot the planting of the Most Powerful or to destroy his vine.[13]

9   Neusner "Formation" 122
10   Martyn *History & Theology*2 52; Cohen "Yavneh" 57
11   *Sib. Or.* 3:702-713: dated by Collins in the period 163-145 BC (*OTP* 1:355)
12   *Sib. Or.* 3:755-808
13   *Bib. Ant.* 18:10, cf 32:9-17, a *midrash* on the Song of Deborah and Judg. 5:20

Pseudo-Philo is particularly interesting in that it seems to represent 'popular' thinking in Palestine in the first half of the first century.[14] It reflects grass-roots — perhaps better *vine-root* — nationalism, a widespread covenant confidence that God would protect
and preserve Israel against her enemies, even if she fell into sin:

> The God of our fathers, when we had sinned against him and he had
> delivered us up before our enemies and we were hard pressed by
> them, was not mindful of our sins but freed us ... Even if our sins be
> overabundant, still his mercy will fill the earth (*Bib. Ant.* 39:4,6).

The blow to this confidence through the destruction of Jerusalem
was severe. The laments in *2 Baruch* and *4 Ezra* quickly turn to
questioning: Why did the presence of many righteous in Jerusalem
not lead to the preservation of the city?[15] Why should God thus
judge Israel, when the Romans are no better?[16] Why should
humankind die off the face of the earth, when God created it for
us?[17]

> Why have I been endowed with the power of understanding? For I
> did not wish to enquire about the ways above, but about those which
> we daily experience: why Israel has been given over to the Gentiles
> as a reproach; why the people whom you loved has been given to
> godless tribes, and the Law of our fathers has been made of no effect

in particular. "Vine" is a frequent image for Israel in the literature of this period (as
also in rabbinic literature: Str-B 2:563f): cf *Bib. Ant.* 12:8f, 23:12, 28:4, 30:4, 39:7; 4
Ezra 5:26; *2 Baruch* 36:3ff, 39:7f. In *Bib. Ant.* 23:12 and 28:4f it is associated with
"flock" as a companion image.

14   So D.J. Harrington in *OTP* 2:300. The popular origin and flavour of *Bib.
Ant.* is underlined by features of the book like **(1)** the special interest in the
legendary and the miraculous (e.g. the stories of Kenaz in chs. 25-27, and the
midrashic expansion of the stories of Jephthah's daughter in ch. 40 and Micah the
idol-maker in ch. 44); **(2)** the downplaying of some of the central religious themes
and symbols of Israel (the law is exalted, but *the study of* the law is nowhere
commended; the festivals receive very brief treatment, 13:4-7 (cf *Jubilees!*), and
circumcision is nowhere mentioned); **(3)** the way no apparent reticence is felt about
Abram lying to his captors in 6:15, or God deceiving Israel by the Urim and
Thummim in 46:1; **(4)** the interest in magic, exorcism and necromancy attested in
chs. 34 (a story unique to *Bib. Ant.*), 44, 60 and 64.

15   *2 Baruch* 14:6-7

16   *4 Ezra* 3:28-36, 6:57

17   *2 Baruch* 14:17-19. The same question is shaped nationalistically in *4 Ezra*
6:59: "If the world has indeed been created for us [Israel], why do we not possess
our world as an inheritance?"

and the written covenants no longer exist; and why we pass from the world like locusts, and our life is like a mist, and we are not worthy to obtain mercy ...[18]

Underlying all these questions, for the author of 4 Ezra, lies the basic enigma: Why did God create the evil *yetzer* in mankind, which has meant that the whole purpose of the covenant has failed? "What good is it to us, if an eternal age has been promised to us, but we have done deeds that bring death?"[19] These are the questions of educated men, but we may be confident that, in essence, this *theological* trauma was felt, to a greater or lesser degree, by every Jew who had paid the Temple tax as an expression of his or her commitment to the covenant centre of Judaism.

It is fascinating to note how, in 2 Baruch and 4 Ezra (though to a greater extent in the former), the specific issue of the fate of Jerusalem is related to wider issues of creation, sin, and death. These are also the great themes of the Fourth Gospel, not least in 8:31-59; and there too we find the issue of theodicy specifically raised, in a way (we shall argue) which must have immediately connoted for Jews the problem caused by the destruction of the Temple. For whose sin was this man born blind — his own or his parents (9:2)? To this question we may relate the agony felt over the death of the righteous alongside the wicked *in* Jerusalem, and the wider agony over the 'death' *of* Jerusalem at the hands of the nations from whom she had been chosen by God.

The rabbinic literature is not such as to record this kind of agonised questioning among the rabbis, but there are plenty of references to their grief over the calamity.[20]

3.2 Explanations of the calamity

Explanations cannot wholly be distinguished from responses, but it is helpful to isolate them, because the explanations formed the heart of the response to the challenge to formulate a theodicy that could adequately account for the disaster.[21] We find that there were essentially three explanations, which underlay the five responses we will survey in the next section.

18   4 Ezra 4:23f
19   4 Ezra 7:49; cf 3:20-27, 4:30, 7:[62]-[72]
20   E.g. *'Abot. R. Nat.* A4:11a; cf Neusner *Yohanan2* 11f
21   There is a helpful survey and discussion in Tom W. Willett, *Eschatology in the Theodicies of 2 Baruch and 4 Ezra* (JSPSup 4; Sheffield, JSOT Press, 1989).

3.2.1 Punishment for sin

This was the dominant explanation of the disaster. As Neusner
notes, it was inevitable, for the alternatives were simply "Either our
fathers greatly sinned, or God is not just".[22] For some the sin was
especially associated with the Temple — for instance, in the
Apocalypse of Abraham, where the climax of the book is the horrifying description of the idolatry of the Temple in chapter 25, which
then prompts the destruction (chapter 27). A similar view is allied to
a strong polemic against the Temple cult in *Sib. Or.* 4, and the same
line of thought is reflected in 2 Baruch 10:18 (the priests have been
found to be "false stewards").[23] But corruption within the Temple
was generally regarded as but one example of a wider corruption
which caused the disaster. For instance, Josephus laid the blame
squarely on the Zealots and the other warring factions in Jerusalem,
adding to general lawlessness the sin of not submitting to Rome.[24]
A focus on the sin of *Jerusalem* (as opposed both to the Temple and
the wider people) is discernible in 4 Baruch (1:1, 8; 4:7f).

Tradition is influential here. The violations of the Temple by
Antiochus and by Pompey are explained as the result of Israel's sin
in 2 Macc 5:17-20 and *Pss. Sol.* 2:1-3, 16,[25] and of course Jeremiah
and Ezekiel make it very clear that the destruction of Jerusalem in
586 BC was caused by sin. R. Yohanan ben Torta, a contemporary of
Akiba, comments on the cause in *t. Menah* 13:22:

> In the time of the Latter Temple we observe that they toiled in the
> study of the Torah and were meticulous in giving the tithes. Why
> then were they exiled? Because they loved money and hated one
> another. This teaches you that hatred between people is grievous in
> the sight of the Omnipresent.[26]

This illustrates an awareness that sin could cohabit even with
meticulous external observance. This may be intended as an explanation of the particular problem posed in 2 Baruch 14:7 (see above),
concerning the indiscriminate suffering of the righteous alongside
the wicked: the answer is that the righteous were not as righteous as
they appeared! However, not all could be as radically self-critical as
Yohanan ben Torta. The 'standard' explanation is offered by

---

22   Neusner *Yohanan2* 12
23   Cf also Josephus *War* 5:402, 412; *Test. Mos.* 2:8f, 5:3f, 6:1
24   See his speech before the walls of Jerusalem in *War* 5:376ff.
25   Cf Stone "Destructions" 196
26   Quoted Urbach *Sages* 675

Yohanan ben Zakkai, in the famous story about the girl on the road
to Emmaus. He saw a girl picking barley-corn out of dung from an
Arab's horse, and commented to his disciples,

> You were unwilling to be subject to God, behold now you are
> subjected to the most inferior of the nations, the Arabs ... You were
> unwilling to repair the roads and streets leading up to the Temple;
> now you have to keep in repair the posts and stations on the road to
> the royal cities ... Because thou didst serve the Lord thy God with
> love, therefore shalt thou serve thine enemy with hatred; because
> thou didst not serve the Lord thy God when thou hadst plenty,
> therefore thou shalt serve thine enemy in hunger and thirst ...[27]

The identity of the "you" or "thou" here is left undefined: was it
the whole people without exception, or the generality of Israel with
the exception of the sages and the righteous? Yohanan was keen, as
we shall see, to make Torah the answer to Israel's need, so he would
certainly reject the view that Torah was *not* effective to combat sin.
But this is what we find in 4 Ezra:

> Though they had understanding they committed iniquity, and
> though they received the commandments they did not keep them,
> and though they obtained the Law they dealt unfaithfully with what
> they received ...[28]

The author is keen to preserve the law itself from taint, like Paul
in Rom 7:7ff:

> We who have received the Law and sinned will perish, as well as our
> heart which received it; the Law, however, does not perish, but
> remains in its glory.[29]

However, as in the case of Paul, this defence of Torah does not
preserve it from being "weak" in the face of the power of human
corruption.[30] The author of 4 Ezra struggles to retain the covenant

---

27 Mekhilta de R. Ishmael, Bahodesh 1, *Lauterbach* 2:194. In other sources (e.g.
b. Ket. 66b) the girl is identified as the daughter of the proverbially wealthy
Naqdimon (Nicodemus) ben Gorion, so part of the pathos is her loss of wealth and
status.

28 4 Ezra 7:[72]

29 4 Ezra 9:36f

30 Rom 8:3. See the comparison of the view of the law in 4 Ezra and Paul in
Longenecker *Eschatology* 272-4. I do not think that Longenecker sufficiently exploits
the notion of the 'weakness' of the law in his treatment of either.

in spite of overwhelming evidence that it has not been effective in saving Israel from the corruption of heart which has produced the disaster, and which will lead to further judgment yet.

3.2.2 The devil

The devil is surprisingly absent from some explanations of the disaster. Josephus never mentions the devil, Satan or Beliar at all. Similarly the Rabbis do not ascribe much significance to the figure of Satan.[31] Even more surprising is his absence from 4 Ezra, for there is a well-established tradition running from *Jubilees* through the *Testaments of the 12 Patriarchs* to the Qumran literature, in which the devil is closely associated with the evil *yetzer*.[32] Even though there is a strong heaven-earth dualism in 4 Ezra, the devil is never brought in as an agent or force behind human sinfulness.

However he was alive and well in other contemporary circles. We may discern a double development. On the one hand, the *Apocalypse of Abraham* clearly stands in the *T. 12 Patr.* tradition, with the corruption of Israel ascribed to Azazel's (the devil's) influence. This gives the 'theodicy' question a particular shape:

> Eternal, Mighty One, why then did you adjudge him [Azazel] such dominion that through his works he could ruin humankind on earth?[33]

The dualism is carefully limited, however: responsibility for evil is ascribed firmly to evil-doers. God's reply to this question is that Azazel was given dominion over "those who desire evil, and all whom I have hated as they commit them" (23:13).[34] On the other hand, other texts externalise this internal, moral conflict, and apply it to the conflict between Israel and her enemies. In *Sib. Or.* 5 the destruction of the Temple is an act of sheer injustice, in no way a judgment on the sin of Israel. The Temple was "made by holy people" who hoped that it would be "always imperishable" (401-2). In it "they honoured the great God, begetter of all who have

---

31   Foerster *TDNT* 7:156 maintains that the rabbinic emphasis on "free decision on the basis of the law ... crowds out the figure of Satan".

32   *Jub.* 1:20f, 11:4-6; *T. Jud.* 25:3, *T. Zeb.* 9:8, *T. Gad* 4:7, *T. Ash.* 1:8-9 — etc; 1QS 3:21-24, CD 12:2-3

33   *Apoc. Abr.* 23:12

34   The final "them" does not make sense: H.G. Lunt notes that the text could be corrupt, since we need a reference to "evil" here (*OTP* 1:701 n. p.). The Slavonic text of *Apoc. Abr.* is apparently quite corrupt.

God-given breath, with holy sacrifices and hecatombs" (406-7). It was destroyed by "a certain insignificant and impious king" (408), who was then killed by God for doing so (411). Though Rome is not specifically identified as Beliar in this text, she inhabits "the lawless nether region of Hades" (178), and this identification is well established in other texts from the period.[35]

3.2.3 The plan and will of God

The desire to understand the disaster as *contributing to* the plan of God for Israel, rather than *negating* it, is the primary impulse in all the texts that address the issue. Ways of doing this are various:

(1) The view that *the suffering was redemptive* is found in 2 Baruch: e.g 13:9-10, 15:7-8. It is *not* found in 4 Ezra, where there is such deep pessimism about the possibility of inducing human beings to goodness by any means at all.

(2) *The inscrutability of God's will* is another line of thought. This is particularly important for us, because it raises the issue of revelation. Is it possible for mystics and apocalyptists to discover the inscrutable will of God? 4 Ezra makes a fascinating study in this respect. In spite of attempts to produce a coherent theodicy out of 4 Ezra,[36] — and without entering into the debate in detail — I do not myself believe that the author ultimately offers anything beyond the answer given at the start:

He said to me, 'You cannot understand the things with which you have grown up; how then can your mind comprehend the way of the Most High? And how can one who is already worn out by the corrupt world understand incorruption?' (4:10-11).

The author does his best to provide a suitable *end* for the story — most notably by producing the ten lost tribes like a rabbit from a hat, so that in the end virtually the whole of Israel is saved (13:39-50) — but he never manages to explain why the story has the agonising *middle* he has just experienced. The dualism of heaven and earth is never overcome: "Who is able to know these things except he whose

---

35 E.g. *Mart. Isa.* 4:1, *Sib. Or.* 3:63-74, and of course Rev 13, 18. The Qumran texts mediate between these two developments, for there too the Romans are identified as "the horde of Belial" (e.g. 1QM 1:4-6, 15:2-3, 18:1-2), and accordingly they believed that the whole world had been given over to Belial, who would rule it until the final judgment when he would be overthrown (esp. 1QS 3:21-24).

36 See the review in Longenecker *Eschatology* 49-57.

dwelling is not with men?" (5:38). In spite of the fact that visions are given to Ezra, there is a fundamental *lack* of revelation. The visions all take place firmly *on earth*, in contrast to those in *Apoc. Abr.*: 4 Ezra 8:20f in fact reads like a polemic *against* the possibility of visions of the *merkabah* like that described in *Apoc. Abr.* 15-18.[37]

There is also a certain coyness about whether Ezra is in fact conversing with God, or with the angel Uriel. Only in 6:18-28 is the voice of God definitely heard, "like the sound of many waters", and there the voice simply announces the final judgment and the signs that herald it: it provides no answers.

Ezra never actually progresses beyond the plaintive "neither did I ever ascend into heaven" (4:8), with which he confesses his inability to answer the questions about "this world" which are the precondition to understanding "the way of the Most High" (4:11). He eschews the heavenly journeys claimed by others. Finally he is inspired to write 94 books, of which the 24 which represent the Hebrew canon are made public, while the other 70 remain hidden (14:37-48). The relative numbers reflect the sense of the author about the extent to which he knows the mind of God. He affirms an answer to his questions by faith, but has no access to it.[38]

He clearly felt the same reluctance as the Rabbis about the possibility of really being transported to paradise: of the four who went, so the story ran, only Akiba came through the experience unscathed. Ben Azzai died, Ben Zoma went mad, and Elishah ben Abuyah became a heretic.[39]

The *Apocalypse of Abraham*, on the other hand, has no hesitation about moving the apocalyptist right into the presence of God. But even here, at the crucial point God's will remains veiled. Cleverly, the author links God's freedom to his emphasis on human responsibility. Referring to Terah's decision to *remain* an idolater, and Abraham's to *reject* idolatry, God answers the central "Why?" question with

---

37   Dunn "John" 325

38   We meet the same use of the heaven-earth, hidden-revealed dichotomy earlier, in the climactic fourth vision (9:38-10:59), rightly regarded as the pivot of the book. He sees Zion *as she really is*, in "the brightness of her glory and the loveliness of her beauty" (10:50), in spite of the fact that she is also mourning the loss of her 'son', the earthly Jerusalem.

39   *t. Hag.* 2:3-6 (*b. Hag.* 14b). Cf also *4 Bar.* 9, where Jeremiah (the prophet) prays to "the true light that enlightens me" (9:3), and then receives a revelation of "the mysteries", apparently dying in the process. Baruch and Abimelech (scribes) are very anxious to "hear in full the mysteries that he had seen" (9:23), and their wish is fulfilled, but the mysteries are not described.

As the counsel of your father is in him, as your counsel is in you, so also the counsel of my will is ready. In days to come you will not know them in advance ... (26:5f).

God, too, is free to act in whatever way he will.

Against this background the claim of the Fourth Gospel that Jesus has descended from heaven to tell "heavenly things" (3:12-13) takes on new relevance. We need to read John carefully against the background of this twin concern for theodicy and revelation.

(3) There is naturally a particular *focus on the Temple* in the attempts to explain the plan of God. We will outline below the various ways in which the rebuilding of the Temple was foreseen in this period. Here we will touch on the interesting hermeneutical devices employed in the attempt to explain its destruction.

In 4 Ezra the loss of the Temple is interpreted as *sheer loss,* simply part of the loss of the vast majority of mankind, over which the apocalyptist mourns, but which he simply has to accept.[40] Even in the great fourth vision of the real Zion, which some have interpreted as a kind of conversion experience supplying a mystical answer to the apocalyptist's grief,[41] no explanation is offered for the death of the woman's son.

The author of 4 Ezra had no hesitation in regarding the destruction of Jerusalem as the work of God. But this actually provides the basis for an expectation of restoration, which will be equally the work of God. This line of thought is particularly clear in 4 Baruch, where emphasis is laid on the fact that *God* destroyed the city before the Chaldeans did (1:6-8, 3:4, 4:1-3). The purpose of this emphasis appears in 4:8f:

Do not let the outlaws boast and say, 'We were strong enough to take the city of God by our power'; but because of our sins it was delivered to you. And our God will pity us and return us to our city.

This is developed further in 2 Baruch. For this author, the disaster was *more than was required* as a judgment for sin,[42] and was in fact carried out by God for his own reasons in pursuance of his universal purpose. "I now took away Zion to visit the world in its own time

---

40   E.g. 4 Ezra 8:1-3, 37-41; 9:19-22
41   So Stone "Destructions" 203; followed now by Longenecker *Eschatology* 112, 149. Cf also *Nickelsburg* 293.
42   14:5-7, 77:8-10, 78:5, 79:1-4

more speedily" (20:2). So it may be reckoned that the suffering was actually "for your good" (78:6), and it is possible to rejoice in present suffering (52:6) because of the certainty of future hope.

This is 2 Baruch's answer to the problem of the destruction of the righteous along with the wicked, but it involves an interesting reinterpretation of the status of the Temple:

> Do you think that this is the city of which I said, 'On the palms of my hands I have carved you?' It is not this building that is in your midst now; it is that which will be revealed, with me, that was already prepared from the moment that I decided to create Paradise (4:2-3).

Here Isaiah 49:16 is applied, not to the physical Temple, but to the heavenly Temple which will be "revealed" in the age to come. The physical Temple is simply part of this age, and stands under the judgment which applies to this age as a whole. The tribulation to come is far greater than that already experienced (32:6), but this final tribulation will be the work of the Messiah (30:1-5), through whom also "the building of Zion ... will be renewed in glory and ... perfected into eternity" (32:4). Then "all that has been ... will become as though it had not been" (31:5).

So the view that the whole *idea* of the Temple must be re-thought is not unique to John. For the author of 2 Baruch, the building of the Temple in the sixth century BC is regarded in retrospect as *not* the real meaning of the verses that promised it, like Isaiah 49:14-26. The destruction, and not the building, of the Temple is what points forward to the age to come.[43]

The author does not apparently face the hermeneutical problem raised by this re-evaluation of the Temple: namely, whether the 'physical' interpretation of Isaiah 49 was in fact a grave *misinterpretation*. He does not suggest this. But there is no hesitation in *Sib. Or.* 4:

> Happy will be those of mankind on earth who will love the great God ... They will reject all temples when they see them; altars too, useless foundations of dumb stones ... defiled with blood of animate creatures, and sacrifices of four-footed animals. They will look to the great glory of the one God and commit no wicked murder (4:24f, 27-31).

---

43   So Murphy *Second Baruch* 86-90. The whole age of the Second Temple is described in positive, but distinctly lukewarm, terms in 68:5-8.

It is intriguing to see the Old Testament commonplace polemic against idols as *dumb* being applied here to the Jerusalem Temple and altar. Presumably this polemic has roots also in the prophetic denunciation of the cult, but this represents a hermeneutical abandonment of the whole cultic heritage which goes further than anything else in contemporary Judaism, so far as we know — except in Christian Judaism.[44]

3.3 Responses to the calamity

We will briefly outline five responses which seem to be distinguishable, although they are not mutually exclusive, as will become apparent.[45]

3.3.1 Rejection of the cult

This is clear in the text just discussed, where it is allied to a strong attack on all idolatry.[46] It is easy to imagine that, for Jews for whom the Temple was already of marginal importance, the events of 70 AD could have underlined the view that temples are "a bane which brings many woes to men" (*Sib. Or.* 4:9). *Sib. Or.* 4 refers to the murders committed in front of the Temple, either by the Romans or the Zealots (115-8) — and clearly makes no sharp distinction between these and the killing of animals inside (cf 29-31). The author commends a universal monotheistic "piety" (162-70) which will lead to "spirit and life and favour" when God acts to judge the world (183-92). We find a similar perspective in the *Testament of Abraham*,

---

44   J.J. Collins in *OTP* 1:383 and at 384 n. c. suggests parallels first with Stephen in Acts 7 and then with the Essenes and Qumran. But Stephen does not pillory the cult, merely suggests that the Abrahamic promise of 'worship in this place' (7:7) has not yet been fulfilled. The Essenes still sent gifts to the Temple (Jos. *Ant.* 18:18), and at Qumran they expected its restoration.

45   Neusner "Destruction" 87-93 describes four responses, including the Christian response which we do not isolate here. His analysis can be refined and extended.

46   Collins is agnostic about the provenance of *Sib. Or.* 4 (*OTP* 1:382), but it is tempting to connect it with the attacks on pagan temples by the Jews during the disturbances in Alexandria, Cyrene and Cyprus in 115-117 AD (*Schürer* 1:529-534). Philo of Alexandria never goes so far as to reject the Jerusalem cult, but the *allegorical* interpretation of the cultic laws was clearly more important for him than the *literal*. In *Quod Det.* 21 he contrasts "noble", spiritual kinds of worship with purely external rituals which try to give gifts to him who cannot be bribed. So also *De Mig.* 89-93, where he also argues against those who go too far and *reject* the literal in favour of the allegorical. It is easy to imagine how the events of 70 AD reinforced the rejection of the literal cult by such people.

which makes no distinction between Jews and Gentiles: all are judged together, and accepted if there is a preponderance of good works over bad (e.g. 12:13-18). Sanders refers to "the lowest-common-denominator universalism of its soteriology".[47] Temple and cult have vanished entirely.

This marginalises Torah in a most extraordinary way. Geza Vermes has suggested that this attitude (though he does not mention *Sib. Or.* 4) is attacked as *minuth* ('heresy') by rabbinic orthodoxy, and that in particular it was the pressure of this vague, pious universalism which led Rabbis to abandon the daily recitation of the decalogue.[48] 2 Baruch shows a similar concern, referring to "many of your people who separated themselves from your statutes and who have cast away from them the yoke of your Law".[49]

The Ebionites breathe a different air from *Sib. Or.* 4, but likewise reject sacrifices. We can only speculate on the extent to which this rejection, inherited from Essenism,[50] was reinforced by the destruction of the Temple. But the 'full' Ebionite teaching, as represented in the second-century *Preaching of Peter*, goes much further than the Essenes as represented in the Qumran literature. Whereas at Qumran they regarded "prayer offered *according to the law*" and "perfection of behaviour" as the equivalent of sacrifices (1QS 9:4-5), the Ebionites taught that the law had been *corrupted* by the addition of the sacrificial legislation. We will suggest below that John 8:31-38 possibly engages with nascent Ebionism.

The Rabbis, of course, would have nothing to do with such rejection of Torah, nor would they support any blurring of the distinction between Israel and the Gentiles. But we find among them an intriguing parallel to this polemic against the cult. It is clearly marginalised, for instance, in the famous exchange between Yohanan ben Zakkai and his disciple Joshua ben Hananiah:

---

47   *OTP* 1:877

48   Vermes "Minim". The vital passage is *y. Ber.* 1:3c, which refers to the use of Deut 5:22 ("These are the commandments the Lord proclaimed ... and he added nothing more") to deny the divine origin of the rest of the Torah: "It used to be proper to recite the Ten Commandments every day. Why then do they not recite them now? Because of the claim of the Minim: so that they may not say, Only these were given to Moses on Sinai". Vermes rejects the view that these *minim* are Jewish Christians (still held by Brooke "Law" 109f), on the ground that no Jewish Christians would have taken such a radical view of the Torah. But Jews espousing an anti-cultic, ethical Judaism could have argued argued in this way.

49   2 Baruch 41:3. Klijn thinks that this refers just to Christians (*OTP* 1:633 n. 41a), but this seems unnecessarily limited.

50   Daniélou *Theology* 57

> Once as Rabban Yohanan ben Zakkai was coming out of Jerusalem, Rabbi Joshua followed after him, and beheld the Temple in ruins. Woe unto us, Rabbi Joshua cried, that this place, the place where the iniquities of Israel were atoned for, is laid waste. My son, Rabban Yohanan said to him, be not grieved. We have another atonement as effective as this, and what is it? It is acts of lovingkindness, as it is said, "For I desire mercy and not sacrifice" (Hos 6:6).[51]

Neusner in several places points out that the Pharisees were ready with a theology which could cope with the destruction of the Temple. Even before 70, they sought to practice Temple purity in the home. So they were well placed to continue and develop that emphasis after the Temple was destroyed. The principle is expressed in *b. Ber.* 55a: "As long as the temple stood, the altar atoned for Israel. But now a man's table atones for him". Because atonement was possible through the practice of piety, "the temple and its cult were not decisive".[52] The selfless practice of lovingkindness became the sacrifice to replace those of the Temple.[53]

The negative converse of this was also developed: impurity and impiety were regarded as having *social* consequences, rather than *cultic*, and so a link was gradually forged between particular sins and particular punishments, *"because the community of Israel now is regarded as the temple"*.[54]

Along with this went naturally a growing emphasis on the atoning quality of suffering. In *t. Ber.* 1:15 an interpretation of Jer 32:31 and Ps 68:16 is developed which allows the destruction of the Temple to atone for its sins: before destruction, the Divine Presence was *not* there, because "This city has aroused my anger and my wrath" (Jer 32:31). But after destruction (which made atonement for it), it became again Salem, where "his abode has been established" (Ps 68:16).[55]

In all likelihood this theology took time to develop, and at first

---

51 *'Abot. R. Nat.* A4, quoted in Neusner *Yohanan1* 142

52 Neusner "Destruction" 92

53 Cf also Neusner *Yohanan2* 193-5; "Formation" 135ff; *Myth* 12

54 Neusner "Destruction" 97, his emph.

55 The view that suffering atones for sin is well embedded in pre-70 thinking (Isa 53; 4 Macc 6:27, 17:21-23), but the *particularisation* of this idea, so that each individual may atone for his own sins by acts of charity, repentance or suffering, seems to derive from the destruction of the Temple: see K. Kohler in *JE* 2:275-284, esp. 278-80. Cf esp. *m. Sanh.* 6:2, and the discussion in Sanders *PPJ* 168-175 (he maintains that "the view that death as such atones for sin was developed after the destruction of the Temple", 173).

did not displace hope for the rebuilding of the Temple. It is interesting that it is only after the Bar Kokba revolt, when all hope of a new Temple was finally extinguished, that this detailed reinterpretation of purity and impurity in social terms really developed. We find hints of it, however, in the Fourth Gospel, both in the discussion about the blind man in 9:2ff and in Jesus' words to the lame man in 5:14, which at first sight seem to point in different directions. Both passages reflect an environment in which questions were being asked about the social consequences of sin — questions prompted both by the belief that Israel's sin was being punished in the destruction of the Jerusalem, and by the emerging view that further disaster could be avoided by the practice of Torah — or, for *Sib. Or.* 4, by the practice of "piety".

3.3.2 Renewed emphasis on 'Torah'

The origins of rabbinic Judaism in the post-70 period have been the object of considerable study. As noted above, caution is now widely felt about the speed with which the distinctive ideas and emphases of rabbinic Judaism became established as the leading expression of Jewish faith. Here the apocalypses are significant, because they enable us to take a sounding into Jewish life and faith at an early point in the process, and thus to gauge the pastoral motivation behind the work and teaching of the Yavneh academy.

In both 4 Ezra and 2 Baruch, the view that the sin of Israel caused the disaster leads to a renewed call for obedience. This is particularly so in 2 Baruch:

> To you and to your fathers the Lord gave the Law above all nations. And because your brothers have transgressed the commandments of the Most High, he brought vengeance upon you and upon them ... If, therefore, you will make straight your ways, you will not go away as your brothers went away, but they will come to you (77:3-6).[56]

Thus the emphasis on personal responsibility implicit in the analysis of the *cause* is carried forward into the prescription for the *cure*. 4 Ezra is distinctly more deterministic (6:1-6) with a clear sense that people *cannot* obey, because "the grain of evil seed" sown at the

---

56   Cf also 32:1, 46:5, 48:22-24 ("we know that we do not fall as long as we keep your statutes", 22), 51:7, 84:6-9, 85:3-4 ("Zion has been taken away from us, and we have nothing now apart from the Mighty One and his Law. Therefore, if we direct and dispose our hearts, we shall receive everything which we lost again by many times")

beginning in Adam's heart (4:30) remains unaltered:

> The inhabitants of the city transgressed, in everything doing as Adam and all his descendants had done, for they also had the evil heart (3:25-26).

But even though a change of heart is not expected until the messianic age (6:26), yet future blessedness is held out to those who "have striven with great effort to overcome the evil thought which was formed with them" (7:[92], cf 9:7), and Ezra's final solution is to re-issue the law to the people "that men may be able to find the path, and that those who wish to live in the last days may live" (14:22). In spite of the evil *yetzer*, we are all in a "contest" which will determine life or death for us (7:57-61).[57]

This is also the emphasis in emerging rabbinic Judaism.[58] If the Pharisaic ideal of Temple purity in the home underlay the view that deeds of lovingkindness were the equivalent of the sacrifices, then this renewed emphasis on personal obedience already had a contemporary theological rationale to support it. Neusner actually finds Yohanan ben Zakkai's "message of comfort" in the dreadful story of the girl on the road to Emmaus quoted above, for he regards as authentic the saying attached to the parallel story in the Talmud:[59]

> Yohanan thereupon exclaimed, "Happy are you, O Israel! When you obey the will of God, then no nation or race can rule over you. But when you do not obey the will of God, you are handed over into the hands of every low-born people, and not only into the hands of the people but even into the power of the cattle of that low-born people" (*b. Ket.* 66b).

The authenticity of this saying is supported by the observation that 'freedom through obedience' is also the prescription of the apocalyptic tradition in part. The author of 2 Baruch even knows how the life of obedience will be encouraged:

---

57 We find the same balance between determinism and responsibility at Qumran, and in the *Testament of Moses*, a work which seems to antedate the destruction of the Temple: everything is "under the ring of his right hand" (12:9), but at the same time "Those who truly fulfil the commandments of God will flourish and will finish the good way, but those who sin by disregarding the commandments will deprive themselves of the good things which were declared before. They indeed, will be punished by the nations with many tortures" (12:10-11).

58 Metzger notes the connection in *OTP* 1:522.

59 Neusner *Yohanan2* 184f

Israel will not be in want of a wise man, nor the tribe of Jacob, a son
of the Law. But only prepare your heart, so that you obey the Law,
and be subject to those who are wise and understanding with fear
(46:4-5).

The figures of Baruch and Ezra represent *scribes*, a tradition
appropriated also by the new rabbinism at Yavneh.[60] 4 Ezra's
determinism and pessimism find no echo in rabbinic Judaism, nor
his emphasis on *eschatological* solutions to contemporary problems.
But the ideal of detailed, individual obedience to Torah as the heart
of the response to the calamity unites them all. This ideal comes
under critical scrutiny in John 5 and is of crucial importance for the
interpretation of 8:31-59.

One particular aspect of the work of the Yavneh academy calls for
our attention. Recent interpretation of John 8:31-59 has been strongly
influenced by what we have called the 'Martyn hypothesis' —
namely that the Gospel reflects a breakdown in relations between
church and synagogue following the introduction of the *birkat ha-
minim* into the synagogue prayers by the Yavneh sages. The view, in
essence, is that the introduction of the curse on *minim* — not
necessarily just Jewish Christians — was part of a policy of expansion by the Yavneh sages, as they sought to consolidate their authority and reinforce Torah 'orthodoxy' against various fringe groups,
among whom the johannine Christians were caught up.

In the seventies this view of things had no rivals, so that Onuki's
Gemeinde, the fruit of research conducted in the late seventies,
devotes only five pages to the historical background of the Fourth
Gospel, even though the picture is fundamental to his thesis.[61] The
same is true of Wengst's *Bedrängte Gemeinde*, published in 1979.

However, by the time Onuki's work was published in 1984, the
tide had turned dramatically:

• The first move towards a reassessment had been made in 1975
when Peter Schäfer argued that the *birkat ha-minim* played no significant role in the separation of Jews and Christians in the first
century.[62]

---

60   Neusner "Formation" 138-143. Scribal guidance is the key to restoration
also in 4 Baruch: "Everything you have heard from the letter observe, and the Lord
will lead us into our city" (7:23): Baruch the scribe had written to tell the exiles to
separate themselves from the Babylonians (6:16f; cf 7:37).
61   Onuki *Gemeinde* 29-34
62   Schäfer "Jabne"

• Then in *1980* the research project at McMaster University on "Jewish and Christian Self-Definition" began to publish its work, and under that umbrella Lawrence Schiffman and Reuven Kimelman argued respectively (*1981*) that post-70 Judaism did not close ranks against the Jewish Christians, and that there is no evidence that the *birkat ha-minim* was directed at them particularly.[63]

• In *1982* Shaye Cohen argued that, far from being exclusivist, the Yavneh sages had a remarkably *inclusive* spirit, playing down their sectarian roots in pre-70 Pharisaism, and only 'cursing' those who were unwilling to commit themselves to ideological *pluralism:* "There is little evidence for 'witch-hunting' in general and anti-Christian activity in particular".[64]

• In the same year William Horbury published a masterly study of the textual development of the 12th Benediction, showing the insecure textual foundation of the 'Martyn' view.[65]

• In *1983* Neusner suggested that Eliezer ben Hyrcanus, one of the Yavneh sages, showed a remarkably eirenic spirit towards groups within Judaism, even towards Samaritans.[66]

• In *1984* Steven Katz argued strongly against the view that Yavneh launched a concerted official attack on Jewish Christianity.[67]

• The result of all this was that, in *1985*, Wayne Meeks declared the *birkat ha-minim* to be "a red herring in johannine research"[68] — a judgment now echoed (1992) by Graham Stanton.[69]

We cannot review the evidence which led to this change. There is now a healthy consensus that (a) the Yavnean sages did indeed introduce a curse on the *minim* towards the end of the first century, but (b) we cannot be sure who the intended *minim* actually were, nor (c) what the precise wording was, and (d) since the curse worked by self-exclusion rather than by expulsion (so that it would only bar from the synagogue those who recognised *themselves* as "*minim*"), it must have functioned more as exhortation to Jews generally than as a specific means of social exclusion. This fits with (e) the insight that the Yavnean sages were more concerned to heal breaches than to reinforce them. When 2 Baruch considers the *minim*, the author's

---

63 Schiffman "Schism"; Kimelman "*Birkat*"
64 Cohen "Yavneh" 59
65 Horbury "Minim"
66 Neusner "Formation" 133
67 Katz "Separation"
68 Meeks "Breaking Away" 102
69 Stanton *New People* 142; cf Lindars "Persecution" 51, Smith "Life Setting" 439, Culpepper "Jews" 281

instinct is not to curse them but to puzzle about them: "What will happen with those? Or how will that last time receive them?"[70]

If there was no widespread movement to break off all contact with Christians in the late first century, then it becomes all the more possible that the johannine reinterpretation of the law could have functioned *within* the context of this range of responses, as an *address to Jews* (rather than as a means of bolstering a beleaguered Christian group). There is a small but significant piece of evidence in Ignatius which supports the hypothesis of wide contact and vigorous debate. In a passage which probably refers to experiences in Antioch before his arrest, rather than on the journey, Ignatius reports,

> I heard some saying, "Unless I find it in the ancient writings, I will not believe in the Gospel". When I said to them, "It is written", they replied to me, "That's the question that lies before us".[71]

Clearly the dialogue partners here are Jews, demanding Scriptural proof of Christian claims. The door had certainly not been shut against such contacts, at any rate in Antioch or Asia Minor around 100 AD. *It is just this kind of Scriptural argument which we find taken up in the Fourth Gospel.*[72]

3.3.3 A resurgence of mysticism and apocalypticism

The evidence is strong that some of the Yavnean sages engaged in *merkabah* mysticism.[73] Neusner, discussing Yohanan's special interest in it, suggests as one reason for it the historical parallel between Yohanan's experience and that of Ezekiel: just as the departure of the chariot from Jerusalem signalled the destruction of the Temple for Ezekiel (Ezek 10), so the destruction of the Temple in Yohanan's day prompted a similar interest in the chariot now located in heaven.[74]

---

70   2 Baruch 41:5. Those in mind here are both those "who have cast away from them the yoke of your Law", and those "who left behind their vanity and who have fled under your wings". The answer is a little obscure, but it seems as though the period *before* conversion (either from or to the law) is to be discounted in the Judgment (42:3-8).

71   Ign. *Phld.* 8:2

72   Frédéric Manns has argued that the Fourth Gospel is a detailed response to the Yavnean decrees (Manns "Réponse", "Jabné"), but supports this contention merely by pointing to possible contacts of thought with material drawn indiscriminately from the whole rabbinic corpus.

73   That is, the use of the chariot (=*merkabah*) vision of Ezek 1 as the basis for mystical reflection and experience.

74   Neusner *Yohanan1* 101-3

We may support this conjecture with reference to the apocalypses, where clearly the destruction of the earthly Temple prompts interest in the heavenly. This is particularly clear in 2 Baruch, where the opening section distinguishes immediately between the earthly Temple, now destroyed, and its heavenly counterpart "preserved with me" (4:6).

Scholars have, I think, unduly distinguished between the *merkabah* mysticism found among some Rabbis and the contemporary apocalypses. Ira Chernus, for instance, in his study of the origins of mysticism among the *tannaim*, does not consider any connection with the apocalyptic literature.[75] There are differences, of course: the Rabbis seem generally to have rejected the eschatology of the apocalypses, emphasising present, practical solutions to the problems of Israel,[76] and the *merkabah* of Ezek 1 does not figure largely in the apocalypses.[77] However, at the level of motivation this interest is really one phenomenon, as Dunn emphasises.[78] It attests *a longing for heavenly knowledge, at a time when the ways of God seemed past comprehension.*

In the case of the Rabbis, the knowledge was sought through meditation on mystical texts, especially Ezek 1, in the tradition of the inspired interpreter of Sirach 39:1-11, who meditates on the "law of the Most High, the wisdom of the ancients" (39:1), and to whom, if he wills, the Lord will give "the spirit of understanding" (39:6) so that he may "know his way among the hidden things of God" (39:7), and lead many to "praise his understanding" (39:9).

In the case of the apocalyptists, the knowledge was sought through the visions and dreams firmly *rejected* by Ben Sirach (Sir 34:1-8), in the tradition of Daniel and Enoch, who brought "a holy vision from the heavens which the angels showed me: and I heard from them everything and I understood" (1 Enoch 1:2).[79]

But whatever the *source* of the knowledge, the *motivation* was the same for both groups: knowledge of the hidden things of God. In

---

75   Chernus *Mysticism* 1-16 (the first chapter of his book, "Revelation and Merkabah Mysticism in Tannaitic Midrash").

76   Cf Neusner *Yohanan1* 145

77   Ezek 1 provides the imagery of the vision described in *Apoc. Abr.* 15-18, but this seems to be the only example. See Stone in *Stone* 417.

78   Dunn "John" 323-5: he underlines "the extent to which these two strands [sc. apocalyptic and merkabah mysticism] ... overlap" (323). These pages of Dunn's article are a brilliant summary of the evidence for and features of this strand in post-70 Judaism.

79   For this distinction between the two types of revelation, see Nickelsburg "Wisdom". He places John firmly in the second tradition (82f).

both groups, too, there was a clear sense of the danger of seeking this knowledge. It could only be imparted to very special people — to Enoch, Abraham, Moses, Baruch, Ezra, Yohanan ben Zakkai, Eleazar ben Arak, Akiba ... Amongst the Rabbis there was reticence about passing the knowledge on, so special was it — a reticence shared by the authors of 4 Ezra and 4 Baruch, but not apparently by other apocalyptists.[80]

We have already considered the relevance of this contemporary movement for understanding the johannine theology of revelation (above, 2.3). As we saw, it is a vital factor in the 'staging' of the Nicodemus dialogue, for he is presented as one seeking precisely this knowledge from a recognised master, under the necessary conditions of secrecy. And this in turn sets the stage for the dialogue in John 8, where the discussion turns on "knowing the truth", and Abraham is presented in terms strongly reminiscent of his treatment in the apocalyptic texts — as we shall see.

3.3.4 Quietist eschatology

It was inevitable that the disaster would prompt eschatologies. Action by God was predicted, to repair the damage apparently done to the special covenant relation with Israel. But the way in which this action was envisaged varied, and in particular we may distinguish between *quietist* and *activist* eschatologies. This distinction is vital for the Fourth Gospel, for once again we shall argue that it engages with this contemporary debate and that its eschatology falls clearly into the former category.

A "quietist eschatology" leaves the solution of the problem entirely in the hands of God, and does not envisage any kind of 'holy war' to solve it. 2 Baruch provides the clearest example of this among the apocalypses, and in this respect it is closer to the Rabbis than to *Apoc. Abr.* As we saw above, Baruch emphasises that *God* was responsible for the destruction of the Temple (6:3-7:1, 80:1-4), as part of his plan for the world; and so *God* will be responsible for the final judgment yet to come (ch. 83), and for the restoration of the world which will follow that (chs. 72-74). There will be vengeance for what has been done to Jerusalem (13:5, 82:2), but this rests entirely in God's hands. "The Most High will cause all these things

---

80   Halperin *Merkabah* 180ff shows how the exposition of the *merkabah* was clearly thought to be the prerogative of the greatest. The famous story in *t. Hag.* 2:1, *b. Hag.* 14b of the exposition of the *merkabah* by Eleazar to his teacher Yohanan underlines the secrecy with which such matters must be discussed (cf Halperin *Merkabah* 120).

to come" (85:12). So the appeal is issued:

> Why do you look for the decline of your enemies? Prepare your souls
> for that which is kept for you ...[81]

Significantly, there is no reference to a reconstruction of the
Temple in the restoration after the judgment, nor to any human
agency in carrying out the judgment.

Frederick Murphy argues that this quietism is polemically directed at the more activist, revolutionary responses to the disaster.[82]
His argument seems well-founded. The failure to envisage a rebuilding of the Temple is particularly interesting, and aligns 2 Baruch
with the Rabbis in this respect. Yohanan ben Zakkai is credited with
a remarkable saying:

> If you have a sapling in your hand, and it is said to you, Behold,
> there is the Messiah — go on with your planting, and afterward go
> out and receive him. And if the youths say to you, Let us go up and
> build the Temple, do not listen to them. But if the elders say to you,
> Come let us destroy the Temple, listen to them, for the building of
> youth is destruction, and the destruction of old age is building —
> proof of the matter is Rehoboam, son of Solomon.[83]

Such a saying might be dismissed as later rabbinic rationalisation,
were it not for the coincidence of thought with 2 Baruch. Eschatological fervour and a desire to rebuild the Temple are connected with
each other, and *both* are countered with the sober judgment that the
destruction of the Temple was actually *a good thing*. It looks as
though Yohanan believed, with the author of 2 Baruch, that the
disaster was a *step forward* in the plan of God, and that messianic
movements should be resisted.

This was not the only form that 'quietist eschatology' took. *Sib.
Or.* 5 likewise leaves the restoration entirely to God, but it will be
brought about by the Messiah ("the best of the Hebrews", 5:258),
who will destroy all evildoers (418f), and rebuild the city with "a
holy temple, exceedingly beautiful in its fair shrine" (422f). 4 Ezra
occupies a mediating position between the 'heavenly temple only'
view in 2 Baruch and this thoroughly earthly construction in *Sib. Or.*
5: here too the Messiah conducts a judgment of the nations (12:31-33,

---

81   2 Baruch 52:6-7
82   Murphy *Second Baruch* 136f, "2 Baruch" 664
83   *'Abot. R. Nat.* B31, quoted in Neusner *Yohanan1* 134

13:37f), in connection with which "the city which now is not seen shall appear" (7:26), "Zion will come and be made manifest to all people, prepared and built" (13:36). The new Temple will simply "appear", as it does to Ezra in his vision (10:25-27).

The eschatology of 4 Baruch is definitely "quietist", but may nonetheless have contributed to the activist fervour that produced the second revolt. Here the restoration is wholly the action of God, but such emphasis is laid on the "sixty-six years" of the exile, at the end of which God steps in (5:2, 4, 27, 6:8), that we may well imagine that this work reflects, or even contributed to, the rise in anti-Roman fervour as the terminus after 70 AD drew near.[84]

The johannine Jesus likewise insists that the kingdom of God is not something for which human beings should fight (18:36): but this saying is set in the context of a realised eschatology to which there is no parallel in contemporary literature. John's remarkable message to his contemporaries was that *God had already acted to rebuild the Temple* and to bring in the messianic age. We will find this eschatological quietism important as background to 8:31-59, when we consider the spiritualisation of the concept of "freedom" there.

3.3.5 Activist eschatology and popular messianism

By "activist eschatology" we mean a response to the calamity which looked for a future restoration in which the people of God themselves would play an active role. The appeal of 2 Baruch 52:6-7, quoted above, may be mirror-read as evidence for the continuing life of the Zealot movement after 70 AD. In fact, one might expect this to be the dominant response, although the literary evidence for it is slimmer than for the 'quietist' response. However there is enough evidence to make it certain that this was a significant factor in the context of the Fourth Gospel.

Scholars have recently pointed to a militarism implicit in the eschatology of *Apoc. Abr.*[85] Here there is a sharp focus on the Temple cult, both in the analysis of the cause of the disaster, and in the prescription of the solution. Tribulation is predicted for the world (29:15, 30:2-8), following which "my chosen one" will be sent to gather "my people, humiliated by the heathen" (31:1). Then

> they will live, being affirmed by the sacrifices and the gifts of justice and truth in the age of justice. And they will rejoice forever in me, and they will destroy those who have destroyed them ... and they

84   So Robinson *OTP* 2:416
85   So Mueller "Apocalypse" 348f; Murphy 2 *Baruch* 137

will spit in their faces (29:17-19).

Here the restoration of the cult is clear, and also the agency of God's people in carrying out vengeance on the oppressing nations. The emphasis on the cult may perhaps explain the remarkable absence of *the law* as a feature of both problem and solution.[86] *Apoc. Abr.* clearly moves in a different world from 2 Baruch and the Rabbis, and that may well be the world of the militarism which looked for a return match with the Romans and eventually produced the Bar Kokba revolt.

Evidence in support of this may be supplied from the pre-70 period by Pseudo-Philo and Josephus, who together illustrate the extent of the *popular* interest in a prophetic deliverer — an interest which must have survived the disaster and may even have been fuelled by it.[87] There is a strong emphasis in Pseudo-Philo on the importance of a *leader* to guide and intercede for the people. Joshua reminds God of his promise, when he himself is about to die:

> Now let the fullness of your mercy sustain your people and choose for your heritage a man so that he and his offspring will rule your people. Did not our father Jacob speak about him, saying 'A ruler will not be lacking from Judah ...' (21:4-5).[88]

And, for this author, such a leader will be a *prophet*. "We have a king, because we are not worthy to be governed by a prophet", the people cry to Samuel when Saul is being appointed (57:4); and remarkably, in that passage, "all the people and the king wept with great lamentation and said, 'Long live Samuel the prophet!'" (57:4). The leaders who are also prophets (Moses, Joshua, Kenaz, Deborah, Samuel) are shown in a very good light, while those who are not prophets (Gideon, Abimelech, Jair, Jephthah, Samson, Saul) all fall into sin and lead the people astray, even though they are appointed as deliverers. The death of Samuel is actually delayed until the end of the book (64:1-2), and we are left with the strong impression that there *is* no replacement for him — even David does not match up.

---

86 Pointed out by Mueller "Apocalypse" 347, *Nickelsburg* 299. It could be argued that the law is implicit in the polemic against fornication and idolatry (24, 25), but one corrupt verse (27:8) is the only possible reference to Torah as part of the solution.

87 See above, note 14, for the evidence for the popular nature of *Bib. Ant.*

88 Later much space is devoted to the difficulty of appointing a judge after the disturbance surrounding Micah the idol-maker, culminating in the appointment of Samuel as an expression of God's mercy to a sinful people (chs. 49-51).

With this may be connected a polemic against the priesthood, visible at several points. Pointedly, immediately after Eli is appointed priest (48:2), the people begin a search for a ruler,

> For perhaps we will find a man who may free us from our distress, because it is not appropriate for the people to be without a ruler (49:1).

Plainly Eli will not do! — even though he is described as *judging* Israel in 1 Sam 4:18.[89] At a time when the Jerusalem priesthood did in fact provide much of the leadership, and when there was no single ruler, but a division of power between several bodies and factions, these features of Pseudo-Philo become especially significant, as reflecting a popular longing for the one *prophetic* leader who will be God's gift and the means of delivering Israel from the enemies surrounding her.

Such a grass-roots longing is confirmed by Josephus *War* 2:259 (early 60's, time of Felix):

> Deceivers and impostors, under the pretence of divine inspiration, persuaded the multitude to act like madmen, and led them out into the desert under the belief that God would there give them signs of freedom.

Then Josephus relates the story of the Egyptian mentioned in Acts 21:38, describing him as a "false prophet" and as "a sorcerer compelling acceptance of himself as a prophet" (*War* 2:261). In Acts his following is numbered at 4,000, in Josephus at 30,000. Even if the lower number is accepted, as seems more likely, this incident well attests the popular readiness not just to believe that a prophetic leader might appear, but also to follow such a figure virtually at a moment's notice to almost certain death. This undoubtedly helps to explain the appearance of the various factions which so undermined the Jewish cause in 68 and 69 AD.

Josephus also confirms the anti-hieratical spirit of this popular messianism in his account in *Antiquities* of the same rebellion.[90]

---

89   Cf also the extended section on the corruption of the sons of Eli (chs. 52-54), the inability of the priest Phinehas rightly to discern the will of God through the Urim and Thummin (chs. 46-47), and the addition to the biblical story of the murder of the sons of Abimelech (1 Sam. 22), which interprets their death as God's judgment for profanation and desecration of the first-fruits (ch. 63). The only priest who leads effectively in Pseudo-Philo is Phinehas, who is also described as a prophet in 28:3 and compared to Elijah (48:1).

According to this account the Egyptian led out "masses of the common people" to the Mount of Olives, where he ordered the walls to collapse before him like a latter-day Joshua before Jericho. Horsley and Hanson suggest that behind this action lay an intention to fulfil the eschatological vision of Zechariah 14, where the Lord stands on the Mount of Olives (14:4) and proclaims judgment on the nations.[91] This is compelling, especially since the Egyptian could have portrayed himself as the spearhead of the international pilgrimage to Jerusalem for the eschatological feast of Tabernacles there prophesied (Egypt is specified in Zech 14:18).

If this is so, then the destruction of the walls of Jerusalem must have been conceived, implicitly or explicitly, as the overthrow of the existing Jerusalem order, which would release the eschatological flow of living water from the city (Zech 14:8), and bring in the messianic age. Following the Egyptian, therefore, meant opposing the Jerusalem cult and the priesthood that sustained it, as well as opposing the Romans,[92] and so it is interesting to find the anti-hieratical stance of Pseudo-Philo at a popular level both confirmed by Josephus and brought together with the ready acceptance of a prophetic deliverer.[93]

If such currents of thinking were prevalent before 70, they will hardly have been less so after the disaster. Undoubtedly for some, the leaderless confusion of the years before the war, and the factionalism which was so disastrous during it, will have produced a climate in which messianic fervour started looking again for the Figure to lead Israel to victory over her enemies. Hugo Mantel argues that the seeds of the Bar Kokba revolt are to be found in the intense

> desire of the Jews for freedom and salvation — a desire which to the Romans and Christians appeared as nothing but a spirit of madness and suicide. But for the Jews, who despised slavery and subjection, there was no other way. The Jews had not ceased weeping and mourning for the loss of their Temple.[94]

90   *Ant.* 20:169-172

91   Horsley & Hanson *Bandits* 169f; cf R.P. Martin, *James* (Word Biblical Commentary Vol 48; Waco, Word Books, 1988), lxiv

92   Horsley and Hanson do not specifically identify an anti-hieratical and anti-Temple impetus behind this revolt, but they illustrate well the tension between the priestly aristocracy and the 'multitude' in this period (e.g. *Bandits* 178f).

93   Josephus points in the same direction with his portrayal of the violence and rapacity of many priests in the period before the War (*Ant.* 20:180).

94   Mantel "Bar Kokba" 278

So when Bar Kokba appeared, he found a nation ready to support him. Even Akiba was touched by this — and of course Akiba started life as an *am ha-aretz*, a member of "the crowd" (in johannine terms). In the unshakable confidence of Pseudo-Philo we are able to feel the pulse of the Judaism in which Akiba was nurtured and which produced both the Jewish war and the Bar Kokba revolt. The song of Deborah and Barak includes the ringing declaration,

> And from this hour, if Israel falls into distress, it will call upon those witnesses along with these servants, and they will form a delegation to the Most High, and he will remember that day and send the saving power of his covenant.[95]

This is all of enormous significance for the interpretation of the Fourth Gospel, where (a) Jesus is portrayed as a (*the*) prophet through whom alone Israel may be saved, (b) he performs signs to attest his status, (c) a polemic against the cult is signalled right at the start (2:14ff) and pervades the whole, (d) the images and slogans of political deliverance are pointedly employed, and (e) special prominence is given to Tabernacles and its fulfilment in Jesus. All these points remain to be developed, but we will argue that they are all vital for the interpretation of 8:31-59, insofar as our focus rests on the way the passage would have been *heard* in the post-70 situation.

3.4 Conclusion

We may summarise our conclusions as follows.

The external evidence is sadly incomplete. There are elements of diversity not represented in the sources we have surveyed, but clearly reflected in the Fourth Gospel: for instance, we know little about either the Samaritan response to the destruction of the Jerusalem Temple, or the shape of incipient gnosticism among Jews in this period[96] — nor indeed that of Samaritan or proto-gnostic Christianity. Here we are wholly in the realm of speculation. But I believe that enough is known about Judaism in broad terms in this period to

---

95 Ps.-Philo *Bib. Ant.* 32:14

96 See Robinson *Library* 6f. Vermes "Minim" suggests that Gnosticism had influenced the Jews who rejected all but the Decalogue (see above, p. 107): they were the "progressive, enlightened and intellectual *elite* of the Mediterranean, and especially Egyptian, Diaspora". Brooke "Law" 184 n. 64, referring to Vermes' view, suggests that the treatment of the Decalogue in the Fourth Gospel may have been designed to appeal to such Jews.

make it possible to discern how the Fourth Gospel would have been *heard,* either in Judea or in the diaspora. And if, when read against that background, it appears that the Gospel 'fits', that is, makes clear and compelling sense, then that in itself will be an argument for the truth of the hypothesis.

What, then, can we say in broad terms? The decades after 70 AD were marked by a continuing remarkable pluralism within Judaism, to which justice is not done by the widespread view that the sages of Yavneh quickly achieved a new and universally effective settlement. A growing consensus in present scholarship is reflected in the title of the essay-collection *Judaisms and Their Messiahs at the Turn of the Christian Era.*[97] We have discovered a wide spectrum, from the non-cultic, ethical universal "piety" of *Sib. Or.* 4, through the Torah-centred religion of 2 Baruch and the Rabbis, with its revisionist attitude to the cult, to the intense, cult-oriented militarism reflected in *Apoc. Abr.* Sometimes the tensions surface: we noted the anti-militarism of 2 Baruch, and its concern about the abandonment of Torah by some. It is no longer possible to maintain, with Witten-berger, that Judaism was actually strengthened by the destruction of the Temple, because of the speed of the rabbinic reconstruction:[98] the trauma was too great.

The internal 'points of sensitivity' traced in chapter 2 come together with this variety in a remarkable way. Shaye Cohen notes how the sectarianism within Judaism before 70 maintained itself *with reference to* the Temple, because the various groups defined their respective positions over against the Temple. Its destruction, he suggests, undermined this sectarianism and led to a rise of individualism, in which individual prophetic voices sought to make themselves heard.[99] I believe that he is right, and that the Fourth Gospel is one of those voices, seeking to bring order into the social chaos and disorientation which resulted from the disruption of the pre-70 groupings — just as, in different ways, the Rabbis, the apocalyptists, and the militants also sought to.

Before the 'new look' on Yavneh, scholars tended to hold that the Fourth Gospel reflected a situation in which all contact between Jews and Christians had been severed.[100] This now seems increasingly

---

97   Edd. J. Neusner, W.S. Green and E.S. Frerichs (Cambridge; CUP, 1987).

98   Wittenberger "Judenpolemik" 322

99   Cohen "Yavneh" 56f

100   So e.g. Hahn "Juden" 430f, Vouga *Cadre* 73-75 ("la porte est claquée"), Leroy *Rätsel* 173, Nicol *Semeia* 144f; *contra* Martyn *History & Theology* 78-82; Fortna "Locale" 94; Manns *Vérité* 105

unlikely, such was the turmoil and lack of central direction in the decades after the War. Into this situation the Fourth Gospel speaks a message of hope and salvation: of a Temple already rebuilt in the resurrection of Jesus the Christ, who is the promised Prophet of deliverance like Moses; of a people living in intimate communion with God through this Christ, who is to them all that they lost when old Israel died in the flames of Jerusalem, and much more besides; of the continuing life of all the great symbols and institutions of Judaism among this people, including the Scriptures and the festivals; of real and regular revelation by the Spirit among this group; above all, of a God who has not abandoned his people in their hour of need, but has visited them and suffered with and for them, so that their agony is his. And it speaks all this in a way designed to *persuade* the victims of the Jewish war and its aftermath to 'come on board' and accept the faith of this Christ.

Following our method, we must now return to the text of the Gospel and begin to explore the exegetical implications of this broad picture. In three chapters we will gradually focus in on our chosen passage, 8:31-59, setting it in its co-text so that we can hear its authentic voice clearly.

Before we do this, however, we will devote a chapter to issues of hermeneutics and method, following on from our discussion in chapter 1. Readers for whom this technical discussion holds little attraction may jump straight to chapter 5 at this point!

4

Thinking Further About Method

In chapter 1 I proposed the interpretative method on which this study will rest, and we have now seen its first two stages in operation. Before we move on to stage 3,[1] we devote a brief chapter to reflection on the hermeneutics of the method. In particular we will discuss:
- (4.1) the relationship between *function* and *plot;*
- (4.2) the definition of the 'implied reader';
- (4.3) the position of 'original' readers over against later readers; and
- (4.4) some features of johannine rhetoric.

In all this our concern is to discover a *rapprochement* between historical and narrative methods of interpretation, following Stibbe's good example (see above, p 32). I am not alone in feeling that, as Johannes Beutler and Robert Fortna put it, "the reciprocal relation between diachronic and synchronic readings of a text" is a "more and more urgent problem".[2] They do their best to point to common ground between the various essays on John 10 in their collection, but in the long run there is no meeting of minds. The advocates of a synchronic narrative approach simply do not believe that the interest shown by the others in the development of the text, or in the history of the johannine community, or in the author's intention, has any real significance for interpretation. In fact one of the contributors, Hartwig Thyen, calls it a "dangerous illusion" to regard the author's intended meaning as the "right" interpretation, and calls for this illusion to be destroyed. The only wrong interpretations, he maintains, are those which are grammatically imposs-ible.[3]

The combined historical / narrative method proposed here holds

---

1   See above, pp 33f.
2   Johannes Beutler and Robert Fortna (ed.), *The Shepherd Discourse of John 10 and its Context* (Cambridge; CUP, 1991), 4
3   Thyen "Johannes 10" 118

that the *hearing* of the Gospel is even more vital a focus of study than its *writing:* in other words, that the *function* and *rhetoric* of the text in its original, 'natural' setting have interpretative priority over all other appropriations of the text, so that later uses of it which do not converge with its original rhetoric can really be judged *misinterpretations.*

This contention is clearly of great significance for a study of John's anti-Judaism which takes its starting-point from later, anti-semitic uses of the text. In this chapter I simply outline the arguments in support of it, and I refer readers to an essay in which I seek to develop the case more substantially.[4]

4.1 Function and Plot

4.1.1 Function

In the description of our method in chapter 1 we touched on the distinction between *context* and *co-text* (pp 31f). This useful distinction points to the two vital ways in which the meaning of a discourse like John 8:31-59 is constrained: by the social context in which it acted, and by the literary co-text in which it is set. The force of each needs to be analysed with as much precision as possible. The need to allow both to exercise a combined weight in interpretation is the burden of this study.

One of the disappointments of existing studies of 8:31-59 is that, generally speaking, they treat the section in isolation from both context and co-text. Manns *Vérité* examines merely John 7-8, and says very little about setting and function. Lona *Johannes 8* is the first attempt to apply literary theory to the passage, but he merely pays lip-service to the function of the text at reader-level. Aker *Merits* only considers John 7-8, and assumes the Martyn hypothesis. Bartholomew *Sermon-Drama* treats it in complete isolation and makes some unsubstantiated conjectures about genre and function. So any emphasis on function will have to be undergirded by the kind of analysis of context we have attempted in the last two chapters, and will have to be as open to co-text as we seek to be in the next three.

Our approach stands in the tradition of 'text-pragmatism', a 'reader response' theory which maintains that the meaning of a text is bound tightly to its function or effect upon a reader or a group of readers. Walter Rebell summarises it sharply:

---

4   S. Motyer, "Method in the Fourth Gospel Studies: A Way out of the Impasse?", *JSNT* forthcoming (1997)

> The principal idea in 'text-pragmatism' is that a text produces effects on its recipients ... It asks after the 'how' and the 'what' of this process: *how* is *what* done to the reader?[5]

In applying this approach to John, Rebell underlines the importance of background historical analysis, if the function of the text is to be clearly discerned.[6] He quotes Thyen to the effect that only by discovering the historical situation of a text can its polysemy be rendered unambiguous.

Similarly the linguist J.P. Louw suggests that discourse analysis must operate at three levels — the *declarative* and the *structural* levels which are concerned respectively with the *data* and *compositional features* of a text or narrative, and the *intentional* level which is concerned with the actual message conveyed by the text (and which gives the text its semiotic quality).[7] In this he is in line with the movements in linguistics which underlie the development of sociological approaches to interpretation, as we saw above (1.1.4, p 18). As soon as speech is conceived as an *act*, then its meaning becomes attached to the relationships within which it 'operates', and its *function* moves to centre-stage.

Louw may be criticised for his use of the word 'intentional' to describe this third level at which discourse analysis must work, if 'intention' is meant to connote the consciousness of the speaker. While 'intention' may often be more or less co-extensive with the function of an utterance, it will not always be so. Utterances may fail in their intention, or achieve unintended effects. Or it may be impossible to know what the speaker intended. In any case, for 'classic' texts like the Fourth Gospel, authorial intention can only be a matter of conjecture. If inference is an insecure guide to the situation of the johannine community (see 1.2), then this is no less true of the evangelist's intention. Culpepper has underlined this point by introducing the distinction between the *real* and the *implied* author. The implied author may wish to convert readers to Christianity (if this is what 20:30f means), but the real author may have had a different intention — one which can best be achieved by a *presentation* of this sort.

Our best access to intention, anyway, will be through an analysis

---

5   Rebell *Gemeinde* 161f, my trans.

6   *Gemeinde* 86-8. Unfortunately his own analysis of John's context is distinctly thin, because he stands so firmly in the Martyn tradition.

7   Louw "Semiotic"

of function, because it is not unreasonable to assume that effects are intended. However we are only too aware that the Fourth Gospel has had 'effects' far beyond the circumstances of its origin. We are particularly concerned about its antisemitic 'effects'. In itself, 'text-pragmatism' does not require us to give particular attention to the *original* recipients: it invites us to give equal weight to the 'reception' of the text in any community, at any time. Whether the original recipients may claim priority is the question which will occupy us in section 3 below.

4.1.2 Plot

The concept of 'plot' is a useful way of focusing, from a narrative-critical perspective, how the *rhetoric* of the text actually serves its *function*. Here again, Culpepper's discussion is foundational for johannine studies.[8] Vital for our purpose is that Culpepper affirms a *functional* definition of 'plot': that is, that 'plot' is not just the way in which a story is structured, but (quoting Abrams) it is "the structure of its actions, as these are ordered and rendered toward achieving particular emotional and artistic effects".[9] He concludes his chapter on John's plot with the words,

> The gospel's plot, therefore, is controlled by thematic development and a strategy for wooing readers to accept its interpretation of Jesus.[10]

It must be said, however, that the functional aspect, the "wooing" of the readers, does not figure largely in the survey which precedes this conclusion. He concentrates on the other element, that of "thematic development". The reason is not hard to find: Culpepper's application of literary theory to John is ahistorical, and therefore he does not try to discover who *in fact* these readers are, or how *in fact* they might be "wooed". And yet the impetus to do this lies, I believe, in the very narrative theory on which he draws.

Culpepper especially associates the "affective power" of the plot with the characterisation within it, which forms the subject of the next chapter of his book. He writes,

---

8   *Anatomy* 79-148 (his chapters on "Plot" and "Characterisation", which he rightly recognises as vitally interwoven with each other). Cf also Staley *Kiss* 50-73; Kermode "John"; Stibbe *Storyteller* 9-29

9   M.H. Abrams, *A Glossary of Literary Terms* (New York; Holt, Reinhart & Winston, 1971), 127: quoted Culpepper *Anatomy* 80

10   *Anatomy* 98

> The characters, who illustrate a variety of responses, allow the reader to examine the alternatives. The shape of the narrative and the voice of the narrator lead the reader to identify or interact variously with each character.[11]

The characters within the plot, therefore, are the focus of its function for Culpepper. They are like a rack of clothes in a boutique: "readers may place themselves in the role of each character successively while searching for the response they will choose" (*ibid.*). However, three objections may be lodged against this analysis of the way the plot "woos":

• Firstly, it tends to isolate the characters from the overall narrative, which presents them as acting and reacting within a *story*.

• Secondly, the Gospel itself locates its "affective power" in the signs (20:30f), and of course it is often in response to these that the characters act.

• And thirdly, Culpepper has presented no evidence to suggest that readers *are* searching for an example to follow in this way. Even if they are, simply illustrating alternative responses will not necessarily move them to follow the *right* example, from the evangelist's perspective.

Merely as story, of course, the Gospel certainly has "affective power", and it is this which has made it the 'classic' text it is: through the gripping intensity and intellectual strength of its theological statements, the vividness of its characterisation, the moving contrast between the rejection of Jesus by "the Jews" and the closeness of his relationship with the disciples in chs. 13-17, and the sheer power-to-move of each of the story-gems within it. Culpepper effectively summarises these features. *But, within the terms of the definition he accepts, what he describes is the Gospel's story, not its plot.* The "affective power" of the *plot* lies, I suggest, in the dynamic way in which the history of Jesus is made to speak to the concerns and agonies of post-70 Jews. Without this essential background, there is no *plot*, because there is no function.

Once again, however, we face the question: why should we give priority to *those* Jews? Wherever and whenever the Gospel "woos" readers "to accept its interpretation of Jesus", must we not accept that the strategies of its 'plot' have achieved their purpose? The answer to this must surely be 'Yes' — and yet I wish to argue that the first generation have a prior claim as the primary objects of the

11   *Anatomy* 148

Gospel's strategies. We return to this point after asking —

4.2 The 'implied reader' — who is it?

The notion of the 'implied reader' is a most useful interpretative device in the context of an emphasis on function. For it helps to 'idealise' the function of the text. I have presented evidence which suggests that the Gospel would have been felt to address the needs of Jews wrestling with the trauma of the destruction of the Temple. But there were thousands of Jews in that situation, and doubtless only a small number of them actually read or heard the Fourth Gospel. And of those who did, probably only a small proportion became Christians as a result. In addition the Gospel exercised a wide appeal among Christians of various types. It was quickly taken up by Gnostics, whose use of it inhibited its popularity in more 'orthodox' circles. Where is its 'real' function amid this diversity? To search for the 'implied reader' of this text enables us to reconstruct its 'implied function', to be distinguished from its *actual* function with *real* readers.

4.2.1 According to Culpepper ...

The first application of the idea of an 'implied reader' to John was by Culpepper.[12] His presentation is notable for the way in which he seeks to hold together the notions of 'implied' and 'intended' readership — in a manner also exemplified by William Kurz, who moves easily between them:

> The only evidence for the intended readership of most ancient texts like the Fourth Gospel is the text itself. Since the text reveals only its implied readers and not its real readers ...[13]

So Culpepper, in a rather traditional way, seeks to build up a picture of the implied = intended readership from the internal evidence of the text. He is particularly impressed by the repeated explanation of Jewish festivals and customs, and the occasional translation of Hebrew terms: "A Jewish audience would not need such explanations".[14] So he comes to a very different conclusion from ours:

---

12   *Anatomy* 205-227. The expression was coined by Wayne Booth in his *The Rhetoric of Fiction* (Chicago; Univ. of Chicago Press, 1961).

13   Kurz "Beloved Disciple" 100. So also Osborne *Spiral* 162f.

14   Culpepper *Anatomy* 219-222 (quotation 220)

It appears that the intended readers are not Jewish, but their prior knowledge of many parts of the gospel story shows that the intended audience is either Christian or at least is familiar with the gospel story.[15]

He is vulnerable to criticism here, not just for importing the notion of 'intention' into the discussion, but also for his assessment of this internal evidence. He himself notes that not all customs or expressions are explained. For instance,

In view of the translations provided in the first chapter for "Rabbi" and "Messiah", it is somewhat surprising that no explanation of "the Son of Man" (1:51) seems to be needed.[16]

The surprise is even greater when it comes to allusions to Old Testament and Jewish texts or themes which play a crucial role in the message of the Gospel, but whose basic contours are assumed — like "the prophet", and the Tabernacles rituals. In fact the puzzle posed by the Hebrew translations in 1:38-42 — three of them in the course of five verses — is greater than Culpepper allows. He restricts himself to the question, 'If the readership is Jewish, why are the translations supplied?' But we must also ask, 'If the readership is Gentile, why are the Hebrew originals used at all?' Clearly something rather odd is afoot. We need the more sophisticated discussion provided by Jeffrey Lloyd Staley:

4.2.2 According to Staley ...
Staley criticises Culpepper for failing to distinguish between 'implied' and 'intended' readers.[17] For him, the 'implied reader' occupies no location in space or time, certainly not in an author's mind. It is a way of describing "a narrative text's manipulation of temporality" which "gives rise to the rhetorical devices of surprise and suspense".[18] A *narrative*, he argues, has an implicit sequential quality which implies an act of reading but which is *a quality of the text whether anyone reads it or not*: and it is this quality which Staley dubs 'implied reader'.

The word 'reader' is thus a metaphor, and has nothing to do with real readers, either ancient or modern. Real readers can be re-

---

15 *Anatomy* 224
16 *Anatomy* 221
17 *Kiss* 13-15
18 Staley *Kiss* 34

readers, and can thus illumine earlier parts of the narrative by later parts; they read it in a particular setting, bring to the text a wide range of experiences and cultural assumptions which shape their reading, and may or may not be persuaded by it. But this 'implied reader' brings to the text only a knowledge of koine Greek,[19] is always reading the text for the first time, with a perfect memory of what has preceded, and always performs the responses the text calls for.

This leads to some extraordinary exegesis. For instance, because the 'implied reader' is a wholly text-internal creature, he (it) cannot supply the geographical and historical information which would enable him to know that the Bethany of 11:1 is not the same as the Bethany of 1:28. So Staley interprets 11:1-18 as if the 'implied reader' is misled into identifying the two — which would mean, of course, that the reader assumes that Jesus is *not* at a distance when the sisters send word about Lazarus' illness.[20]

But this distinction between Greek (which the implied reader 'knows') and local history, geography, culture, and traditions (which it does not know) is hardly tenable. It is a commonplace of linguistic theory that language and culture (in the broadest sense) are mutually self-referring and reinforcing.[21] Should the 'implied reader' not be permitted to know whatever the text seems to take for granted? We need an approach which mediates between Staley and Culpepper, if possible — and Staley in fact points us in the right direction, for he fails to carry through his definition of the 'implied reader' consistently. He simply cannot resist the pressure to allow his 'implied reader' to have some historical dimensions, beyond mere linguistic competence.

We see this in the stimulating answer he gives to the puzzle about the interpreted Hebrew expressions and customs. He suggests that the purpose of these notes is to establish the reliability of the narrator. The narrator shares knowledge of the meaning of these terms with the implied reader, who is thus reassured about the narrator's

---

19   *Kiss* 36

20   *Kiss* 105-7

21   This insight goes back to Saussure's distinction between *langue* and *parole*: *langue* is the language-capacity of a language-group, thus involving all that makes them a social unit; *parole* is an individual utterance, a concretization of *langue* in a particular instance (Saussure *Course* 11-15). Koester *Symbolism* 15-17 emphasises the close interplay between johannine symbolism and its cultural background. He illustrates his point with "shepherd", which is loaded with literary, cultural and affective overtones in a first-century Hellenistic context.

competence as he sees him handling the language accurately and correctly explaining Jewish customs.[22] Doubtless Jews were frequently called upon to supply such explanations, and their presence in the text would signal not only the narrator's trustworthiness, but also the relevance of this Gospel to Gentiles. Staley's insight helps to explain both the *selective* nature of these explanations overall, and the further particular puzzle about 1:38-42.

But here we see the 'implied reader' taking on a cultural identity! It has become more than the mere temporality of the text. It is looking like a first-century Jew. For all Staley's determination to keep the distinction between real and implied readers watertight, little breaches in the dyke let the water of history seep through into the world of the text.[23]

4.2.3 Our definition ...

Rather than define the 'implied reader' through a narrative theory, like Staley, I find a particular 'reader' implied by the dynamics of the relationship between this narrative which aims to persuade, and the situation within which it speaks. At a handful of crucial places, the *narrator* and the *narratee* of the Fourth Gospel put in an explicit appearance, and these must figure prominently in our definition. We have already identified 20:30f as signalling a 'point of sensitivity' for the Gospel, and this is one such place:

• At 1:14, 16 we meet the "we" who have seen the glory of the one and only Son, and received from his grace. From this point on, the Gospel assumes the character of personal testimony to experience of the divine in Christ.

• This relates to 20:31, which is anticipated by 19:35. Here the "we" directly address the "you" whom they hope to draw into the same experience of life through faith in Christ.

• Finally 21:24 is meant to secure the reliability of the story told by this "we". They refer allusively to the un-named source on which their testimony rests, who turns out to be none other than the 'Beloved Disciple'. The "you" of 20:31 are the implicit object of this statement of reliability.

Who is this "you"? From a narrative perspective, they cannot be the *intended* readership, because the notion of intention is too slippery to be helpful in a definition. They must also be other than

---

22 Staley *Kiss* 38

23 In fact Staley admits the connection between language and its wider context when he writes that "most of the allusions and socio-historical contexts of the language are not lost in translation" (*Kiss* 36). This seems inconsistent with his point about "Bethany" in his exegesis of John 11:1-18.

the *real* readership, because this must have included (as it still does) countless readers who already believe that Jesus is the Christ, and who thus recognise that, though it shines on them, they are not at the focal point of this text. So I define the "you" of 20:31 as the *implied* readership, that is, as *that imaginary amalgamated group of types of reader who are the objects of persuasion by this text.*

My hypothesis is that the "you" is made up of all Jews of the late first century who would have felt themselves to be specifically addressed by this text, whether they read it and were persuaded by it or not. They are life-like, but exist only in theory. They are people with a wide knowledge of the language, culture, traditions and history which shaped the late first-century Jewish world.[24] Above all they have experienced and are trying to come to terms with the loss which had befallen all Jews, whether Christian or not, in the destruction of the Temple.

I believe that the text will support my contention that such an address would have been heard right across the wide spectrum of *types* of Judaism 'on offer' at that time (including Samaritanism). The implied readers are more than life-like also in that they are presumed to be co-operative, that is, to be willing to listen, open to persuasion, and ready to assume honesty and consistency on the part of the narrator (a vital assumption which is well and truly tested in the course of the narrative). They have flesh and blood, but cannot be identified with any particular group, because they have characteristics which in sum would not be found in real readers.

4.3 The original readers — do they have priority?

As we noted above, an emphasis on the function of the text does not in itself highlight its *original* function — that is (in our terms), its function among its 'implied readers', those who occupy the same socio-cultural world as the text and who supremely might have been persuaded by it to believe in Christ. If there is an argument which gives the original implied readership a privileged status over all other (later) readers, then this will be of considerable significance for us. We will be able to exclude as illegitimate all anti-Jewish appropriations of the Fourth Gospel, if these do not cohere with its original functionality. But is there such an argument?

24   It is fascinating to see how the metaphor becomes personified for Staley, rather like Philo's *Logos:* so much so that he interprets the "you" of 20:31 (which of course is *plural*) as a direct address by the narrator to his *implied* reader (*Kiss* 112).

I believe that there is. I seek to develop it more fully elsewhere,[25] but in essence it has two elements and runs like this:

4.3.1 The Gospel's 'natural' setting

Stibbe uses the word "natural" when describing his own hermeneutical approach to the Fourth Gospel:

> I choose instead to analyse NT narrative against its natural background, which is primarily OT narrative, and secondarily those Greek narrative forms whose presence can be clearly felt.[26]

He is defining "natural background" in purely literary terms here. It would be open to us to widen the definition, so as to cover all the 'background' we have surveyed in chapters 2 and 3. But we still need to ask what the word 'natural' means in this context, and how appropriate it is.

We must of course take seriously the *Wirkungsgeschichte* of the Fourth Gospel — that is, the history of the effects that it has exerted through the centuries. This whole study is motivated by one particular aspect of that *Wirkungsgeschichte*. We must equally allow full room for appropriations of the Gospel which do not concern themselves with analysis of its historical roots — in art, drama, liturgy or personal devotion. But *finally* we must recognise (I contend) that it has a 'natural' setting to which due attention must be given, however often it has been transplanted into different soil.

It is that 'you-plural' address in 20:31 which signals dramatically for us this 'natural' rootedness of the Gospel. Here is a group — definable by historical investigation — to whom this text is actually addressed. They are the ones who might be persuaded by *this* text, rather than by another, to believe that Jesus is the Christ. Finally, therefore, a narrative-critical approach to John cannot do justice to it, if it ignores the historical rootedness signalled by this "you". We may develop this argument further:

4.3.2 The Gospel's natural 'owners'

The concept of 'ownership' has some hermeneutical currency. Croatto employs it in his *Biblical Hermeneutics* to argue that interpretation should be wrested from the hands of powerful professionals and returned to the poor:

---

25 See the essay mentioned above (n. 4).
26 *Storyteller* 22f

It is not difficult to recognize that the most adequate "ownership" of the Bible, the most adequate "pertinency" for rereading the kerygma of the Bible, is with the poor. That kerygma belongs to them "preferentially" — first and foremost.[27]

He argues for this on the ground of the *content* of the Bible — that it consistently portrays "God's preference for the oppressed, the marginalized, the sick, sinners, and so on". This overall tendency confers rights of interpretative 'ownership', he suggests, on those who 'fit' the obvious concern of the text.

A 'classic' text like the Fourth Gospel belongs, of course, to all who value and use it. But all texts, even classics, are 'owned' by a person or group, implied or real, who have a natural priority in interpretation, even if this is not exercised or asserted. And quite clearly the Fourth Gospel 'belongs' in this sense to its *implied* readership, to those who have the right to say what the precise force of its arguments are, as they exert pressure on *them* to make the suggested response.[28]

If plot is defined functionally, and if the final rights of 'ownership' of this text are invested, not in all readers, but in a historically identifiable group, the "you" of 20:31, then the plot will be revealed as we discover the strategy of this text to affect *this group*, as distinct from all others. This is the aim which we will pursue in the following chapters.

4.4 Some features of johannine rhetoric

Before we move back to the text, we touch briefly on some important features of its *rhetoric*, that is, the techniques it employs in order to exercise persuasive power. Recent studies have focused upon many such devices, like irony and misunderstanding, symbolism, *double entendre*, repetition and pairing of episodes, as well as inclusion, chiasmus and 'dramatic' techniques. Rather than survey them all, it seems best to discuss them *ad hoc* as we encounter them in the text in the course of the next three chapters. However, three particular topics ask for a preliminary discussion, because of their special importance and relevance.

---

27   J.S. Croatto, *Biblical Hermeneutics. Toward a Theory of Reading as the Production of Meaning* (Maryknoll; Orbis, 1987), 62f

28   I am conscious that my argument is condensed here. I pursue it more fully in the related article (n. 4).

4.4.1 'Discontinuous dialogue'

This is a newcomer to the scene. It is an interesting literary device described by A.D. Nuttall, David Jasper, Martin Warner and Mark Stibbe, who have all used it to illumine the dialogue between Jesus and Pilate in John 18:33-38.[29] Stibbe refers to "the systematic absence of logical fit between Pilate's questions and Jesus' answers",[30] and quotes Nuttall's description of the 'discontinuity' as "a technique of deliberate transcendence", a way of conveying a sense of "an enormous mystery".[31]

This approach is of significance for the exposition of 8:31-59, although I want to refine this definition of 'discontinuous dialogue'. It is not so much the absence of "logical fit" which constitutes it, as the *unexpectedness* of Jesus' responses, the *sideways* logic which both he and the narrator employ. As Jasper notes, this unexpectedness throws the reader off balance, makes her look for the logic, and thus compels her to become

> involved in the text, adjusting the focus and pitch, negotiating the implications of discussions carried out under such odd conditions.[32]

"Transcendence" may be an element of the reader's conclusion, as a result of this negotiation: but *the technique itself* does not imply transcendence. It is a "process of imaginative demand" (Warner), a down-to-earth narrative device aimed at gripping — and hopefully fascinating — the reader.[33]

We see this happening, not just in the dialogues, but also in the narration. In the first sign (2:1-11), the story reaches an impasse at the end of verse 5: the problem has been introduced, but extraordinarily Jesus has refused to act in response to his mother's prompting, and has even given her a rather rude brush-off (2:4).[34] How

---

29   A.D. Nuttall, *Overheard by God: Fiction and Prayer in Herbert, Milton, Dante and St John* (London; Methuen, 1980); Jasper *Imagination* 43-46; Warner "Persuasion" 168f; Stibbe "Elusive" 27f.

30   "Elusive" 28

31   Nuttall *op. cit.* 131, 134, quoted Stibbe "Elusive" 28

32   Jasper *Imagination* 44

33   Rebell discusses this feature of the johannine narrative, but describes it differently. He underlines the *didactic function* of the narrative, and analyses its technique in terms of "provocative gaps in the narrative" ("Reizwort-Leerstellen"): by this he means that the reader is faced with a narrative which challenges and tempts him by leaving certain vital elements unexpressed, so that he has to supply background knowledge essential to understand the story (for instance, the knowledge of Old Testament 'well and betrothal' scenes which fill out the meaning of 4:1-42): e.g. *Gemeinde* 200f.

can the story progress from this point? Amazingly, Jesus' mind is apparently changed by the sight of the stone jars "provided for Jewish purification" (2:6). This sideways lurch in the narrative — so unexpected — has the effect of moving the issue of 'purification' into the centre of interest, where it stays for the next three chapters.

A similar technique is employed also with Nicodemus, with the Samaritan woman, with the Galilean crowd in ch. 6, with the brothers of Jesus in 7:1-13, and with "the Jews" in 8:31-59, as we shall see.

4.4.2 Indeterminacy and openness

As a way of exercising "imaginative demand", this discontinuous dialogue is an instance of the general *openness* of the johannine narrative. Responses are not prescribed, but the implied reader is made to realise that a response is necessary. Staley illustrates this at several points in the narrative. We may mention again the wedding at Cana. Here the challenge to the implied reader is underlined by what Staley calls the "underdetermining of the text's symbolic code" — i.e. the miracle is presented as *sign*ificant, but the *what it signifies* is not specified:

> The implied author destabilises the implied reader's 'earthly' reading of the story without giving him all the tools he needs to reconstruct its symbolic, 'heavenly' significance.[35]

In other words, we are told that the event reveals the glory of Jesus (2:11), but are not told *how*, nor what the content of the disciples' responsive faith is. Similarly Bassler calls the Nicodemus episode "an unsatisfying encounter", in that so many questions are left unanswered.[36] He seems to be in just the same position as the disciples, believing on the basis of the signs (cf 2:11), and yet he is treated sharply by Jesus. Nicodemus' response is left unclear — and his later appearances in 7:50-52 and 19:39-42 do nothing to clear up the uncertainty. Is he a believer, or not? Bassler regards the ambiguity as deliberate:

> Nicodemus creates a cognitive 'gap' in the text that the reader must

---

34   Staley *Kiss* 89 comments that the story is 'destabilised' by the addition of "my" to "hour": "It just doesn't fit with the story as the story has developed thus far ... the implied reader is thrown off guard and must reevaluate his understanding".

35   Staley *Kiss* 87f

36   Bassler "Nicodemus" 637

fill ... the struggle to resolve Nicodemus's indeterminacy forces the reader to wrestle with the contours of Johannine faith.[37]

We will have occasion to notice the use and effects of this indeterminacy at several points in John 7-8. When the 'implied reader' is conceived as a third party experiencing the narrative from 'outside', this effect becomes apparent.

One feature of this indeterminacy only appears when we reflect that, frequently, reading of texts like the Fourth Gospel was a public rather than private event.[38] The exigencies of book-production meant that often it would be read out loud to a group (whether in worship or not). This is significant for interpretation at points where the *tone of voice* in delivery has a strong effect on the meaning: for instance, the text does not prescribe with what tone of voice Nicodemus' question "How can this be?" (3:9) should be read: with scornful scepticism, puzzled incomprehension, frank astonishment, or wistful longing?[39] The (public) reader would have to make this decision 'on the hoof', and the hearers would appreciate the dilemma.

In a text like 8:31-59, full of direct speech expressing apparent hostility, tone of voice in delivery will make an appreciable difference to meaning.

4.4.3 Structure

We need briefly to consider this issue from a theoretical perspective, before embarking on our treatment of the text. Recent literary criticism has an ambivalent attitude towards analysis of *structure*. Such analysis has always been a feature of commenting on John, even if it amounted only to a rudimentary division into broad sections.[40] However alongside this rather minimal approach there have been many attempts to show that the Fourth Gospel has a highly developed structure, often employing chiasmus to a high

---

37 "Nicodemus" 644

38 See Stanton *New People* 73-76, citing B.M.W. Knox, "Silent Reading in Antiquity", *GRBS* 9 (1968), 421-435.

39 The commentators, of course, try to resolve the uncertainty: *incomprehension* (the majority option: e.g. Bernard 1:108, Bultmann 143f, Sanders 126, Barrett 211, Bruce 86, Becker 138, Michaels 40, Painter *Quest* 162); *scepticism* (Lindars 154, Schnackenburg 1:374, Beasley-Murray 49, Carson 198); *astonishment* (Godet 2:55); *wistfulness* — no candidates (why not?).

40 So e.g. Barrett 11-15; Lindars 70-73. Apart from his tables of Contents, Schnackenburg devotes no attention to literary structure aside from the question of possible textual displacements and evidence of editing (1:44-58).

degree. George Mlakuzhyil reviews all such attempts in his own massive contribution to this debate,[41] which proposes a complex analysis with five main sections, all but the third of which have detailed chiastic structures. He criticises Culpepper for restricting his interest to plot development and ignoring the presence of "Semitic literary devices" like "inclusion".[42] Culpepper never discusses the issue, but we may imagine that he would regard such detailed analyses as incompatible with a functional understanding of plot: what affects the reader is not a chiastic structure teased out after multiple readings, but the powerful impact of the developing story.

In contrast to Culpepper, Staley proposes an elaborate structure for the whole Gospel, in which the chiastic pattern of the Prologue is repeated in four following main sections.[43] He follows Matthias Rissi in ascribing pivotal significance to the journeys of Jesus, which are taken to mark the boundaries between sections.[44] But when he turns to the discussion of the "rhetorical strategies" employed to 'manipulate' the implied reader in the first section, 1:19-3:36, the chiastic structure of the section is not one of them. In fact, he then gives a different analysis of the section altogether.[45] So there is considerable ambiguity in his use of the word 'rhetorical', which he employs to describe both the chiastic literary analysis, and the way in which the text seeks to persuade.[46] The word does not mean the same in the two applications, and its use in connection with both conceals a substantial lack of coherence in his book. He does not explain how the repeated chiastic pattern contributes to the *functional force* of the Gospel.

I argue therefore that *the strategy of the story to persuade* must be the governing principle in the analysis of its structure. Only when this principle is allowed precedence can we have confidence that structural analysis will not fall prey to subjectivity. *"How is what done to the reader?"* is the basic question,[47] so answers to the ques-

---

41   Mlakuzhyil *Structure*. His review does not include Ellis *Genius*, nor the more recent (1991) contribution of Gunnar Østenstad ("Structure"), which proposes a magnificent concentric structure with seven sections, all focused around 10:24-39 at the heart of section four.

42   Mlakuzhyil *Structure* 62

43   *Kiss* 50-73

44   Rissi "Aufbau". This focus on the structural significance of the journeys has been now taken up by Stibbe, e.g. *John* 123. Stibbe's interest in Jesus' journeys is more theological than structural, however: he underlines the elusiveness of Jesus in John, something signalled by his constant movements (cf Stibbe "Elusive").

45   *Kiss* 74-94

46   E.g. *Kiss* 74f

47   See the quotation from Rebell above, p 107.

tion "How?" must fall within the reasonably presumed range of the reader's perception. Nothing will be "done to" her by literary structures which fall outside her perception. This is not to say, of course, that such elaborate concentric and other structures *do not exist*. The Fourth Gospel has mysteries that only disclose themselves on multiple readings. However in this study we are concerned with the direct rhetorical effect which an initial (or second) reading would have had on our 'implied reader'.

We return now to the text of John, in order to apply the third stage of our method, and to seek out its function among the implied readers whom we posit.

5

Hearing 5:1-12:50:
its literary and rhetorical structures

We now return to the text of John in order to 'hear its voice' within the setting we have proposed. This is an imaginative exercise, in which we seek to 'step into the shoes' of late first-century Jews and listen to the Gospel through their ears. Of course, we are not trying to imagine whether readers would have made a *faith*-response. Our aim is simply to discern in what ways the text would have been heard to *address their needs, desires and ideas*.

Our survey has underlined the wide spectrum of 'types' of Judaism in this period. Potentially, many different Jewish ears might have responded to this text. We have suggested a particular engagement with the Torah- and Temple-centred religion of Judea, and with the special trauma caused to such Jews by the loss of the Temple, and clearly we must test this suggestion. But the argument from 'fit' will be important as we bear in mind the whole range of needs, desires and ideas felt and expressed in this desperate period of Jewish history.

The focus of our interest is 8:31-59; but because its meaning is shaped by its co-text, we preface our examination of it with two short chapters in which we approach it through two concentric circles, first looking at its place within John 5-12 (this chapter), and then within John 7-8 (chapter 6). Our aim here is not to provide an exegesis of these chapters, but to carry on the process of discerning the 'points of sensitivity' signalled by the text itself: in other words, to identify and describe those features of the text where its quality as *address* seems particularly clear. As we conduct this broad survey of John 5-12, four features of the story clamour for our attention: the festivals, the law, the 'division' motif and the signs. Our method will prove its value as it enables us to identify certain facets of their treatment which have been missed by less focused approaches.

5.1 The Festivals

5.1.1 The festivals and the structure of John 5-12

At 5:1 there begins a long sweep of text structured around a successive treatment of the festivals, beginning with the unnamed 'feast' of 5:1, and including two Passovers (6:4, 11:55). As first sight the festival in ch. 5 seems to be no more than a staging device, designed just to move Jesus to Jerusalem. But there is more than meets the eye. Just when the attention of all is focused on the Temple, Jesus bypasses it and seeks out a man who is marginalised from the cult — who in fact was not permitted to enter the Temple because of his disability,[1] and who has put his faith in a pagan-sounding superstition beside one of the many *mikvoth* in the area behind the Temple.[2] Such a man finds in Jesus the full answer to his need, even though his response seems inadequate. The narrative gently pokes at the inadequacy of the Temple cult, for readers would all accept the connection (granted in 5:14) between the man's condition and his sin. But he is helpless, even though he lies under the shadow of the Temple where sin is dealt with — until Jesus the new Temple appears.

The main 'hinge' between the sign and the discourse is, of course, the Sabbath and its associated 'working' motif. This provides the evangelist with the opportunity to develop the great christological claims of 5:19-30. But when the discourse reaches its climax with the claim that "Moses wrote of me" and its converse that "Moses accuses you" (5:45-6), Jesus' behaviour at the festival is also connoted. He is addressing those who have scrupulously observed both the festival and the Sabbath, while he has been lax — certainly about the Sabbath, possibly about the festival too.

Lindars 233 rightly points out that 5:46 forms the agenda for

1   In 1QSa 2:5-10 no one who is "lame in his feet or hands, limping or blind or deaf or dumb or afflicted with a visible blemish" is permitted to appear in the congregation. This appears to rest on the theology which Neusner ascribes to the Pharisees before 70, namely the extension of Temple purity regulations to the whole of life: see Lev 21:16-23. Later rabbinic Judaism took this up: in *m. Hag.* 1:1 "a lame man and a blind man" are barred from the three pilgrim festivals.

2   Davies *Land* 311-313 maintains (following Duprez) that pagan cults flourished in this area of cosmopolitan Jerusalem, and that the lame man was possibly putting his faith in a healing cult dedicated to Serapis. We do not need 5:4 (almost certainly not original) to reveal that a healing cult was associated with this pool (5:7 is sufficient for this). Fringe Judaism was remarkably capable of absorbing elements of paganism in this period. Jesus steps out of the religion of Judea, strictly defined, in reaching out to such a man.

chapter 6. However the 'agenda' is not just the presentation of the evidence that Jesus is the 'prophet like Moses' of Deut 18. We also need to know how Jesus can play fast and loose with the Mosaic law (apparently), while still retaining the 'witness' of Moses in support. And as a motivation this extends beyond ch. 6, as we shall see: in fact it is the fundamental concern of these chapters.

Chapters 6-12 are structured chiefly around the great pilgrim festivals of Passover (ch. 6, 11:55ff) and Tabernacles (7:1-10:21), with Dedication given a special role (10:22-11:54) because of its particular significance for the Temple into whose place Jesus steps. Each festival is hijacked in turn for Christian faith, as Jesus is portrayed as its 'true' or 'real' counterpart.

That the whole of 7:1-10:21 can be placed under a 'Tabernacles' rubric is disputed,[3] but seems right. The festival is not mentioned after 7:37, but the 'light' imagery (8:12) recurs in 9:5, and Siloam (9:7) featured in the daily water-ritual.[4] The specifically Tabernacles imagery is bound up with other themes *connoted* by celebration of the feast, most notably the law, the flock of God, and (of course) the problem of theodicy caused by the destruction of the Temple: "Who sinned ...?" (9:2). We will consider these themes below.

Similarly the thematic significance of Dedication (Hanukkah — the festival celebrating the re-dedication of the Temple in 164 BC after the Maccabean victory) is usually limited to 10:22-42, and in particular to the use of ἁγιάζω ("dedicate") in 10:36.[5] But the significance seems much greater than this. Not only do commentators generally miss the connection with 2:19-22 (Jesus *is* the renewed Temple), but they also fail to spot the evocative Maccabean imagery in 10:22-42 and in ch. 11. In seeking to take direct action against blasphemy (10:33), the Jews are standing in the tradition of the Maccabean heroes who opposed Antiochus IV Epiphanes, the pagan king who also "being a man, made [himself] God".

But on the other hand *Jesus* is portrayed in Maccabean terms when Thomas declares "Let us also go, that we may die with him!" (11:16); and as the story proceeds we realise that the deliverance of

---

3   E.g. by Schnackenburg 2:187

4   The way in which the johannine narrative silently presumes knowledge of the Tabernacles ceremonies is well known (e.g. Brown 1:326-8, 344). Jesus' claim in 7:37-39 alludes to the daily water-ceremony, in which a procession passed from the Temple to draw water in the pool of Siloam, and then returning marched around the altar, pouring the water down the steps and reciting Ps 118:25. On the first evening four great lamps were erected in the Temple, whose light was said to shine out into the streets of Jerusalem (*m. Sukk.* 5:2-4)

5   So e.g. Beasley-Murray 173, 177; Brown 1:405

Lazarus from death is undertaken at the cost of Jesus' own life. Ironically, he will lose his life because the Jews are afraid that, because of him, Antiochus' contemporary equivalent will come and try the same again (11:48). But in fact this Maccabean self-sacrifice by Jesus will lead to the *restoration* of the people (11:51f) and their deliverance from a great oppressor who *already* holds sway over them — *death*.

The use of imagery drawn from the festivals throughout this section creates its own irony, inevitably reminding readers of what they have lost, and of their need to find something to fill the gap. Setting Jesus' ministry in this context is a persuasive strategy, making Jesus directly relevant to these deeply-felt needs.

But it is not just the use of familiar (and poignant) imagery which makes the message relevant. The evangelist employs a particular dramatic technique to press readers towards a decision about Jesus:

5.1.2 Participation or not?

The theme of *violation of the law* by Jesus continues through these chapters. It would be possible to argue that in ch. 5 he violates not the law but Jewish Sabbath *halakah* ('moral teaching') — though this distinction would appear unreal to our 'implied reader'. But the same cannot be said of 6:53-58, where Jesus flouts the prohibition against eating blood (cf Lev 17:10-14). No Jewish reader would be surprised at the reaction of some of the disciples (6:60, 66). Far more surprising is Peter's, "You have the words of eternal life ... You are the Holy One of God" (6:68f). How can this be the case, when Jesus has just deliberately rejected one of the precepts of Torah?

Something similar happens in connection with the festivals. First, Jesus apparently does not go to Jerusalem to participate in the Passover mentioned in 6:4. In fact, the response of "the twelve" in staying with him (6:68) seems to mean that they, too, remain in Galilee (7:1) when many of their fellow-Jews (those who *leave* Jesus) are obeying the command to present themselves before the Lord in Jerusalem (Deut 16:16, Lev 23:33ff).

Matters are made worse by Jesus' direct refusal to go to Jerusalem for Tabernacles in 7:6-8. Surprisingly, I cannot find a single commentator who remarks on the breach of Torah which this involves — let alone on the significance of this within a narrative in which Moses is being claimed as a witness on behalf of Jesus.[6] Jesus' refusal is so worded that participation in the Feast could even be among the

---

6   Hahn "Juden" 431 n. 12 actually lists 7:2ff amongst references indicating that Jesus participated in festivals!

"works" which he calls "evil" (7:7).[7]

The attention of commentators naturally focuses on the "contra-diction" (Lindars 285) between 7:8 (where Jesus refuses to go) and 7:10, where he changes his mind and goes. Schnackenburg reviews and rejects five interpretations, and then proposes an equally unlikely solution of his own.[8] For Staley, this is another example of the "victimization" of the implied reader, whereby the relation of trust between narrator and reader is suddenly violated by something totally unexpected.[9] And certainly, this is another instance of *discontinuous* narrative, in the sense discussed above (4.4.1, pp 117f). Since Jesus has been portrayed as a faithful festival pilgrim (2:13, 5:1), the last thing the reader expects is this extraordinary refusal followed by an equally extraordinary change of mind.

But we have presupposed a relationship of co-operation between narrator and 'implied reader'. The reader will not jump to the con-clusion drawn by Porphyry, that Jesus was simply irresolute.[10] He will assume that there is a coherent reason for Jesus' behaviour — and when a reason is observed, the spirit of co-operation is streng-thened and the reader takes a step further towards *faith*.

Staley maintains that no reason is given: "the implied reader ... only comes up with confusion".[11] But this is unduly pessimistic. The distinction between "openly" and "in secret" (7:10) would have held a particular connotation for our 'implied reader' (as opposed to Staley's) which makes it coherent. Jesus refuses to participate in "this feast" (7:8), which represents a "time" for his brothers but not for him (7:6). Even when he goes to Jerusalem — late — it is clearly *not*

---

7   Of course attendance at the festivals was not universal: but more went to Tabernacles than to any other, according to Josephus *Ant.* 8:100, and any who aspired to leadership would have to be as scrupulous as possible. Cf *m. 'Abot.* 3:16: "R. Eleazar, the Modiite, said: He who profanes holy things and despises the set feasts [and shames his associate in public], and makes void the covenant of Abraham our father, and discloses meanings in the Torah which are not according to the Rule, yea, even if he have [Torah and] good works, he has no portion in the world to come" (trans. Herford, *APOT* 2:701). Herford suggests that the chief objects of this saying were Jewish Christians, but they were by no means the only Jews at whom it could have been directed (see above, 3.3.1).

8   Schnackenburg 2:142f: Jesus is simply acting out of his own "sovereign consciousness". On the one hand, he "must contradict his unbelieving relatives", but on the other he must go to Jerusalem because of the state of division amongst people over him. But this does not solve the problem: why does Jesus contradict his unbelieving relatives, when they are telling him to obey the law?

9   Staley *Kiss* 103-105

10   Cited by Bruce 173

11   *Kiss* 104

as a participant, because no one could participate "in secret". Tabernacles was a public occasion.

Rather, Jesus has another "time" in mind for himself — one which begins half-way through the feast (7:14), when he *does* start to reveal himself to the world (7:4). Then the reader hears Jesus proclaiming himself as the centre of an *alternative* Tabernacles, a spiritual one in which the water of the daily ritual is replaced by the Holy Spirit (7:37-39), and the Temple lamps are replaced by Jesus himself as the light of *the world* (8:12, 9:5).

So Jesus never participates in "*this* feast". His apparent vacillation is a vivid means both of distancing himself from the Jerusalem celebration, and of remaining in contact with it in order to proclaim its fulfilment (and therefore replacement).

But here is the 'crunch' question: In refusing to participate, is he a law-breaker and deceiver, or "a good man" (7:12)? The reader is brought face to face with this dilemma. The question can only be answered by the means to which the discussion in 7:16-24 points: by "right judgment", an open-minded willingness to re-read the Scriptures in the light of Jesus' claim (as we will see below).

We encounter disruption of the 'normal' festival procedures later in the section also. Davies maintains that walking in Solomon's Portico (10:23) implies that Jesus has distanced himself from the Dedication celebration.[12] And in the case of the final Passover (11:55-12:19), there are many such features. Jesus is again late (11:56); he does not go to the Temple to "purify" himself like everyone else (11:55), but instead undergoes his own ceremony of consecration in the house at Bethany,[13] which itself begins to look like a Temple (12:3b), and becomes a focus of pilgrimage *out of* Jerusalem (12:9-11, cf 18); and when Jesus eventually enters the city, events take place (12:13) which are typical not of Passover but of *Tabernacles*, and strongly reminiscent of the founding of the festival of *Dedication* as described in 2 Macc 10:6-8.[14]

As we have seen, attitudes to the cult varied widely in the post-70 period, across the whole spectrum from those who thought the end of the Temple was to be welcomed, through those who sought to adjust to its loss in various ways, to those who longed for its reconstruction. For all such, this narrative in which *non-participation by*

---

12   Davies *Land* 292f

13   Bornhäuser *Missionsschrift* 65-67

14   The waving of the *lulab*, the palm-branch, and the crying of Ps 118:25 are typical of Tabernacles. The original Dedication was likewise celebrated "in the manner of the festival of booths" (2 Macc 10:6).

Jesus and his followers is not only made a virtue but claimed as fulfilment of the Scriptures would constitute an appeal which addressed the central concern of the age. But the narrative forcefully poses a question, as we have seen: can Jesus' attitude actually be *supported* by Moses? This leads us to the next point:

5.2 The Law

It is clear that, underlying the portrayal of Jesus as the replacement of the Temple and festivals, there is an engagement with the Scriptures as the foundation upon which they rested. Here we return to the issue discussed in 2.7 above, where we argued that the Fourth Gospel does not employ a private Christian 'in'-language, but uses public arguments and seeks to rest its presentation of Christ on interpretations of Scripture which could appeal to Jews as *right*. As we look broadly at chapters 5-12, does this contention hold good? We explore this under three headings:

5.2.1 The Exodus gifts — images of the law

Over thirty years ago T.F. Glasson pointed out how the three 'Exodus gifts' of bread, water and light are developed in turn in John 6, 7 and 8.[15] Jesus is the source now of *true* bread (6:32), of *living* water (7:38), and of light *for the world* (8:12). In all these, of course, the imagery and rituals of Passover and Tabernacles are connoted: Jesus is their replacement. But Glasson did not note how each of these is also a *contemporary image for the law*, so that Jesus is being presented in polemical terms, as *greater than* what is on offer through Moses.

Many commentators note the ironic background to 6:35 in Sir 24:21, where Wisdom (there identified with the law) says "Those who eat me will hunger again, and those who drink me will thirst again".[16] In the same passage Wisdom invites people to "come to me" (24:19, cf John 6:35b) and claims to be more nourishing than "honey", which was a regular image for manna (24:20).

It is typical of the Fourth Gospel that allusions like this are not marked, but speak powerfully to those who notice them. Jesus not only identifies himself with Wisdom and with the law, but pointedly claims to surpass Torah in what he gives. Similar material may be

---

15   Glasson *Moses* 62-64. The three are combined in Neh 9:12-15, Ps 105:39-41 and in several rabbinic texts cited by Glasson.

16   E.g. Lindars 259, who uses the allusion to explain the addition of "thirst" to a context in which only bread has been offered.

found to illustrate the use of light and water as images for the law.[17]

Israel had just been through an appalling experience in which the inadequacy of Torah and cult to deal with sin had become painfully clear to many. Against this background, the dialogue in ch. 6 gains new resonances. Readers would know well *why* "the fathers" died in the desert, even though they had the manna to sustain them (6:49) — in fact, John has reminded them of the reason in 3:14: they rebelled against God. Now, once again, sin has led to death for Israel, on a massive scale. But Jesus is the answer! — the one who can deal with sin and bestow life on those who believe in him. At the level of *claim*, therefore, this presentation is certainly *comprehensible* to late first-century Jews: maybe even *compelling*.

5.2.2 The decalogue in John 7-10

Against this background it is intriguing to turn to George Brooke's significant essay on the law in John 7-10, and to observe with him the extent to which the decalogue plays a role in these chapters. He maintains that there are allusions to each of the ten commandments: to nos. 1-3 in 10:30, 10:33 and 10:25 respectively (so that the 'Dedication' passage is marked by allusions to the commandments concerning God),[18] and to nos. 4-10 in the Tabernacles passage, 7:1-10:21:

- Sabbath: 7:23 (cf 5:18)
- Honour father: 8:49 (cf 5:23)
- Murder: especially 7:19, 8:40, 44 (cf 5:18)

---

17   LIGHT: *T. Levi* 14:4, 19:1; also Pseudo-Philo *Bib. Ant.* 9:8, 11:1, 22:3 (in 11:1 the law is described as "a light to the world"); frequently in 2 Baruch: 17:4, 18:2, 54:5, 78:15-16; "light" is an image for prophetic revelation in *Sib. Or.* 5:238f, Pseudo-Philo *Bib. Ant.* 28:3, 51:4-7, 4 Baruch 9:3.

WATER: "Living water" is an expression found at Qumran, referring to the law. The full phrase "a spring of living water" (Myiy.axah Miyam r");b.) appears in CD 19:34, referring to that which has been abandoned by those who have left the Community. From CD 6:4 (cf also CD 3:16) it appears that the spring is an image for the law which nourishes and sustains the life of the community, in particular for the law as interpreted and applied by the "wise men", the founders and teachers of the community (they are the ones who have dug the well, CD 6:5-6).

Odeberg 155 compares Sir 15:1-3, where wisdom, Torah, water and bread appear together.

In addition it is possible that "light" would have connoted the Temple: it is used as an image for the Temple in *Gen. Rab.* 3:4, 59:5 ("Jerusalem is the light of the world"), and also in the first-century (probably) *Lives of the Prophets* 12:10-13. In this passage "a light in the Temple" marks the end of the Age.

18   Brooke "Law" 105, 108

- Adultery: 8:41[19]
- Theft: 10:1, 8, 10
- False witness: 8:14, 8:44[20]
- Coveting: 8:44 (the only occurrence of ἐπιθυμία, "desire", in the Fourth Gospel)

These allusions seem clear and compelling. From this list it is apparent that *no fewer than five of the commandments figure in 8:40-49*. We shall return below to the significance of this interesting fact, which so far as I can see has only been observed by Brooke;[21] but it is clear immediately that this must have a bearing on the meaning of the challenge in 8:46, "Which of you convicts me of sin?". The desire of some to interpret "sin" here without reference to the law looks unlikely.

This interaction with the decalogue is part of the strategy to bring Moses in on the side of Jesus, to use the law as positive testimony in support of his claim. A debate is set up with "the Jews", the fervent representatives of orthopraxy: who obeys the law? As we shall see, this question focuses on the issue, Was the execution of Jesus the *legal penalty* rightly exacted on a blasphemer, or was it *murder*? But for the moment we observe simply that *this is public argument*, not internal Christian 'Sondersprache'. It could convince.[22]

5.2.3 "Right Judgment"

The challenge to "right judgment" in 7:24 is vital in this connection. This challenges underlies the mere *presentation* of Jesus as the replacement for Temple and cult, for this is a challenge to *hermeneutical second thoughts*. Jesus broke the Sabbath *halakah* in healing the lame man. But the reader is challenged to read this act within a wider appreciation of the scriptural plan for human beings. After all, the man was made "whole" — which, after all, is the real purpose of circumcision, in respect of which the *halakah* permits the suspension of the Sabbath regulations.[23] Barrett 319 rightly explains

---

19   Brooke "Law" 107 provides evidence to support the closeness of the association between fornication and adultery, especially in the prophetic tradition in which both are treated as symbols of idolatry and unfaithfulness to the Lord.

20   Brooke does not give this second reference but it may be added.

21   Brooke points out the concentration here, but for some reason does not mention the references to *murder* and *false witness* in 8:44, so lists only three ("Law" 107).

22   This is Brooke's conclusion also: "The appealing use of the decalogue ... might have been sufficient to convert some, once they had admitted that Jesus and his followers had neither broken nor abrogated the law" ("Law" 112).

23   Thomas "Judaism" 173f, following Neusner, argues for the antiquity of the

the difficult διὰ τοῦτο ("for this reason") in 7:22 by referring it forward to the idea of complete health in 23b: by healing the man, Jesus has fulfilled the purpose of his circumcision. "Right judgment" will discern this.

Whitacre suggests that the argument here depends on Christian presuppositions: "the author's use of the Torah to vindicate Jesus" is "dependent on a correct appreciation of Jesus' identity, his union with the Father".[24] But this is surely not so. Rather, Dodd calls 7:23 "an argument which is barely intelligible outside its Jewish context".[25] When "rightly judged", *the law itself* supports the action Jesus took, because he has achieved something more important than strict Sabbath observance.[26]

It is fascinating to note the same distinction between peripheral matters of *halakah* and basic Scriptural principles in the traditions about Hanina ben Dosa. In a story recorded in *b. Ber.* 33a,[27] Hanina deliberately breaks rabbinic regulations (*b. Hul.* 127a) when he carries the corpse of a snake he has just miraculously killed. As he carries it, he declares, "It is not the snake that kills, but sin". Vermes comments,

> The question of historicity is far less important than the fact that such an attitude was accepted as not only possible, but credible.[28]

The argument underlying Hanina's action is exactly that deployed in John 7:22-24, and illustrates the truth of Dodd's remark quoted above.

The vindication of the claim that "Moses wrote of me" is linked to a comparable use of the prophets in this section. It is balanced by the statement that "Isaiah spoke of him" in 12:41, and in between Ezekiel (ch. 10) and Zechariah (12:15f) play particularly important roles. The

---

teaching in *m. Sabb.* 19:1 about the priority given to circumcision over the Sabbath. In fact, Eliezer ben Hyrcanus was very lenient over the activities permitted on the Sabbath in order to fulfil the law of circumcision: he even allowed the wood to be cut in order to make the charcoal with which the forge the knife!

24 Whitacre *Polemic* 37
25 Dodd *Tradition* 333
26 So Pryor *John* 34, Derrett "Circumcision". Derrett mounts a strong case for the intelligibility of the argument in a Jewish context, including an interesting observation about the irony implicit in "I made a *whole* man *healthy*": the man was supposed to be "whole" because of his circumcision, but manifestly was not ("Circumcision" 217).
27 Quoted Vermes "Hanina" 185
28 Vermes "Hanina" 186. But Vermes also illustrates the bad odour that his name evoked in later rabbinic circles, because of attitudes like this.

need for "right judgment" is (deliberately?) underlined by the complicated citation in 7:38, which seems to draw upon an amalgam of Old Testament texts, mainly prophetic.[29]

5.3 "There was a division among them"

The repeated references to *division among the people* in this section are structurally and rhetorically significant. Division first appears implicitly in 6:60ff, although there the disagreement does not lead to debate about Jesus, as it does in 7:12, 7:40-44, 9:16, and 10:19-21. Division about Jesus is implicit in the whole section, and 12:37-43 finally picks up and comments on this feature of the narrative.

The references to division in 7:40-44, 9:16 and 10:19-21 are structurally important. *In each case, the succeeding narrative focuses in turn on each 'half' of the division, beginning with those who reject Jesus' claim,* as follows:

(1) 7:40-44 (cf 7:31):
• A: those who want to arrest him (7:44): 7:45-8:29 (NB 7:45, 8:20)
• B: those who think he is "the Prophet" (7:40): 8:30ff
(2) 9:16:
• A: those who think he is a sinner: 9:17-34 (NB 9:24)
• B: those who think he may not be a sinner: 9:35-10:18
(3) 10:19-21:
• A: those who think he is demon-possessed (10:20): 10:22-39
• B: those who think the signs make that impossible (10:21): 10:40-11:54

The alternation of the narrative between hostile and more open encounters keeps the reader on the move, and constantly poses the question of the reasons that prompt these varying reactions to Jesus.

Observation of this alternation helps to explain the extraordinary reaction of the Pharisees in 9:40. Duke claims that their question is "sneering ... the kind we have come to expect",[30] but we have certainly not come to expect Pharisees to ask whether they are spiritually blind. These Pharisees do not misunderstand 9:39 to refer to literal sight (as undoubtedly they would, if they were total unbelievers); and suddenly we realise, that, from a narrative perspec-

---

29   The imagery begins with the water from the rock of Exod 17:6-7 / Num 20:11, which provides the raw material for rich prophetic development: e.g. Isa 28:16 (Reim *Hintergrund* 56-88 argues that this is the chief "Scripture" in mind), 43:19-21, 44:3, 55:1, Jer 2:13, Ezek 47:1-12, Zech 14:8. The last-named text applies the imagery explicitly to Tabernacles. This whole development seems to be cited here.

30   Duke *Irony* 124

tive, they have accompanied Jesus while he has searched out a man just expelled from the synagogue, and have watched without murmur while the man has worshipped him. *These Pharisees are the "others" of 9:16b*, who are open to the possibility that Jesus may not be a sinner, and who are now "with him" — a phrase which elsewhere denotes at least interested association, and usually discipleship: 6:66, 11:16, 12:17, 18:26. "Where I am, there also my servant will be" (12:26): these Pharisees are moving in that direction, and are ready to hear the stern words that follow about the false shepherds who have actually plundered the flock instead of feeding it — the words which may enable them to *become blind* (i.e. to realise that *they* are the thieves and robbers), so that they may see.

This insight will be of considerable help in the exegesis of 8:30ff, where likewise the focus turns from those who reject Jesus to those who "believe in him". The faith mentioned in 8:30-31, I will argue, is best understood as *faith in Jesus as the Prophet*, the conviction expressed in 7:40. But — as always with faith in John[31] — their faith is immediately challenged to grow, in a way paralleled by the treatment of the Pharisees "with him" in 9:40-10:18.

We must note the rhetorical significance of this see-saw between opinions and reactions, for it is particularly significant for John 8. By this means the evangelist is able

> to present the case of Jesus Christ to his readers and challenge them — as the world has been challenged ever since — to reach their own verdict.[32]

It is remarkable that the evangelist presents arguments *against* the messiahship of Jesus (e.g. 7:27, 41; 10:33), as well as for it. By such means he allows the 'implied reader' to be *cooperative* without also being a *believer*, for the objections to faith are not simply pilloried. The intratextual characters who question his messiahship because they know where he is from (7:27) are shown wrestling, in a very human way, with conflicting impressions and indications. Yet the narrative gently takes up their objection and replies to it — (a) by challenging them to see their very lack of faith as an admission that they do not know his origin (7:28-29), and then (b) by referring ironically to Jesus' origin in *Bethlehem* (7:41f).

We will develop these thoughts further in the next chapter.

---

31 See above, 2.6.
32 Harvey *Trial* 17

5.4 Prophetic Signs

In the rhetorical strategy of these chapters — that is, their design to *persuade* — a special role falls to the three signs (chs. 6, 9, 11). Readers are expected to accept that these things really happened, a reasonable assumption in the first century. So the concentration of the narrative rests on *interpreting* the signs in support of Jesus' claim. How would these signs have struck our 'implied reader'? We may summarise their rhetorical force under three headings:

5.4.1 Jesus the Prophet like Moses

The miraculous feeding is interpreted not by the narrator but by the intratextual observers of the event (6:14): "This is truly the prophet who is coming into the world!" This refers, of course, to the 'prophet like Moses' of Deut 18:15-18 — the identification which John the Baptist refused for himself (1:21), and which the Samaritans have already decided upon for Jesus (4:42).[33]

Placing this acclamation in the mouth of "the people" has the effect of signalling to the reader the existence of some inherent quality in the sign which makes this extravagant response appropriate: and there can be no doubt that it is the 'Exodus' quality of the sign which is meant to do this. Following 5:46, Jesus' action in feeding this crowd of Passover pilgrims is even meant to be *predictable*. The question to Philip in 6:5 sets a test for the 'implied reader', too, and conveys a sense of inevitability: Jesus cannot but act in a way that makes him *look like Moses*, because he *is* the Prophet like Moses.

Reim finds at least twenty-two references to the eschatological prophet in the Fourth Gospel,[34] and underlines in particular the 'Moses' background to the signs, finding several detailed points of correspondence.[35] Martyn similarly emphasises this feature of John,

---

33   That the confession in 4:42 amounts to recognition of Jesus as the "Taheb" — the Samaritan name for this prophet — is widely agreed. Undoubtedly the identification of Jesus as the "Prophet like Moses" would be compelling for Samaritan readers of the Fourth Gospel. In the Samaritan Pentateuch, Deut 18:18-22 is included after the decalogue in Exod 20: Bowman "Samaritan Studies" 310f and Brooke "Law" 110 lay emphasis on the importance of the Samaritan version of the decalogue for the interpretation of John.

Deut 18:18 does not figure much in Jewish sources (Reim *Hintergrund* 111-113), perhaps in reaction against the Samaritan emphasis, but it is used at Qumran (4QTestim 5ff, 1QS 9:10f; *Vermes* 50 finds 'the Prophet' also in 1QS 4:20-26).

34   Reim *Hintergrund* 119-129

underlining the popular nature of the expectation of the eschatological prophet — but also the way in which the johannine Jesus does not match the categories of contemporary expectation, instead doing something *new* and unexpected.[36] The material gathered above in 3.3.5 supports the contention that, both before and after 70 AD, 'prophet' was a highly charged designation, capable of quickly arousing dramatic political expectations at a popular level — and this is precisely what is reflected in 6:15. Immediately the reader receives a clear signal that *Jesus does not offer that kind of solution to Israel's troubles.* He flees before the attempt to make him King. Like the Egyptian of Acts 21:38, he announces the eschatological Tabernacles, but it is a *spiritual* one.

Meeks emphasises the relevance of the 'false prophet' passage in Deut 13:1-11, which forms a pair with the promise of Deut 18:15-18. The problem voiced in Deut 18:21, "How can we know when a message has not been spoken by the Lord?" is basic to the johannine presentation of Jesus, as Meeks acutely observes:

Jesus' hearers [*we may also say: John's readers*] are placed before a dramatic decision, for while they are commanded to heed the true prophet upon pain of divine judgment (Deuteronomy 18.19), they are also commanded to put the false prophet to death (Deuteronomy 18.20; 13:6). The crowd therefore divides.[37]

The truth and importance of this observation is indicated by allusions to Deut 13 and 18 throughout John 6-12. The identification by the crowd in 6:14 is matched by the closing words of Jesus in 12:48-50, which specifically allude to "I will put my words in his mouth" (Deut 18:18) and the warning which follows (18:19). In between, we may point

• (a) to the further identifications at 7:40 and 9:17,

• (b) to the repeated claim by Jesus to speak the words given him by God (7:16; 8:26, 28), and

• (c) to the highly ironic use of "gods you have not known" (Deut 13:2, 6) in 7:28, 8:19 and especially 8:55: when "the Jews" attempt to stone Jesus in 8:59, in obedience to Deut 13:10, they are indicating their ironic *agreement* with his charge that they "do not know" the God he has been proclaiming to them.

This all puts the reader dramatically on the spot: who is right?

---

35 *Hintergrund* 132-140: manna, water from the rock (background to John 7:37f), bronze snake, the "signs" of the Exodus ...

36 Martyn *History & Theology2* 102-128

37 Meeks *Prophet-King* 56

Was Jesus a false, or a true prophet?

5.4.2 *Exodus symbolism*

This is so prominent in these signs that our 'implied reader' would undoubtedly be struck by it. By underlining the parallels and contrasts between Jesus and Moses, the signs point to *Jesus* as the one who really knows God and speaks from him. Martyn is right: the feeding sign goes far beyond a mere repetition of Moses and the manna.[38] It is interpreted as signalling a whole new Exodus, far greater than that celebrated at Passover: "Moses did *not* give you bread from heaven, but my father gives you the *true* bread from heaven" (6:32)! God is now acting to give Israel *true* bread, as opposed to the manna which was much less than "true" in comparison with Jesus.[39]

Exodus symbolism appears also in 8:12 and 8:31f, an observation vital for interpretation, as we shall see: Jesus claims to lead an Exodus from the slavery of *sin*. This is further matched in 11:43f by Lazarus' dramatic Exodus from the slavery of *death*. The narrative of Lazarus' emergence from the tomb resonates with Exodus overtones as an 'intertextual echo' which might be quite subliminal in its effect on the reader:[40]

• Jesus has been "sent" (11:42) to deliver in this way (Reim interprets the "sending" of Jesus as a Mosaic motif[41]);

• he overthrows the enemy with a mighty word of prophetic command (11:43);

• Lazarus "goes out", and is immediately released from bondage (11:44).[42]

---

38   Martyn *History & Theology2* 125-128

39   Hahn "Prozeß" 71 n. 20 is on the right track, I believe, when he comments that Jesus' words in 6:32 are a straight denial of Ps 78:24 just quoted (6:31). The emphasis falls on the final τὸν ἀληθινόν, "true"; and the striking present tense (δίδωσιν, "gives") reinforces the contrast between the two breads. In comparison with the *true* bread given by God *now*, the former bread was not really from heaven at all, in spite of Ps 78:24 (and Exod 16:4).

The point of the verse is thus not the contrast between Moses and God. What would be the point of reminding them that God is the subject of the sentence they have just quoted?

40   Richard B. Hays has added the 'intertextual echo' to the tool-kit of those who explore relationships between texts: *Echoes of Scripture in the Letters of Paul* (New Haven & London: Yale University Press, 1989). This tool explores the subliminal imagistic and connotational relationships which can exist without any formal quotation or even verbal allusion.

41   *Hintergrund* 130-132

42   The motif "the Lord, who brought you out of the house of bondage

The story thus exercises an emotional as well as a cognitive appeal — the former reinforcing the latter, to present Jesus as the prophet *who surpasses* Moses.

5.4.3 Exile, restoration and theodicy

Something similar happens in the narrative of ch. 9, although here it is exile and restoration which is imaged. The argument between the man and "the Jews" concerns *sin*. Their answer to the question posed in 9:2 is unhesitating: "you were born totally in sin!" (9:34)[43] — i.e. his parents sinned grossly, he inherited the sin, and his blindness was the result. *Their* response to the man's sinfulness is to throw him out (9:34b). But *Jesus'* response is to make him an occasion for revealing "the works of God", first by healing him, and *then by finding him and restoring to him the worship from which he has just been excluded* (9:35-38).

As with Lazarus and the Exodus, so the climax of this narrative mirrors an exile-restoration pattern which makes the man a symbol of Jesus' whole ministry to Israel. This theme is carried through into ch. 10, with its evocative use of Ezekiel 34, where the reason for the exile is laid at the door of the false shepherds of Israel (e.g. 34:5), and a new shepherd is promised — the Lord himself — who will "search for the lost and bring back the strays ... bind up the injured and strengthen the weak" (34:16), just as Jesus has done for the blind man. The specific use of exile-restoration language in 10:16 and in 11:52 confirms this line of thought.

It is fascinating to relate the 'sign' of ch. 9 to the situation of Judaism in the post-70 period, when (a) the motifs of exile and restoration were readily applied to Israel,[44] and (b) the question raised in 9:2 was extensively debated. As we saw above (3.1), 2

(slavery) with a mighty hand" appears (with variations) nine times in Exodus and Deuteronomy, including twice in the 'false prophet' passage (Deut 13:5, 10). Deut 13:5: "That prophet or dreamer must be put to death, because he preached rebellion against the LORD your God, who brought you out of Egypt and redeemed you from the house of slavery": how can Jesus be a false prophet if he performs exactly such a release on Lazarus?

43   The connection is noted by Bultmann 337; Barrett 364; Duke *Irony* 123.

44   The parallel between 70 AD and 587 BC (when Jerusalem was destroyed by the Babylonians and the nation carried into exile) supplies 4 Ezra, 2 Baruch, and 4 Baruch with their rationale, because they adopt the *personae* of figures from that era. 4 Baruch is particularly interesting in this respect, because a narrative about the BC situation is issued into the parallel AD situation without any hermeneutical aids, such as the visions of the future in 2 Baruch which specifically enable the message to be extended to the present.

Baruch in particular agonised over the injustice of the death of the righteous alongside the wicked. There is more to the question "Who sinned, this man or his parents?" than immediately meets the eye. If his parents sinned, then is it not unjust that he is punished for a fault not his own? But how could he himself be guilty of sin prior to birth? The man blind from birth is a 'difficult case' within the current theology of retribution. The destruction of Jerusalem is another such case: by all means judge her for her sin, but *total destruction?* For 2 Baruch the problem was that the disaster was *more than was required as a judgment for sin.*

So the question of 9:2, and therefore also Jesus' reply, relate directly to the agony of Israel in this period. The basic causal connection between sin and disaster has already been affirmed in 5:14, and is not retracted here, because this question concerns the special case in which one cannot discern precisely who is to blame, or which sins are being judged. So Jesus' reply ("neither this man sinned, nor his parents, but (it happened) so that the works of God might be revealed in him", 9:3) in fact handles the question in just the same way as 2 Baruch. It answers the problem by pointing to a wider, more important purpose of God than merely the exacting of retribution. The man's blindness serves God's purpose of revealing his "works" — that is, the works which Jesus is about to perform on him, first by healing him, and then by *restoring his worship outside the synagogue.*

The function of the healing of the blind man as a *sign*, therefore, depends upon this dynamic resonance between the narrative and the situation it addresses. The message is clear: those who recognise their blindness and lostness, and in that state are "found" by Jesus and come to worship him, are caught up in a restoration from exile on the Ezekiel 34 model, with Jesus as the "shepherd" of Israel. For them, the light-ceremony of Tabernacles is no longer lost, because they worship the Son of Man, the Light of the world. On the other hand, all others who think that they "see", who have their own answers to the problem of Israel's fate — and especially the Pharisees, the "disciples of Moses" (9:28), who still judge sin by *halakah* (9:16) and persecute the followers of Jesus (9:22b, 34) — must give up their 'sight', abandon their own answers and position, and listen to the voice of the Good Shepherd.[45]

The rightness of this overall approach to the blind man might be confirmed by the use of a similar device in 4 Ezra 9:38-10:59, the

---

45   It is interesting that "blindness" is used as an image for Israel/Jerusalem in relation to the Babylonian exile: Isa 42:16-20; 43:8; Lam 4:13f, 4:17, 5:17f.

vision of the bereaved woman who turns out to be a symbolic representation of Jerusalem. Thinking that she is just an ordinary woman grieving for her dead son, Ezra reprimands her:

> Zion, the mother of us all, is in deep grief and great humiliation ... you are sorrowing for one son, but we, the whole world, for our mother (10:7-8).

Then he tries to encourage her that "if you acknowledge the decree of God to be just, you will receive your son back in due time" (10:16). Zion's troubles are so much greater than her individual sorrow — and the Lord will comfort her (10:19-24). But then Ezra is staggered when the woman is suddenly transformed into a city — the future Jerusalem yet to be built by God.

The sign in John 9 is not explicitly interpreted as in 4 Ezra, but the fact that the events of 70 AD called forth this kind of allegorical treatment strengthens the suggestion that John 9 might be 'heard' in a similar way. The blind man does not, however, represent Jerusalem or the Temple, but Judaism, blind and then transformed, exiled and then restored.

The signs in John 5-12, therefore, are the centrepiece of the strategy whereby the implied author seeks to persuade the reader that Jesus is the prophetic revealer and deliverer of Deut 18. These signs, especially the last, make it impossible for the reader to escape from the question, "Who is this Jesus?". Just as Jesus leaves the Temple in 8:59, having been rejected by "the Jews", so many of "the Jews" leave Jerusalem in 12:11 and "go" to believe in Jesus. Jesus is presented as the "true" cultic centre of Judaism, drawing people away from the celebration of the Temple festivals, in which he himself does not participate, while at the same time bringing the deepest intentions of the law to fulfilment. He is a Pied Piper, whistling a new melody which descants the deep tones of law and cult, and summons Israel to a new following which means eternal life *now* — signalled dramatically by Lazarus' obedient exit from the tomb.

Every reader must take sides, just as "the Jews" do. "Look — the world has gone away after him!", the Pharisees complain (12:19). Will the reader likewise "go away" after Jesus, leaving the Jerusalem cult behind? After 70 AD there was no option about such an abandonment, anyway. The portrayal of division among "the Jews" in these chapters sets up the options vividly, and reaches a climax in 11:45-54: there "many of the Jews ... who saw what he had done believed in him" (11:45), but on the other hand the Sanhedrin decides that, *for Israel's sake,* he must die (11:50).

Who is right? The reader cannot remain neutral, unless she withdraws the co-operation which we have presupposed for our 'implied reader'. The view of the narrator, expressed through the triple irony of 11:48-53,[46] is clear: the death of Jesus is God's means of rebuilding Israel after the disaster. The sin of destroying the Temple *of Jesus' body* anticipated the sin which led to the destruction of Herod's Temple — and provides atonement for it.

---

46   See above, 2.1 (p 41)

6

Hearing 7:1-8:59:
its literary and rhetorical structures

The breadth of our focus now reduces, and we look at the immediate co-text of 8:31-59. Our aim is the same, to sense the 'points of sensitivity' which would have addressed the needs, desires and ideas of our 'implied reader', so as to prepare the way for the close examination in the next chapter. If it is right to explore the text as a *consecutive reading experience*, then we need to define the state of play, as it were, at 8:30, so as rightly to discern what our passage then contributes. That is what we seek to do in this chapter.

6.1 Structure and genre

That 7:1-8:59 constitutes a literary unit is indicated by (a) Jesus' entry into the Temple at 7:14 and departure from it at 8:59, marked particularly by his retreat into *hiddenness* at that point;[1] and (b) the new narrative start at 9:1 (change of place and actors).

There is fairly wide agreement about this,[2] but about the internal structure of this unit there is no consensus at all. Dodd calls it

a collection of miscellaneous material ... a series of controversial dialogues, often without clearly apparent connection.[3]

Many scholars claim to have discovered order in this apparent chaos, but the sheer variety of proposals depresses and bewilders. The long footnote which follows discusses some of the sugges-

---

1   ἐν κρυπτῷ (7:10, "in secret") is picked up by ἐκρύβη in 8:59, "he hid himself". The Greek words are cognate.

2   So e.g. Ibuki *Wahrheit* 66; Manns *Vérité* 16-22; Schenke "Szene" 186; Mlakuzhyil *Structure* 202; Dodd *Interpretation* 345; Beasley-Murray 100; Stibbe *John* 96f

3   *Interpretation* 345. Cf Pryor *John* 34: "a confused mass of sayings with nothing to hold them together in unity".

tions.[4] But such a question is radically affected by the distinctive method we are employing. In asking about the *hearing* of the text, we are seeking its *rhetorical effect,* and therefore — regardless of what might be discovered by another reading which looks for concentric or other literary structures — we focus on what might be felt to persuade the 'implied reader' we have defined. And this means that the question of *form* must take second place to that of *genre.*

The notion of 'genre' helpfully combines function with form in the right relative balance — the latter serving the former. The genre of an utterance is decided by the *hearer* on the basis of her linguistic competence, and serves to provide her with an interpretative framework which guides her response.[5] She may discover that her initial choice of genre was quite wrong, when she laughs at what she took to be a joke and receives a black look; in every case the chosen 'extrinsic' category will have to be revised in the light of its 'intrinsic'

---

4   Mlakuzhyil *Structure* 203f analyses the material into unequal sections around the time-notices in 7:14 and 7:37 — 7:1-13, 7:14-36, 7:37-8:59 (so also Hahn "Prozeß" 75); Stibbe *John* 90, 97 finds a five-unit chiastic arrangement in each chapter, more strongly marked in ch. 7; Manns, Crossan and Ellis find a chiastic structure in the whole unit 7:14-8:59, but respectively with eight, seven and five paired sections (Manns *Vérité* 59-62; Crossan "Anti-Semitism" 195; Ellis *Genius* 135). Manns calls his analysis "un schema très souple" (*Vérité* 62), and even Ellis confesses that this section "appears to lack unity" (*Genius* 139). Ibuki *Wahrheit* 68-71 simply emphasises the way in which themes introduced in ch. 7 are paralleled in ch. 8. And Kern "Aufbau" argues on purely formal grounds for an analysis of five strophes in 8:12-59, arranged concentrically around the third strophe, 8:31b-41a. His analysis of ch. 8 more or less coincides with Stibbe's.

Some of these suggestions rest on compelling observations. For instance, the opening and closing paragraphs of ch. 7 (7:1-11 and 7:40-52) have clearly chiastic structures, and there are other similar structures in 7:21-23, 8:31-38 and 8:42-47. However, though we may affirm these analyses in some respects, their sheer variety bewilders, and in particular illustrates confusion about the relative weight of *formal* and *thematic* considerations:

On the one hand, Kern excludes thematic considerations altogether from his analysis of "tones", "stichs" (lines with two or three tones), "groups of stichs", "strophes" and "groups of strophes" — the five formal units he describes in ascending size. In order to make his analysis work he leaves out narrative connectors and the "Jewish objections" (e.g. 8:19a, 52f), so the actual *content* of the debate serves no role at all.

But on the other hand, Ibuki employs no formal considerations whatever in simply listing "parallels" between chs. 7 and 8 and asking how themes are developed between them.

Clearly a better approach will combine formal and thematic observations. In fact the best approach will start, as we do, with the issues of *genre* and *rhetoric,* and analyse the structure of a text from the perspective of its power to communicate.

5   I am drawing on the discussion of genre by E.D. Hirsch, *Validity in Interpretation* (New Haven/London; Yale Univ. Press, 1967), 68ff.

function in a particular conversation or written communication.

Dealing with a text like John 7-8, the choice of genre by the hearer is extremely subtle. We have touched on this issue already — first in criticising Martyn for suggesting a genre for which there was no literary precedent,[6] and then in commending him for his treatment of what he calls 'midrashic discussion' in John.[7] I suggested that the best description of the johannine dialogues sees them as a kind of *parody* of rabbinic 'midrashic discussion'. The element of *parody* is what compels the reader to adjust the extrinsic genre in the light of what he actually experiences. Even though Jesus is recognised as a γραμματεύς (scribe, 7:15), he does not speak like one, and the differences are what compel attention.

In the next three sections we will analyse three ways in which our 'implied reader' would be forced to make such a genre adjustment.

6.2 Forensic tone

The first adjustment concerns the *tone* of the discussion. Because of the growing opposition to Jesus, which reaches a climax in these chapters, the discussion takes on a thoroughly controversial tone. Throughout this section, questions and counter-questions are exchanged (7:15, 19, 20, 23, 25, 28, 35f, 42, 47, 51; 8:19, 22, 25, 33, 43, 46, 48, 53, 57) which increasingly become accusations, the aim of which "is to shift the *onus probandi* to one's opponent".[8] From a reading perspective, this controversial tone determines the shapes of the text, and relativises some of the possible structural analyses of it.

We may illustrate this process of relativisation by comparing 8:12-20 with 8:51-59. These paragraphs have an identical structure, which can be analysed in some detail. Each follows a statement about Jesus' geographical origin, with that in 8:48 ironically recalling 7:52.[9] Then they develop as follows:

---

6   Above, 1.2.4 (pp 28-30)

7   Above, 2.2 (pp 42-45)

8   Trites *Witness* 82

9   Jesus cannot be both Galilean and Samaritan! The contradiction both underlines a basic *unwillingness to listen* on the Pharisees' part, and ironically confirms Jesus' contention that they do not know where he is from (7:28, 8:14).

A 12 Jesus' claim - overcoming darkness	A' 51 Jesus' claim - overcoming death
Call to discipleship	Call to discipleship
B 13 Objection by the Pharisees,	B' 52-53 Objection by the Jews,
based on the law.	based on the law (and greatly
	increased in force)
C 14-18 Jesus' reply, justifying his	C' 54-56 Jesus' reply, justifying his
claim on the basis of the law.	claim on the basis of the law.
"I AM"	"You do not know him, I know him"
D 19 Brief exchange	D' 57-58 Brief exchange (more hostile)
"You know neither me nor my father"	"I AM"
E 20 Temple location, Jesus	E' 59 Jesus leaves the Temple, attempt
not apprehended	to stone him.

For all its attractiveness to literary critics, however, this parallelism would not be apparent to most readers. Far more prominent is the basic pattern *statement* — *objection* — *response* which appears twice in each paragraph (12-17, 18-19, 51-55, 56-58), and recurs throughout ch 8, as many have seen.[10] The repetition of this pattern forces itself upon the reader, reinforces the sense of a cut-and-thrust debate, and makes it impossible to avoid taking sides.

Neyrey has rightly seen the connection between structure and genre, I believe, in linking an analysis of this repeated pattern to his description of 8:21-59 as a "forensic process". He rightly illustrates the way in which ch. 8 reflects contemporary Jewish forensic procedures, and in so doing extends A.E. Harvey's treatment of this idea.[11] But even so we must object that this passage is *not* "struc-

---

10   E.g. Neyrey "Process" 518f; Stibbe *John* 97f: also in 8:21-24, 26-29, 31-37, 38-40, and 41-47. In all but two cases the final part of the "response" clearly forms the "statement" to which the next "objection" is made (8:18, 24b, 38, 41a, 47b, 51, 56).

Neyrey and Stibbe prefer the terms "statement — misunderstanding — explanation", influenced by Leroy *Rätsel*, who finds 4 of his 11 johannine misunderstandings in ch. 8 (21-24, 31-33, 51-53 and 56-58). Of course, from the evangelist's point of view, the objections do indeed rest on misunderstandings; but within the narrative, they are for the most part reasonable objections with which readers might sympathise. Calling them "objections" is therefore important for an analysis of the *function* of the narrative — and also allows the pattern to be found much more widely.

11   Unfortunately Harvey *Trial* does not consider 8:21-59 to any extent. And for some reason Neyrey does not develop one of Harvey's key ideas, the forensic significance of *calling God to witness*, although it illumines 8:29 as well as 8:16-18.

Neyrey's central contention does not hold water: he argues that the contradiction between 8:15 and 8:26, with Jesus first *refusing* to judge and then doing so, can be explained by the forensic reversal whereby plaintiff could become judge and *vice versa*. But Jesus does *not* say that he "judges" in 8:26. The ἀλλά ("but") in 26 makes it clear that he is saying the same as in 8:15-16 — he *could*

tured as a typical forensic process" (Neyrey's summary of his hypo-thesis[12]). We do not know whether there were ancient Jewish equi-valents of Law Reports, nor, if there were, whether John 8:21-59 would have looked "typical" — but this must be deemed highly unlikely on both counts. What we actually have is a 'midrashic discussion' which has become highly combative, and within which both sides have started to use forensic language prominently, so that the dialogue has taken on features of a *trial*, without being formally constituted as such. This conclusion is of some significance for our argument.

6.3 The Lord's complaint

A.A. Trites well supplements Harvey's interpretative use of Jewish legal procedure with his suggestion that the forensic language of John should be interpreted against the background of the pro-phetic theme of Yahweh's "complaint against the nations" (or against Israel).[13]

We cannot prescribe that any individual reader would catch subtle echoes of the Old Testament. But we can be confident that a cooperative Jewish reader, used to hearing the prophets read, would 'hear' the allusions to which Trites points. The same probing, ques-tioning style is typical of the so-called 'trial scenes' of Deutero-Isaiah (41:2, 4; 41:26; 43:9, 13; 44:7, 8; 45:21; 46:5).[14] In particular, the 'trial scene' in Isa 43:8-13 seems especially important for John 8, with its emphatic use of the ἐγώ εἰμι ("I am") and of the 'witness' theme to which 8:18 seems specifically to allude.[15] Stibbe describes the effect of this background as follows:

> The implicit commentary throughout [8:12-59] supports the narra-
> tor's defence of the divinity of Jesus and the concomitant satire of

---

"judge", but will not.

12   "Process" 509

13   Trites *Witness* 78ff. For the prophetic theme, see especially Gemser "rîb" and Limburg "Speeches". Harvey *Trial* 16f points to the relevance of this background but does not develop it.

14   Trites *Witness* 82

15   Ball "My Lord" 54f notes the relevance of the fact that the LXX adds the Lord himself as a third witness, alongside the Servant and Israel. Stibbe *John* 99 lists 7 "parallels" between John 8 and Isa 43:8-13; Coetzee "EGO EIMI" 171-3 similarly lists 6 "issues" common to John 8 and Isa 42f, only three of which coincide with Stibbe's; Trites *Witness* 88 finds a particular parallel between Isa 43:9f and John 14:29.

the diabolism of the Jews. Jesus takes on the role of Yahweh whilst the Jews take on the role of the false, pagan gods. This accounts for much of the irony in the chapter.[16]

The ἐγώ εἰμι of 8:12, 18, 24, 28, 58 is, I am sure, rightly interpreted against this Isaianic background. However, Yahweh's lawsuit against *Israel* provides a better background than that against *the nations*. Against this background, "the Jews" can stay in character — they do not need to "take on the role of the false, pagan gods". It may be illustrated in Ps 50:7-23, Jer 2:5-19, Isa 1:2-4, Mic 6:1-5, and in particular in Hosea (2:4-15 (MT), 4:1-4, 12:1-3 (MT)). In these passages, too, a questioning style is employed as Israel is charged with abandoning Yahweh. Without reference to this broader issue of genre, G.A.F. Knight cites Isa 1:2-4 as a prophetic parallel to John 8:44: "Through the lips of Isaiah, God had long before called 'the Jews' virtually 'children of the devil'".[17]

6.3.1 Comparing John with Hosea

In fact, a broader comparison between the language of Hosea and that of John 8 helps us, I believe, to 'hear' the controversy between Jesus and the Jews with authentic first-century ears. Hosea's language presents detailed parallels to John 8, particularly the language of sonship (8:41f),[18] sin (8:21, 24, 34f),[19] adultery/πορνεία (8:41),[20] murder (8:37, 40, 44),[21] untruth (8:44),[22] death (8:21, 24, 51),[23] knowledge of God (8:19, 55),[24] and 'seeking' God (8:21).[25] In Hosea, also, political enslavement is a prominent idea,[26] and the uselessness or termination of the festivals and the cult is proclaimed.[27] The decalogue seems to play in Hosea the

---

16   Stibbe *John* 99. This is also the view of Blank, who underlines throughout his book (*Krisis*) the importance of the *Rechtstreit* (lawsuit) of the Lord with the nations as background to John.

17   Knight "Antisemitism" 86

18   Both allowed and denied: Hos 1:8-9, 10; 11:1-4, 10f. (In this and the following notes the references are to the English text of Hosea.)

19   Hos 4:7f, 7:1f, 8:1, 9:7, 9:15 ("because of their sinful deeds I will drive them out of my house" — cf John 8:34f), 10:9, 13:2, 13:12, 14:1

20   Hos 1:2, 2:2, 4:2, 4:10-18, 6:10, 7:4, 9:1

21   Hos 4:2, 5:2, 6:8f, 12:14

22   Hos 4:2; 7:1, 3, 13; 10:4, 13; 11:12

23   As judgment: 13:1; deliverance from: 13:14

24   Hos 2:20; 4:1, 6; 5:4; 6:3, 6; 8:2f

25   Hos 3:5, 5:6 ("they shall go to seek the Lord, but they will not find him — cf John 7:34-6, 8:21), 5:15, 7:10, 10:12

26   Hos 8:13; 9:3, 6; 10:10, 13-15; 11:5

same role as in John 7-10. Hosea does not accuse Israel of being children of the devil — but something very close: as children of God they have abandoned their father (11:2) and have given themselves to another, the Baals. At root, of course, lies the idea of the covenant, mentioned twice in Hosea (6:7, 8:1) and not specifically in John 8, but underlying the whole content of both.[28]

So in Hosea we find an example of prophetic polemic closely akin to that in John 8. The style in John is different, (a) because it is a dialogue, and (b) because Jesus is speaking his own "I", and is not simply passing on God's "I" prophetically (though he claims, of course, that these amount to the same thing: cf 8:43 and 47). But these thematic coincidences make it vital for us to seek to move surefootedly in the thought-world in which these themes cohered.

This challenge is particularly important because of the relationship between *threat* and *hope* in this prophetic polemic. The two sit together almost inconsistently. The threats read like final destruction and abandonment, and it seems impossible that there can also be love and restoration — and yet Hosea (to continue with him) alternates between them without hesitation. The two 'lion' passages illustrate this feature intriguingly, for the same image is used to reinforce both threat and promise:

I am God, and not man — the Holy One among you. I will not come in wrath. They will follow the Lord; he will roar like a lion. When he roars, his children will come trembling from the west. They will come trembling like birds from Egypt, like doves from Assyria. I will settle them in their homes, declares the Lord (11:9-11).

When I fed them, they were satisfied; when they were satisfied, they became proud; then they forgot me. So I will come upon them like a lion, like a leopard I will lurk by the path. Like a bear robbed of her cubs, I will attack them and rip them open. Like a lion I will devour them; a wild animal will tear them apart (13:6-8).

What makes this possible is a particular understanding of the role of *the prophetic word*. Here Hosea helps us greatly in our appreciation of John 8. For Hosea, the Lord's attack upon Israel is not just expressed through the physical assault of a human enemy. It *also* —

27   Hos 2:11; 4:15; 5:7; 7:5; 8:11-13; 9:4-6; 10:2, 5; 12:9 (Tabernacles to be restored); 12:11

28   Other thematic coincidences could be similarly illustrated: judgment, word, light, glory, Egypt/Exodus, life. And looking beyond John 8, we could add theft, vine and fruit/fruitlessness, shepherd/sheep, water, love, 'king of Israel' ...

perhaps *primarily*, certainly *first* — comes through assault by *the prophet himself*:

> What can I do with you, Ephraim? What can I do with you, Judah? Your love is like the morning mist, like the early dew that disappears. Therefore I cut you in pieces with my prophets, I killed you with the words of my mouth; my judgments flashed like lightning upon you. For I desire mercy, not sacrifice ... (6:4-6).

The prophetic attack is the first part of the judgment. In Hosea it consists of a jolting assault on religious certainties, decrying the cult as a focus of sin, predicting disaster, and apparently announcing that, in spite of the covenant, *Israel can no longer be sure of God*. He may in fact be her enemy. If Israel continues unrepentant, he *will* be her enemy. But there is hope, if she will "acknowledge no God but me, no Saviour except me" (13:4). The "killing" with the prophetic word, therefore, is meant to give life by prompting repentance.

6.3.2 Interpreting the polemic

The relevance of this to John is clear. Here too we have an attack on the cult, which is intensified in 8:31-47 into an apparent assault on Israel's whole covenant status: obedience to Torah does *not* give life in the age to come! Being seed of Abraham does *not* liberate from sin. Those who are confident in being children of God — encouraged by verses like Hos 11:1 — are actually *children of the devil*. We may make three points about this attack, against this background in prophetic rhetoric:

(1) It is quite wrong to interpret it in absolute terms. Very many scholars are inclined to regard 8:44 as a final judgment on "the Jews", consigning them to the dark side of the johannine dualism.[29] In the tradition of this prophetic language, the address itself is a

---

29 So e.g. Lona *Johannes 8* 280, 324f; Ibuki *Wahrheit* 102, 114f (in 8:44 the final judgment falls); Gräßer "Teufelssöhne" 164f; Strathmann 152 (8:44 is John's "Gesamturteil über das Judentum"; the opposition between Christians and Jews is now "völlig unüberbrückbar", and John no longer hopes for their conversion); Bultmann 318-22 ("hostility to life constitutes the very nature of the 'Jews'", 321); Blank *Krisis* 229f; Baumbach "Gemeinde" 124; Onuki *Gemeinde* 34-37; Ruether *Fratricide* 111ff; Hellig "Negative Image" 44.

As we have seen, for some the dualism has a social dimension, the breach with the synagogue: so Meeks "Man From Heaven" 67; Wengst *Gemeinde* 47; Wittenberger "Judenpolemik" 325; Freyne "Vilifying" 137 ("The strategies of vituperation are combined ... with ... the absoluteness of cosmic dualism"); von Wahlde "Discourses" 581f; Johnson "Jews" 114f.

judgment out of which restoration may be born. "You are of your father the devil!" is no more absolute a judgment than "your prince is Satan!", addressed to the sons of Jacob by the patriarch Dan.[30] We will argue below that it is essentially a *moral accusation*.

(2) Luke Johnson has done much to explain the context of such polemic.[31] He emphasises how widespread and normal such language was, in both pagan and Jewish circles:

> By the measure of Hellenistic conventions, and certainly by the measure of contemporary Jewish polemic, the NT's slander against fellow Jews is remarkably mild.[32]

Such language could be used quite lightly — as it is, for instance, in 7:20, where the crowd's "You have a demon" seems to be little more than "You're crazy!".[33] But it could be serious also, as it is when "You have a demon" is repeated in 8:48. This second accusation is every bit as severe as that in 8:44a, to which it responds. It is certainly remarkable that the Fourth Gospel includes the opposition polemic, in its presentation of the dialogue: this makes it without parallel in the contemporary examples cited by Johnson.

(3) Read in the post-70 situation, this prophetic polemic would work ironically. *It would be heard as a warning which had not been heeded.* The presupposition which our reader brings to the text is that Israel has just been severely judged by God for her sin. The record of a prophetic denunciation addressed to and ignored by Israel *before* the judgment, gains authenticity *after* it. This is why Josephus includes the story of Jesus ben Hananiah, whose prophecy was ridiculed until it came true.[34] With these prophetic denunciatory motifs worked into it, the johannine narrative would have a similar force after 70 AD.

This force is made to serve the *Christian* message: "You will die in your sins! — unless you believe that 'I am' ... If *the Son* sets you free, you really will be free ... If God was your father, you would love *me* ... Because you are not 'of God', you don't hear *me* ... Whoever keeps *my word* can be sure of life in the age to come ... You do not know God — but *I* know him!" (8:24, 36, 42, 47, 51, 55).

---

30   ὁ ἄρχων ὑμῶν ἐστιν ὁ Σατανᾶς, *T. Dan* 5:6. From the context it appears that "your" indicates the sons of Jacob generally, and not just the sons of Dan.

31   Johnson "Polemic"

32   Johnson "Polemic" 441

33   So Brown 1:131, Duke *Irony* 73, Hahn "Prozeß" 75 n. 40. As Johnson puts it, such language is chiefly "connotative rather than denotative" ("Polemic" 441).

34   Josephus *War* 6:300-309

With this refocusing of the prophetic message onto Christ, the impression is strongly created that the judgment fell because Israel failed to believe in Jesus, and rejected him as "the Jews" do in 8:59. This may be why the story of the blind man follows. Certainly it counterbalances this impression, emphasising that blame must not be apportioned, and underlining the positive power of Jesus to bring light to the blind and hope to the exiled.

6.4 The Public Debate

A third way in which 'genre adjustment' takes place in chs. 7-8 concerns Jesus' conversation-partners. It is in chs. 5-6 that 'midrashic discussion' becomes the genre-choice that makes most sense of what is happening: Jesus is debating the interpretation of the Scriptures with "the Jews" — albeit in a most unusual way which creates sharp opposition on the part of some. When, therefore, Jesus enters the Temple again and starts "teaching" (7:14), the reader expects the same kind of thing to continue. But instead of debating *with* him, "the Jews" make a comment *about* him and his teaching (7:15), and this then becomes the focus of discussion for the next two chapters.[35]

Further, the discussion is developed across exchanges with a variety of different groups, rather than just with "the Jews" or with Jesus' disciples, the setting we might expect. Stibbe suggests that five groups are introduced in ch. 7: Jesus' brothers, the Jerusalem crowds, the Jews, the chief priests and Pharisees, and the Temple guards.[36]

Actually it is necessary to distinguish between "the crowd" and "the Jerusalemites", because "the crowd" is best understood as the *pilgrim* crowd present for the feast. 7:49 might suggest that they are the *'am ha'aretz*, regarded with contempt by the 'teachers of Israel' in the Sanhedrin,[37] but all other references to them except 11:42 have a particular connection with a festival. 7:49 is in any case unique: out of 20 references to the crowd, this is one of only three in reported speech (cf 7:12, 11:42), and this is the only occurrence on the lips of the Pharisees, used in opposition to "the law" in this

---

35   It is interesting to observe how much of the discussion in chs. 7-8 is actually *meta-language,* that is, language about language: apart from the crucial proclamations in 7:37f and 8:12 which form the heart of Jesus' alternative Tabernacles, the discussion is *about* Jesus' words, his right to speak as he does, and the effects of believing him.

36   Stibbe *John* 92

37   So Ashton "Identity" 74; Manns "Jabné" 100

way. It should probably not be used to determine the reference of all other occurrences of "crowd". The "Jerusalemites", in fact, are probably the closest to being *'am ha'aretz*, with their disrespectful attitude to the authorities (7:26) and their espousal of a popular messianic expectation (7:27) — in conflict with the Scriptural approach of some of "the crowd" (7:41f).[38]

At the same time, Jesus' brothers effectively merge with "the crowd", because they are pilgrim visitors to the festival. So we end up with five groups:

- The crowd, including Jesus' brothers
- The local inhabitants of Jerusalem
- "The Jews"
- The chief priests and Pharisees (i.e. the Sanhedrin)
- The Temple guards[39]

Each group interacts with Jesus; and topics which might have been thought to be the preserve of "the Jews", as those especially concerned with orthopraxy and the right interpretation of Torah, are widely debated. *The crowd* is challenged to develop a "right judgment" about the meaning of circumcision and its relation to Jesus' healing of the lame man (7:24), and *the crowd* discusses the criteria for recognising the Messiah (7:40-42) — as indeed do the Jerusalemites (7:27). The Temple guards likewise reach their own judgment — and decide not to obey their orders to arrest Jesus.

At the same time, each group is shown as divided in its response to Jesus. Division among "the Jews" is signalled in that the violence implicit in 7:1 (as in 5:18) is not expressed in 7:15; and then division becomes explicit in 8:30f, 59. The "crowd" is hopelessly divided — from Jesus' brothers who do not deny his "works" but deliberately encourage him to go where his life is endangered, to others who want a formal examination of him (7:30, 44), to others who think he is the Christ (7:31, 41a), while yet others think he is the Prophet but not the Christ (7:40, 41b).

---

38 Painter *Quest* 252-4 underlines the contradictory responses in 7:27 and 41f: the Messiah is supposed both to come from Bethlehem and have an unknown origin.

39 If this analysis is correct, then one of the main reasons for regarding 7:15-24 as transposed from the end of ch. 5 falls away (see the reasons given by Schnackenburg 2:130f). For "the crowd" which speaks in 7:20 are to be distinguished from "the inhabitants of Jerusalem" (7:25), and the apparent contradiction over awareness of the plot to kill Jesus is explained. Pilgrim crowds would not be aware of something the locals knew but kept quiet about (7:13). In fact, the references back to ch. 5 receive a narrative explanation, because the "crowd" is recalling the incident that marked an earlier visit to Jerusalem.

The Jerusalemites wonder whether Jesus could be the Christ, but then feel that this is incompatible with the expectation that the origin of the Christ will be unknown (7:26f).[40] The Temple guards express this division dramatically by their aborted mission (7:32, 46). And the Sanhedrin has Nicodemus, who at the very least feels that Jesus cannot be rejected out of hand, without a proper hearing — unlike many of his fellow-Pharisees (7:50-52).

The effect of all this is to create a debate which extends out of the text and embraces the reader. In this confused situation, everyone is asked to judge for themselves where the truth lies: a good man, or a deceiver? the prophet, or demon-possessed? 'Midrashic discussion' has been thoroughly de-professionalised, both within the narrative, and outside it.

6.5 The Rhetoric of the Trial

The reader is gripped and drawn into the discussion not just by being presented with this bewildering variety of responses. Further techniques are employed — and in this final section we will survey some of these, particularly in the material up to 8:30. This will prepare the way for the next chapter.

Although so many participate in it, the narrative of the debate has been structured in such a way that the topic (essentially "Who is Jesus?") develops connectedly across the various exchanges. There is a narrative flow which needs careful attention. We will look at it consecutively:

6.5.1 7:14-24: murder or execution? Right judgment ...
This section concerns the "sign" of 5:1-9. Jesus asserts that what he did was in harmony with Moses, and questions his opponents' capacity to judge his claim, since they intend to break the law of Moses by murdering him (and thus do not "will to do his will", 17). The final challenge to "judge with right judgment" (24) carries the reader forward, and underlies the whole debate in chs. 7-8.

This paragraph introduces an issue which takes centre-stage from this point onward, by bringing the intention to kill Jesus into connection with the law (7:19). The reader is not allowed to escape reaching a judgment on the question: was the execution of Jesus murder? If it was *not* murder, then the judgment of "the Jews" about

---

40 The tradition of the Messiah's unknown origin is well attested, though in several different formulations (reflecting popular variety): *1 Enoch* 48:6, 4 Ezra 13:52, Justin *Dial* 8:4. Cf De Jonge "Messiah" 255-7, Freed "8:58" 55, Barrett 322.

him is confirmed — Sabbath-breaker, sinner, false prophet, blasphemer. If it *was* murder, then conversely Jesus' claim is confirmed: *they are the sinners*, they do *not* do the will of God, and they show this rejection of the will of God precisely in their rejection of him, who speaks the words of God.

For some readers, the reference to murder at the festival might be highly evocative, if any credence may be attached to Josephus' account of the activities of the *sicarii* at the festivals in the early 60's AD.[41]

6.5.2 7:15-52: origin, attestation and Scripture

The rest of the chapter concerns the *origin* of Jesus and its *attestation*. Should his claim to be from God be judged on the basis of popular belief (27), or by his signs (31), or by the sheer prophetic power of his speech (40, 46), or by Scripture (42, 52) — or indeed by the Sanhedrin (32, 51)?

Jesus himself, followed by the narrator, emphasises the fulfilment of Scripture in what he offers (38-39), and this becomes a chief focus of the debate in ch. 8. But how are the Scriptures to be interpreted? Nicodemus, speaking for the Sanhedrin, claims that "our law" judges people — that is, of course, the law as interpreted and applied by the Sanhedrin. Many, especially in Judea, accepted the final authority of the Sanhedrin, both in Jerusalem and at Yavneh, to judge a matter like the claim of Jesus, and those who did not grant its authority were nonetheless aware that it claimed it. By asserting his freedom from the arresting party, therefore (7:33f), Jesus refuses to submit to the judgment of the Sanhedrin, and *thus throws the issue of the interpretation of the Scriptures wide open.*

That this is the issue is confirmed by the reaction of "the Jews": "will he go to the diaspora and teach the Greeks?" (7:35). Many commentators understand this as an ironic reference to the Gentile mission,[42] and this may play a part: but it is tempting to read this response as alluding to the *jurisdiction* of the Sanhedrin (something

---

41   Josephus *War* 2:254-7: the *sicarii* were "murdering people in broad daylight and in the middle of the city" (μετὰ ἡμέραν καὶ ἐν μέσῃ τῇ πόλει φονεύοντες ἀνθρώπους), which they did "especially during the festivals", because of the crowds. He describes an atmosphere of panic, which is undoubtedly overplayed, but readers' memories could well have been prompted with recollections of the charged atmosphere at those pre-War festival gatherings. Such memories would have the effect of giving the action of the Jewish authorities against Jesus a very distinct poignancy and flavour.

42   So Strathmann, Lindars, Brown, Schnackenburg, Bruce, Beasley-Murray, Carson; also Hengel *Question* 122.

which none of the commentators explore). In the diaspora, Jesus would be beyond its authority to control his teaching and to prescribe *halakah* in interpretation of the Scriptures.

The extent of the jurisdiction of the Jerusalem Sanhedrin before 70 AD is unclear, but the current consensus seems to be that it was not until after the Bar Kokba revolt that the authority of its successor at Yavneh began to be widely recognised beyond Palestine.[43] In the late first century readers would readily have granted that there was no Jewish 'orthodoxy' in the diaspora, merely a general orthopraxy, and that "the Jews" of Palestine did not possess authority to regulate what happened elsewhere.

In any case, "the crowd" are exercising their *own* judgment about what the Scriptures mean (7:41f) — albeit not in Jesus' favour; and the narrator plays a subtle card in 7:50 by putting the case for a hearing on the lips of Nicodemus, whom we already know to be inclined to the view that Jesus *is* "from God" (3:2) — and who therefore must feel that "our law" will not condemn him.

His fellow "rulers", however, feel differently. The narrator plays another card — a most important one — by portraying them as now *unwilling* to hold a formal 'hearing'. What Nicodemus asks for is actually what was intended when the Temple guards were sent to "arrest" Jesus. But now it appears that they have already decided against him: he cannot be "the prophet",[44] in spite of the reaction of the guards (perhaps *because of it?*), and so the arresting party is not despatched again.

Pancaro argues at length and to little effect against the view that "hear" in 7:51 indicates a judicial 'hearing'.[45] In this context, and with lexical precedent for this meaning, this must be its sense.[46] But one of Pancaro's arguments against this interpretation is the observation that

> [John] does not report an official 'hearing' or 'trial' of Jesus by the Jews ... The hearing before Annas (Jn 18:19-23) is not meant to be understood as an official hearing.[47]

43   So e.g. Neusner "Destruction" 93; Meeks "Breaking Away" 102; Mueller "Apocalypse" 341

44   That anarthrous προφήτης in 7:52 refers to *the* prophet particularly, is indicated not only by the fact that this is the identification under discussion (7:40), but also by ἐγείρεται, the verb used of "the prophet" in Deut 18:15 (so Reim *Hintergrund* 123). So also Schnackenburg 2:161 (accepting the reading of p 66, which includes the article).

45   Pancaro *Law* 138-149

46   So Barrett 332

This is undoubtedly correct — though it does not support Pancaro's contention about 7:51. The 'hearing' by the law which is refused at this point in the narrative *never takes place,* even though "the Jews" insist that "we have a law, and by that law he must die" (19:7). When Jesus finally appears before the High Priest and is questioned about his teaching (18:19), he follows proper procedure and calls as witnesses "those who heard what I said" (18:21).[48] But he is immediately rebuked by one of the "servants", who according to 7:45f are precisely those who reported to the Sanhedrin, "No one ever spoke like this!"

Jesus' words to this man clearly recall that report: "If I spoke wrongly, bear witness to my error. But if I spoke well, why do you strike me?" (18:23). But the servant refuses to act as a witness, and remains silent — just as the "servants" in ch. 7 do not report *what* Jesus said. And so *no 'hearing' takes place.* Jesus is sent straight on to Caiaphas, and then straight to Pilate (18:24, 28).[49]

The fact that no formal examination of Jesus' teaching in the light of the law takes place, is vital from a narrative and rhetorical perspective. For this means that *the trial of Jesus is left open in the Fourth Gospel — left, in fact, to the reader,* who is provided with the raw material in dialogues which are replete with legal terminology and which *specialise* in relating the claim of Jesus to the "testimony" of the law.

At this point in the narrative (7:52), the co-operative reader feels that the Sanhedrin has failed in its duty, possibly because of prejudice against Galileans.

6.5.3 8:12-30: trial, self-testimony and God as witness

There is no narrative break after 7:52.[50] "Again" (8:12) probably refers back to 7:37f, and indicates the identity of substance between these two dramatic appropriations of Tabernacles imagery (water, and now light). The connecting οὖν ("therefore") perhaps points to a particular connection between 8:12 and 7:52: those who deny that

---

47   *Law* 140

48   Barrett 528: Jesus' reply is in effect a request for a formal trial, by asking that witnesses be heard.

49   Again, I cannot find a commentator who draws out this narrative bond between 18:19-24 and 7:45f, which is surprising: for many emphasise the way in which the trial of Jesus takes place throughout the Gospel.

50   The textual evidence for the exclusion of 7:53-8:11 is so great that we pass over it without discussion.

the Prophet can come from Galilee now hear words strongly reminiscent of the prophecy of a "great light" which will shine in "Galilee of
the Gentiles" (Isa 9:1-2).[51]

But such a connection would simply heighten the problem posed
by the whole introductory clause "therefore Jesus spoke to them
again" and the specification of "the Pharisees" as his dialogue partners (8:13). Jesus apparently addresses the Sanhedrin, to which he
has not been admitted. Once again, the narrative throws up a discontinuity which makes the reader pause and search for coherence.

The coherence appears as the paragraph proceeds. The point is
subtly made that Jesus is able to address the Sanhedrin, *but on his
own terms* and without surrendering to their authority by being
arrested. Furthermore, the conversation which now takes place with
the Pharisees has all the hallmarks of the trial just refused by the
Sanhedrin. The Pharisees judge what Jesus says according to the
formal rules of evidence drawn from the law (13), and then Jesus
seeks to justify his contention in like manner, appealing to the law of
two witnesses and repeating the legal step of *calling God to witness
on his behalf* (8:14ff, cf 5:37) — which, as Harvey has shown, is a
most significant act in the context of Jewish legal practice.[52] It has
the effect of putting pressure on those who doubt or dispute Jesus'
claim: Jesus is willing to face the judgment of God, should his claim
be false, so those who reject his claim will also face God's judgment,
should it be true. At the end of the paragraph it is emphasised that
this conversation, which looks so much like a formal hearing without
being such, took place at the initiative of *Jesus* (8:20).

These thoughts shed light on the difficult verse 15, "you judge
according to the flesh, I judge no one" (ὑμεῖς κατὰ τὴν σάρκα
κρίνετε, ἐγὼ οὐ κρίνω οὐδένα). It is tempting to interpret this to
mean, "Your administration of the law is guided by 'the flesh': I do
not participate in a formal legal process". The possibility of Jesus
'judging' relates, as Harvey has shown, to the way in which the
tables could be turned on one's opponents in court by appealing to
God as witness; this Jesus refuses to do — even though by this
means he could deliver a "true" verdict on them, because of the
presence of God with him (8:16).

His charge that they judge "according to the flesh" is ironically
and amply confirmed by the Pharisees' response in 8:19, "where is
your father?" — for they clearly take him to mean his human father,
whose evidence would be inadmissible as a close relative.[53] They

---

51   So Lindars 315. He suggests that this passage may be in mind at 7:41, also.
52   Harvey *Trial* 48, 57-59 (on 8:16)

do not seem to realise that he has appealed to God. But of course the reader realises this, and so is put in the dilemma that the Pharisees would be in if they understood Jesus' words: *will he accept this self-testimony or not?* — *remembering that he could be flying in the face of God if he rejects it.*

This illumines 8:30, "as he was saying these things, many believed in him". Several scholars point out how incongruous this faith seems, just after Jesus has spoken so sharply to "the Jews".[54] This incongruity was Brown's original reason for regarding the references to faith in 8:30 and 31 as a late redaction.[55] But, against the legal background sketched by Harvey, "faith" here takes on a particular force: impressed by his appeal to God as witness, "many" are prepared to accept his claim.[56]

This line of interpretation is supported by reflection on the *content* of the claim they are prepared to accept. The reference to Jesus' speech ("as he was saying these things ...") makes it natural to fill out this faith with the confession in 7:40, "This is truly the prophet". This is confirmed not only by our observations about the structure above (5.3), but also by the allusions to Deut 18:18 in vv. 26b, 28c: Jesus speaks what he has heard from God.[57] Disbelieving "the Prophet" also has a sanction specifically attached to it (Deut 18:19). So the "many" who believe are those who accept that Jesus is "the Prophet", prompted to faith by his calling God to witness, and moved by the warnings attached to rejecting both.[58]

Deut 18:20 contains an equivalent warning for the *false* prophet. Risks attach to both sides — both to Jesus himself and to those who dispute his claim. Our implied reader is put on the spot, too, but for her the dilemma is different. Essentially, the question is this: *on whom has the sanction of Deut 18:19f fallen?* On Jesus, rightly executed as a false prophet, or on Israel, who in the events of 70 AD has been "called to account" for failing to heed the words of the Prophet? Jesus lays it on the line: "unless you believe that I am, you will die in your sins!" (24). The fact (a) that Israel *has* died in her

---

53 Harvey *Trial* 58

54 E.g. Haenchen 2:28

55 Brown 1:351

56 Harvey himself does not make this suggestion.

57 Reim *Hintergrund* 106 finds in 8:28 a "probable allusion" to Exod 4:12, rather than to Deut 18:18. There God promises Moses himself that he will be taught the words of God to speak. Whether Exod 4 or Deut 18, the force is clear: like Moses, Jesus speaks the very words of God to Israel (and, we may add, leads Israel in Exodus).

58 See the quotation from Meeks in 5.4.1 above (p 135).

sins,[59] (b) that this warning was issued by someone who claimed to be the Prophet *before it happened,* and (c) that the fulfilment of prophecy is made the test of the Prophet in Deut 18:21f — all this combines to put pressure on the implied reader to adopt the same verdict as the "many" in 8:30.

Even though the conversation-partners change at 8:31, the whole chapter retains this 'trial' flavour. The statement — objection — response pattern continues throughout. Though Jesus refuses to "judge", "the Jews" finally try to carry out the sanction appropriate to a false prophet (8:59). They have decided that Jesus' death would *not* be the sin of murder. Once again, at that point the response of other actors in the drama is left open: what about the believing Jews of 8:30f? Jesus has said some extremely surprising and difficult things to them. Do they support the attempt to stone him, or not? And the same decision faces that fly on the wall, our implied reader. If he were there, would he support the verdict of his fathers on Jesus, or not?

The final ἐγώ εἰμι ("I am") in 8:58 illustrates the way in which the reader is taken through a 'learning curve' by this dialogue. This is the last of five or six occasions on which Jesus has used this expression of himself in this chapter.[60] Commentators, following Bultmann, tend first to classify usages of ἐγώ εἰμι in John, and then to ask into which class particular occurrences fall.[61] So, for both Schnackenburg and Brown,[62] 8:24, 28 and 58 are all "absolute" usages, which reflect the divine name, while in 8:12, 18 and possibly 23 "the formula does not appear in such a 'pure' form", but even so it is still an "Old Testament revelation formula" which has been transferred to Jesus.[63]

The problem with this procedure is its failure to analyse the rhetorical force and effect of this expression in relation to each occurrence. *None* of the previous uses of the "formula" need have caused any excitement. Even that in 6:20 could be heard simply as an identificatory "It is I". 8:18, like 4:26, connotes a particular passage in Isaiah,[64] and an alert reader might catch the allusion. But the usages in 8:24 and 28 are different, in that here for the first

---

59   Strathmann 147 alone (apparently) sees a connection between "you will die in your sins" and the catastrophe of 70 AD.

60   Cf verses 12, 18, 23, 24, 28. The doubt attaches to 23, ἐγώ ἐκ τῶν ἄνω εἰμί.

61   Bultmann 225 n. 3

62   Schnackenburg 2:80f, Brown 1:533f

63   Schnackenburg 2:81, 88

64   Cf above, p 145

time the expression is used 'oddly', in a way that commands attention.

René Robert has successfully expounded this 'oddness', I believe, in arguing that the usage in these verses is deliberately ambiguous, and that the ambiguity is part of a dramatic purpose which carries the debate forward until the misunderstanding is cleared up in 8:58. In 8:25 the response "who are you?" signals the fact that a predicate is missing from Jesus' bald "I am".[65] Jesus' reply is equally elusive (25b): Robert argues — rightly, I think — that it is best taken as a statement, meaning "Precisely what I told you".[66] The natural reference would be to "I am the light of the world" in 8:12, and beyond that back to the great christological statements of 5:19-30: Jesus is the Son who gives life and speaks the judgment of God.

Then in 8:28 ἐγώ εἰμι is simply repeated, again without a predicate. But in 8:58 the overtone of the divine name is unmistakable, and so not only provokes a hostile reaction from "the Jews", but also requires all previous occurrences of the expression to be re-read.[67]

The effect of this is to take the reader through a learning experience identical to that of "the Jews" in the text. But will her response be the same? Is Jesus indeed guilty of blasphemy? We are now ready (at last!) to look closely at the rhetorical strategies in 8:31ff which — we will argue — are designed to produce the opposite response to that of "the Jews" within the text.

---

65 Robert actually suggests that "the Jews" heard ὅτι as ὅ τι, "unless you believe *what* I am ..." ("Malentendu" 281f). But this is not necessary for his case.

66 Robert "Malentendu" 282-7; so also Lindars 321, Beasley-Murray 125, von Wahlde "Discourses" 579 (though with differing evaluations of the difficult τὴν ἀρχήν).

67 For this understanding of the relationship between 8:58 and 8:24,28, cf also Neyrey "Process" 535

7

8:31-59: A Prophetic Appeal

We come now to look more closely at 8:31-59, the passage whose exegesis has motivated us throughout. We will find that our approach allows this passage to play a significant role in the overall persuasive strategy of the Gospel. Rather than make it impossible for the Gospel to function evangelistically, the polemic and the *irony* of this passage actually play quite a crucial part in urging its message upon the reader.

We will examine 8:31-59 in three sections, and in each case focus on its rhetorical force in the post-70 situation. But first we must consider some introductory issues.

7.1 Structure, Abraham and dialogue partners

7.1.1 Structure

Overall, 8:31-59 consists of a basic appeal (31f), followed by six exchanges between Jesus and "the Jews", as follows:
- 31-32 The appeal to become disciples
- 33-37 First exchange: the nature of freedom
- 38-41a Second exchange: kinship with Abraham
- 41b-47 Third exchange: kinship with God or the devil
- 48-51 Fourth exchange: Jesus the giver of life?
- 52-56 Fifth exchange: Jesus greater than Abraham?
- 57-59 Sixth exchange: the final alternatives

There are some quite elaborate chiasms here too, most notably in 31-37[1] and in 42-47.[2] But because it is unlikely that these would be immediately apparent to the reader (or rather, *listener*[3]), we will concentrate on the structure supplied simply by these exchanges between Jesus and "the Jews". The tone becomes increasingly more hostile, marked particularly by the long speech of "the Jews" in 52-

1   Culpepper "Pivot" 27; Lindars "Slave" 274
2   Brown 1:365f
3   See above, p 119.

53, so that the degeneration of speech into hostile action in 59 is not a surprising climax.

It is not surprising also that *the identity of Jesus* becomes a focus in the last three exchanges, where "we know" in 52 is matched by "you do not know ... I know" in 55. We realise at the end that Jesus' *hiddenness* (59) has a symbolic import for the evangelist.

7.1.2 Abraham

Abraham features prominently in the first two and the last two exchanges: in 33-40 his relationship to "the Jews" is discussed, in 52-58 his relationship to Jesus. The appearance of Abraham — only here in the Fourth Gospel — signals the extent to which Israel's status as the covenant people is the focus of discussion.

A parallel interest in Abraham is to be found, as we have seen, in contemporary literature, with two late first-century pseudepi-graphies to his name, and a string of references in other works.[4] The prominence of Abraham in Pseudo-Philo illustrates his impor-tance at a popular level earlier in the first century, as the sign and guarantee of the covenant that sustains Israel[5] (and this of course was the confidence so radically undermined by the disaster of 70 AD). So far as I can see, the significance of Abraham in John 8 has not been explored from this perspective.[6] And yet we may regard it as certain that this is the background against which the text would have been 'heard' in the late first century. Hopefully, our 'implied reader' will guide us into hitherto unexplored features of John 8.

7.1.3 Dialogue partners

This is a most important question for the interpretation of our passage. Who are "the Jews" with whom Jesus speaks? We need to

---

4   The *Apocalypse* and the *Testament* are both given first-century dates by their editors in *OTP*: the former much more securely than the latter. Cf also 2 Baruch 4:4, 57:1, 78:4; 4 Ezra 3:13-15, 6:8, 7:[106]; 4 Baruch 4:9f, 6:21.

5   E.g. *Bib. Ant.* 6:3-18, 7:4, 18:5, 23:5-7, 32:1-4, 61:5.

6   The latest 'trajectory' study of Abraham, Jeffrey S. Siker's *Disinheriting the Jews*, devotes a chapter to John 8, but does not touch upon any of these sources. Ashton *Understanding* 142-5 suggests that *Apoc. Abr.* is important for the interpretation of 8:56-8, but (as we shall see) more because of the angelic guide Iaoel who conducts Abraham to heaven, than because of Abraham himself.

Lona *Johannes 8* 292-313 offers the fullest exploration to date, suggesting that the Fourth Gospel may have arisen among Jews who shared the vision of *Apoc. Abr.* for the restoration of Israel. This seems unlikely, in view of the striking militarism of *Apoc. Abr.*, but at least Lona sees the relevance of this contemporary text for the 'Abraham' passages in John.

consider this from two perspectives — first intratextually, and then with reference to evidence from outside the text.

(1) *Who are they within the text?* One of the most challenging problems facing interpreters is that "the Jews who have believed in him" (31) are very quickly accused of wanting to murder Jesus (37, 40), of being children of the devil (44, implied in 38), and indeed of *not* believing him (45); and then "the Jews" accuse him of being demon-possessed (48). It looks as though a change of interlocutors takes place — but where?

Scholars respond in a variety of ways:

• Bultmann 314 finds evidence for textual dislocation in the discrepancy between 8:31 and what follows, but in the event he keeps 30-40 as a unit and so leaves the problem intact (though not the text!).

• Some scholars solve the problem by removing the phrase πεπιστευκότας αὐτῷ ("who had believed in him") as a late redaction.[7]

• Bornhäuser suggests that the change takes place immediately: Jesus addresses believing Jews, but unbelieving Jews reply in 33.[8]

• Bartholomew turns the problem to exegetical advantage, and theorises that the purpose of the discourse is precisely to turn believing Jews into murderers: that is, to undermine and destroy the faith of Christian Jews who retain allegiance to the synagogue.[9]

• Several scholars effectively ignore the reference to faith in 31, treating the discourse as in substance an argument with non-Christian Judaism.[10]

Help in this dilemma may be obtained by comparing this discourse with the several earlier ones in which *a dialogue partner of Jesus is treated as representative of a wider group.* This is the case with Nicodemus, with the Samaritan woman, and with the royal official in 4:46ff: Nicodemus represents the Jerusalem authorities, the

---

7   So e.g. von Wahlde "Jews" 50f, Brown 1:354f (though he changes his mind in *Community* 77 n. 141), Lindars 323, *Behind* 80n.

8   *Missionsschrift* 55. There would surely need to be some textual indication of the change of partner.

9   *Sermon-Drama* 104-110. This motivates his proposal that 8:31-59 is a "sermon-drama", dramatically picturing this change in one group in order to bring it about in another. But he provides no documentation for this new genre, isolates it from its co-text, and fails to propose how realistically such a "sermon-drama" may have functioned.

10   So e.g. Aker *Merits;* Brown 1:362; Hahn "Juden" 438; Manns *Vérité* 103-5; Lindars "Discourse" 97; Beasley-Murray 133; Painter *Quest* 256-60

Samaritan woman her fellow-Samaritans, and the royal official his household (cf 4:53). In each case, the wider group is signalled by the sudden appearance of a 'you-plural' address (3:7, 11f; 4:21f; 4:48).[11]

The same is true, I suggest, of the discourse before us, although here the wider group cannot be indicated grammatically, because the dialogue-partner is already plural. Just as (believing) Nicodemus represents all his fellow-rulers, so in 8:37 the limited address to "the Jews who had believed in him" is widened to include those plotting to kill Jesus, as it becomes clear that these believing Jews are no more prepared to accept Jesus' word than their plotting fellow-Jews. This will be confirmed by the exegesis below.

Then in 8:48 a formal change of interlocutor occurs, marked by the new introduction, "The Jews replied and said to him ..." The wider group, already in fact addressed, now speaks up. We have here another example of the structure we noted above (5.3), whereby an expression of *division* is followed by engagement with each side in turn — except that, in this case, the positive response is treated first. 8:30 does not express the division directly, but it is implied by mentioning the faith of "many". Then the groups are addressed in turn — first the believers (31-47) and then the unbelievers (48-59).[12]

At 6.5.3 above I suggested that the faith of "the Jews" in 8:31 is *acceptance of Jesus as the Prophet*. Nothing that these Jews say in 8:33, 39 and 41 is inconsistent with that faith (in the terms in which they hold it), but "you have a demon" (8:48) is quite incompatible with it. In fact it asserts the opposite: Jesus does not speak from God, but from the devil.

This understanding of their faith is essentially an intratextual definition, which comes forward within the developing dynamic of the text itself.[13] But who are these Jews? We must devote some

---

11 Koester *Symbolism* 12 suggests that the sudden use of plural forms of speech in addressing individuals "introduces an element of incongruity into the narrative" and thus signals a symbolic role for the individual concerned (he focuses on Nicodemus).

12 The proposal of a change of interlocutor at 8:48 is supported by Siker *Disinheriting* 132 and apparently by Dunn *Partings* 157.

13 Neyrey "Process" 518f makes an interesting and different proposal which finally fails to convince. He explains the faith of 8:30 as essentially a plea of "not guilty" to the charge Jesus has just made against the Jews, namely that they do not believe in him because they are "from below" (23). So the Jews attempt to prove him wrong, by believing in him. The agenda is thus set for the rest of the dialogue, Neyrey suggests, for Jesus now seeks to prove that they have not *really* believed. This at least gives priority to an intratextual understanding of this 'faith'. But forensically, 8:30 is far more likely to mean that some of Jesus' opponents have accepted the rightness of his case. And, as we saw above, this makes sense following

pages to seeking any extra-textual referents behind Jesus' dialogue-partners.

(2) *Who are they outside the text?*

Scholarship diverges radically in answer to this question. At the level of principle, Lona holds that the reference to faith in 8:30f *cannot* be explained from within the text, and therefore must relate to the situation of the reader (which he then does not explore).[14] On the other hand, Gräßer thinks that the picture of "the Jews" in this passage is *historically impossible*, and is thus wholly text-internal (theological) in motivation.[15] They cannot both be right! The majority build on the assumption that these intratextual characters must also be an identifiable 'group' within the environment of the evangelist (an assumption we challenged above[16]), but the proposals are depressingly numerous.[17]

Our intratextual definition of their faith produces an interesting question: Was there a specific group in the evangelist's environment who acclaimed Jesus as "Prophet", in distinction from other believers? It is tempting to point to the Ebionites, the Jewish-Christian group who, according to Epiphanius, accepted Jesus as the "prophet of truth" who became Son of God "by promotion, and by his connection with the elevation given to him from above".[18]

---

his appeal to God as witness (a forensic feature of the passage ignored by Neyrey). Yet we may agree with Neyrey that in 32-38 Jesus seeks to destabilise their theology and to undermine their profession of faith.

14 Lona *Johannes 8* 394
15 Gräßer "Teufelssöhne" 167f
16 In the introduction to ch. 2 above.
17 We may identify eight suggestions:
   • (1) Jewish Christians who are still members of the synagogue: Martyn "Glimpses" 168, Whitacre *Polemic* 19, Bartholomew *Sermon-Drama* 104-110, Brown "Sheep" 13f, Siker *Disinheriting* 139;
   • (2) Jewish Christians with a 'judaising' theology: Dodd *Tradition* 379f, Goulder "Nicodemus" 164f, Rensberger *Community* 125, Pryor *John* 37f;
   • (3) Jewish Christians in danger of lapsing back into Judaism: Schnackenburg 2:204f;
   • (4) Former Jewish Christians who have already abandoned their faith: Culpepper "Jews" 278;
   • (5) The heretical 'believers' of 1 John 1:8, 2:4: Manns *Vérité* 84;
   • (6) New converts from Judaism in need of instruction: Leroy *Rätsel* 70f;
   • (7) Jewish Christians of weak, untrustworthy faith: Meeks "Man From Heaven" 55, Brown *Community* 76-8, Neyrey "Process" 541;
   • (8) Jews of fickle faith — who feel momentarily inclined to believe, but never really do: Strathmann 143, Ibuki "Viele" 128-138, Urban & Henry "Philo" 161, Carson 347f.

Epiphanius locates the origin of the Ebionites in the flight of the Jerusalem Christian community to Pella during the War (*Panarion* 30:2:7), and this seems to be confirmed by the clear elements of Essene theology which appear in Ebionite teaching. Schoeps and Daniélou both trace the origins of Ebionism back to the mix of ideas in this area in the late first century, "where from of old time Jewish minority groups opposed to civilization and the cultus had settled"[19] — in other words, to the broad area in which we have tentatively located the Fourth Gospel, with its interest in issues of law, Temple and cult.

But we must exercise caution. For no writer earlier than Irenaeus identifies 'Ebionites' as a distinct group, and there are quite wide divergences in the various descriptions of their teaching. According to Epiphanius they believed that

> Jesus was begotten of the seed of a man and chosen, and thus named Son of God by election, after the Christ who had come to him from on high in the form of a dove (*Panarion* 30:3:1).

But Irenaeus does not mention a prophet-christology in his brief description of their views.[20] Similarly Justin describes simply an adoptionist christology without any 'prophet' overtones, when he mentions Jewish Christians who believed that Jesus was just a "man born of men".[21]

On the other hand, the Pseudo-Clementine *Recognitions*, parts of which many regard as emanating from second-century circles later called 'Ebionite',[22] clearly espouse a prophet-christology, yet it is not adoptionist: Christ is a pre-existent divine being, greater than all angels, who "became man" (*Rec.* 1:45:4). There is no assertion of ordinary human generation.

In fact Epiphanius specifically mentions various "conflicting accounts of Christ" among the Ebionites: "they get all giddy from supposing different things about him at different times" (*Panarion*

18   Epiphanius *Panarion* 30:18:5, trans. Williams *Panarion* 134. The quotations below are all from Williams.

19   Schoeps "Ebionite Christianity" 223, Daniélou *Theology* 56f; also Strecker "Jewish Christianity" 257f

20   Irenaeus *Adv. Haer.* 1:26:2

21   Justin *Dialogue* 48:4

22   E.g. Daniélou *Theology* 59; Schoeps "Ebionite Christianity" 219; Strecker "Jewish Christianity" 257f; Martyn "Persecution" 60 In particular Ps.-Clem. *Rec.* 1:33-71 is held to be essentially the early work mentioned by Epiphanius as the *Ascents of James* (so Strecker, Martyn).

30:3:1, 3:6). So Strecker helpfully emphasises the variety and fluidity of Jewish Christian groups and views in the first and second centuries — something we might in any case have expected. Bearing this variety in mind, there are three features of this nascent Jewish Christianity which may help us to understand the 'sensitivity' of our text within its environment:

(a) *'Prophet' and law?* A central feature of Ps.-Clem. *Rec.* 1:33-71 is the affirmation of Jesus as "the true Prophet", who reveals the future of the world to Abraham (1:33) before he "comes, bringing signs and miracles as his credentials by which he should be made manifest" (1:40). At the same time, this group is aware of a fundamental affinity between themselves and Jerusalem Judaism. The only point of difference is the prophethood of Jesus,

> for on this point only does there seem to be any difference between us who believe in Jesus, and the unbelieving Jews.[23]

Recognition of Jesus as a prophet, and continuing loyalty to Torah, do not necessarily entail each other. But we find them combined, both in the dialogue-partners in the Fourth Gospel, and in this stream of this Jewish Christianity. In John 8:31-59 we meet believing Jews who are only distinguishable from unbelieving Jews by their acceptance of Jesus as prophet. This debate, therefore, would exercise an effective voice in a situation in which the prophethood of Jesus was a point of argument within a fundamental commitment to Torah. But what it says is very striking: confession of Jesus as 'prophet' in such company is a completely inadequate response. Such believers are accused of conniving at Jesus' murder — even though in the *Recognitions* their grief over his crucifixion and over the unbelief of their fellow-Jews, are very clear.[24]

(b) However the *Recognitions* reflect a situation in which an *open debate* about the identity of Jesus is taking place. In an idealised picture of the early church, the author describes how the Jerusalem authorities

> often sent to us [*i.e. Peter and the other apostles*], and asked us to discourse to them concerning Jesus, whether He were the Prophet whom Moses foretold, who is the eternal Christ.[25]

---

23   Ps.-Clem. *Rec.* 1:43:2 (cf 50:6): trans. Thomas Smith, *Ante-Nicene Christian Library Vol 3* (Edinburgh; T. & T. Clark, 1868). The quotations below are all from this translation.

24   Ps.-Clem. *Rec.* 1:40:2-3, 41:2

25   Ps.-Clem. *Rec.* 1:43:1, cf 53:3-4

And then an extended debate is described (*Rec.* 55-69), which almost leads to the conversion of the Jewish leaders, but for the violent intervention of the pre-Christian Saul (*Rec.* 70). The use of Deut 18 in the initial sermons in Acts (3:22, 7:37) supports the contention that *the identification of Jesus as the Prophet was one of the chief foci of the first-century debate with Jews,* as Martyn himself maintains in his *History and Theology.* He gathers eight texts from various sources (Jewish and Samaritan) to illustrate "the strands of eschatological hope" gathered around the figure of the Mosaic Prophet.[26] We may surely realistically imagine that the prophet-hood of Jesus was intensely debated in those trans-Jordan (and indeed Judean) communities from which Ebionism emerged.

(c) One consistent and surprising feature of these groups was *their opposition to the cult.* It may well be right to discern the influence of Essenism here,[27] but in the *Recognitions* this belief is related directly to the destruction of the Temple. One of the Prophet's chief messages is that the sacrifices were basically *wrong,* allowed by God for a time (*Rec.* 1:36), but now abolished by him (1:39:1, 54:1) and replaced with baptism (1:39:2, 55:3). All who are baptised in the Prophet's name

> shall be kept unhurt from the destruction of war which impends over the unbelieving nation, and the place itself; but ... those who do not believe shall be made exiles from their place and kingdom, that even against their will they may understand and obey the will of God [*i.e. his will to abolish sacrifices as evil*][28]

— and Peter predicts the coming destruction of the Temple "because ye will not acknowledge that the time for offering victims is now past" (*Rec.* 1:64:2). Now a second coming of the Prophet is expected, when he will "give the kingdom to those who believe in him" (1:69:4).

We may detect echoes of the debate over causes of the disaster here. Opposition to cult is very clear in the *Recognitions,* but Iren-aeus points to a different stream within Ebionism in his description of those who "are so Judaic in their style of life, that they even adore Jerusalem as if it were the house of God".[29] Perhaps reflected here

---

26   *History & Theology*2 106-111. Meeks *Prophet-King* is foundational in its gathering of evidence for the widespread expectation of the Mosaic Prophet.

27   Schoeps "Ebionite Christianity" 223, Daniélou *Theology* 57f

28   *Rec.* 1:39:3

are two of the options debated in those early years: one which looked for a restoration of a reformed cult in Jerusalem, and another which saw the cult completely replaced by 'baptism' (that is, a christianised purity rite). The 'replacement' theology of the Fourth Gospel clearly relates to this debate. And the offer of freedom from sin apart from cult holds no surprise in itself.

Both these attitudes to cult could be described as politically 'quietist', in the terms discussed above (3.3.4). Employing the distinction made by Horsley and Hanson, the Prophet of the *Recognitions* is an "oracular prophet" like John the Baptist and Jesus ben Hananiah, who simply spoke words from God — to be distinguished from "action prophets", like Theudas and the Egyptian, whose word from God was a command to lead the people into political deliverance.[30]

In all likelihood 'activist' expectations predominated in the post-70 situation, and so it is interesting to note the emphasis in John 8 on Jesus as a *heavenly revealer.* Just as Nicodemus echoes one of the great concerns of the late first century when he recognises Jesus as a "teacher from God"[31] and looks to him for heavenly revelation, so the claims of Jesus in 8:32 and 38 underline his status as Revealer. And since "light" is a frequent image for such revelation, Jesus' claim to be "the light of the world" (8:12) will have connoted in part a claim to be the source of heavenly knowledge and truth.[32] Jesus is a prophet who offers Israel "freedom", but the crucial accusation directed at those who recognise him is that "my *word* finds no place in you" (ὁ λόγος ὁ ἐμὸς οὐ χωρεῖ ἐν ὑμῖν, 37).

So the "faith" of the Jews in 8:30 connotes all the hopes and longings which gathered around the idea of "the Prophet" — whether of an 'activist' (cf 6:14) or a 'quietist' stamp. Such hopes, dealt a cruel blow by the events of 70 AD, yet sustained very many Jews in the following decades. As we shall see, these connotations are vital as background to Jesus' use *and adjustment of* politically loaded language in 8:32-38.

---

29   Irenaeus *Adv. Haer.* 1:26:2, trans. Roberts & Rambaut, *Ante-Nicene Christian Library Vol 5* (Edinburgh; T. & T. Clark, 1868)

30   Horsley & Hanson *Bandits* 135ff, especially 160-187

31   This is not as lavish an identification as "the Prophet", but it is moving in the same direction: contra Martyn *History & Theology2* 116.

32   So e.g. *Sib. Or.* 5:238f, Pseudo-Philo *Bib. Ant.* 28:3, 51:4-7, 4 Baruch 9:3. In this last reference Jeremiah, praying for revelation, addresses God as "true light that enlightens me". In both these Pseudo-Philo references "light" and "truth" appear together in connection with prophetic revelation.

7.2 8:31-38, the Appeal and the First Exchange: Freedom from Sin

We will now survey the substance of the exchange between Jesus and "the Jews" in 31-38. In the post-70 situation, several features of this passage have a highly ironic effect which lends the argument the force of pathos. At the same time, a clear polemic against some of the other responses to the disaster is discernible. The main features of our 'hearing'-based reading are the following:

• *7.2.1:* Jesus challenges those who regard him as a Prophet to *accept what he says.* He then puts his word on a level with Torah in offering "freedom" — an Exodus image — to all who will commit themselves to following him.

• *7.2.2:* "Freedom" was a highly charged political slogan, both in the Jewish War and later in the Bar Kokba revolt. In using it the evangelist claims that the longing for freedom can only be fulfilled through following Jesus.

• *7.2.3:* The reply of the Jews in 33 is highly ironic. For many, a simplistic confidence in the inviolability of Zion because of the covenant with Abraham was exploded in 70 AD. The fact that Jesus' conversation-partners *feel that they are free already and so turn down Jesus' offer* works powerfully in those who have experienced the traumatic loss of that freedom. At the same time, v. 33 accurately voices the conviction of those who adjusted to the tragedy by emphasising a spiritual understanding of "freedom", based on the study of Torah.

• *7.2.4:* Jesus' words in 34 deny that this Torah life-style can deliver people from *sin,* which was the problem that caused the disaster: the prescription has already been shown not to work. Because they were slaves to sin, they were expelled from "the house" (35): but Jesus is able truly to deliver (36).

• *7.2.5:* Their intention to murder Jesus — an intention which can be shared by the reader, even though the deed is long since done — reveals the true quality of their obedience to Torah and radically qualifies their right to call Abraham their 'father' (37). Jesus hints that they have a different 'father' (38).

We will develop each of these points in turn.

7.2.1 Jesus, Exodus and Torah (31-32)

That the content of the Jews' faith is *Jesus as Prophet* is confirmed by the challenge they receive: "if you abide in my word ..." Those who recognise Jesus in this way are faced with a call to live by his word. This is the first of five references to "my word" in 31-59 (also 37, 43b, 51, 52; cf "my speech" in 43a), accompanied by four significant references to Jesus "speaking" (the truth, 40, 45, 46; what he has seen with the Father, 38). As so often in John, faith alone is not enough, and needs to be supplemented by positive, obedient discipleship.[33]

The background to this is, as Reim has shown, the "Mosaic prophet" passage in Deut 18:15ff.[34] In Deut 18:15, 19 it is reiterated that Israel has a responsibility to "hear" this Prophet: and this is essentially what Jesus challenges his hearers to do (cf especially the use of ἀκούειν, "hear", in 43).

This self-designation as the Mosaic Prophet fits with the Exodus imagery in 31f. "Freedom" is an Exodus idea, probably to be understood here as overlapping semantically with "redemption".[35] And "you will truly be my disciples" picks up and reiterates the call to discipleship in 8:12, where Jesus portrays himself as the Exodus gift of light, and calls Israel to "follow" just as she followed the pillar of fire in the wilderness.[36]

So the claim in 31 is dramatic indeed. "My word", *rather than Torah*, becomes the focus of discipleship and the yardstick of "truth". And it is as *Jesus' disciples* that "the Jews" will experience "freedom". Dale Bisnauth is nearly correct with his comment that the believers of 8:31

> refused to become disciples. They were prepared to give assent to Jesus' teaching but not to put that teaching into practice.[37]

---

33   See above, 2.5

34   Reim *Hintergrund* 110ff

35   So Manns *Vérité* 78, Dodd "Behind" 46 n. 1 (though he also finds Stoic content in it). Lategan "Truth" 78 suggests that the use of ἐλευθερόω in 32 alludes to "the one great saving act of God in the past, viz the liberation of his people out of the slave-house of Egypt".

In the Old Testament "freedom" is not used of the Exodus, but the equivalent negative (deliverance from *slavery*) is frequent: e.g. Exod 13:3, 14; 20:2; Deut 5:6, 6:12, 7:8 — etc (14 times in total). In Pseudo-Philo *Bib. Ant.* 23:9, 12 "freedom" is used both of the Exodus and of Israel's secure settlement in her land.

36   Glasson *Moses* 61-64

37   Bisnauth "Liberation" 327

However the gap is not between acceptance of the *teaching* and the necessary consequent *obedience*, but between acceptance of Jesus as a *prophet*, and the consequent acceptance of his *teaching*.[38]

7.2.2 "For the freedom of Jerusalem!"

Klaus Berger, in his essay on the methods by which the views or slogans of "opponents" may be discerned in the New Testament, finds special significance in

> words which only appear in certain contexts ... and which are attested outside the New Testament in texts close to the 'opponents'.[39]

Several scholars have pointed to the sudden and surprising appearance of "freedom" language — only here in the johannine literature.[40] Lindars infers from its restricted appearance that "there must have been a certain constraint upon [John] to use it in the first place", and suggests a source-critical answer: John was constrained by the use of the word in the traditional material which underlies this dialogue, especially (he suggests) in the little parable quoted in 35 (from which, he further suggests, the word "free" has actually been removed).[41] However it is tempting to follow Berger's lead and to find here engagement with a contemporary slogan of deep significance to our 'implied reader'. This is certainly "attested outside the New Testament", which makes the proposal much less speculative than Lindars'.

"Freedom" and "slavery" are frequent metaphors in Josephus for political subjugation and independence.[42] In addition, coinage both

---

38   It is interesting that, in the passage from Ps.-Clem. *Rec.* examined above, "a certain Pharisee" charges the apostles with putting Jesus "on a level with Moses" (1:59:1). The response to this is, "we do not only say that Jesus was equal to Moses, but that he was greater than he" (1:59:2).

39   Berger "Methode" 373

40   E.g. Strathmann 149; Lindars 324

41   Lindars "Discourse" 91f

42   The usage is very common. We have already noted *War* 2:259, with its reference to the "signs of freedom" (σημεῖα ἐλευθερίας) given by prophetic deliverers; cf also e.g. *War* 2:264, 346; 4:95; 5:389; *Ant.* 18:23 (the definition of Zealot philosophy). "Freedom" and "slavery" are frequently used in combination: e.g. *War* 2:348f, 355f; 3:357, 367; 5:395f; 7:255 (the passage which describes the violent hostility of the *sicarii* to all who wanted to submit to Rome after the defeat); *Ant.* 18:4 (Judas the Galilean's revolt against the Roman census).

This is not a distinctively Josephan usage, although "freedom" is only rarely used with a political sense in LXX: cf 1 Macc 2:11. (See above, n. 35.)

from the War and from the Bar Kokba revolt testifies to the use of "freedom" as a powerful slogan. The mottos on Bar Kokba's coins were "Jerusalem", "for freedom of Jerusalem", "the redemption of Israel", "the freedom of Israel", used alongside many symbols of Jerusalem and of the Temple.[43] With this potent contemporary usage so strongly attested, the appearance of this terminology in John 8:32-36 would *certainly* be 'heard' to relate to the longings and agonies connoted by this word.

The basic message is clear: only through Jesus is this "freedom" really to be found.

7.2.3 Faith, Realism — and Irony (33)

"We are the seed of Abraham and we have never been enslaved to anyone" (Σπέρμα Ἀβραάμ ἐσμεν καὶ οὐδενὶ δεδουλεύκαμεν πώποτε) is so worded as to point up an ironic contrast between happy pre-70 confidence (which was even then unrealistic), and post-70 disillusion and division.

To "we have never been enslaved to anyone" it could have been objected even before 70 — as indeed the Zealots loudly did — that Israel had often been enslaved, and in fact *was* enslaved to the Romans. But after 70 this claim would have seemed hopelessly unrealistic, if not positively treasonous, to the many who could not give up the concrete, earthly expression of Israel's theocracy. "We are the seed of Abraham!" is the glorious conviction underlying Israel's whole existence as an independent nation, expressed so vividly in Pseudo-Philo's *midrash* on Gen 11:

> Before all these I will choose my servant Abram, and I will bring him out from their land and will bring him onto the land upon which my eye has looked from of old ... There I will have my servant Abram dwell and will establish my covenant with him and will bless his seed and be lord for him as God forever (*Bib. Ant.* 7:4).

The irony involved in evoking this naive, pre-deluge confidence creates "a community of believers" between the implied author and those who feel deeply the blow to their covenant faith. The phrase "a community of believers" was used by Wayne Booth to describe the way in which irony gives readers a sense of fellowship with an author whose mind they read and whose instincts they discover they share. For this reason, Gail O'Day (who quotes Booth's phrase) calls

---

43   Mantel "Bar Kokba" 279f. For Mantel, the Bar Kokba coins express passionate hope for the rebuilding of the Temple.

irony "a mode of revelatory language".[44] And one revelation may prepare the way for others: here those who realise that the author is gently exposing what they, too, regard as *unrealistic* covenant confidence may be further drawn to accept the prescription for freedom presented here — or at any rate to give it serious consideration. "Community of believers" may be a more than metaphorically appropriate expression.

Yet, as we have seen (3.3.2), there were indeed voices proposing a spiritual understanding of freedom as the answer to the disaster. They became the dominant force, but initially they were not powerful. We noted Neusner's observation that the very fact of the Bar Kokba revolt shows how little influence was wielded by such advocates.[45] Yet great names were attached to these voices:

> R. Akiba said, Even the poorest in Israel are considered as freemen who had lost their estates, for they are the sons of Abraham, Isaac and Jacob.[46]

In particular, of course, it was the study of Torah which gave this freedom:

> R. Nehunia b. ha-Kanah said: Everyone who receives upon him the yoke of Torah, they remove from him the yoke of the Kingdom and the yoke of worldly occupation.[47]

Similarly, boldly (polemically?) in *m. 'Abot* 6:2: "none is your freeman, but he who is occupied with the study of Torah." We find a remarkable parallel to this in 2 Baruch:

> Zion has been taken away from us, and we have nothing now apart from the Mighty One and his Law. Therefore, if we direct and dispose our hearts, we shall receive everything which we lost again by many times ... And these things which I have said earlier should be before your eyes always, since we are still in the spirit of [*v.l.: and in*] the power of our liberty.[48]

In spite of the destruction of Zion and the scattering of the people,

---

44   O'Day *Revelation* 31

45   Neusner "Destruction" 93

46   *m. B. Qam.* 8:6, quoted in connection with this verse by Schlatter 212 (he wrongly gives the reference as *m. B. Qam.* 8:9).

47   *m. 'Abot.* 3:7: this Rabbi is dated early second century.

48   2 Baruch 85:3f, 7

there is hope if Israel will hold on to the law, for she is "still in the spirit ... of our liberty". Though the law is not mentioned in John 8:33, it is surely connoted within this environment.

The appeal to Abraham, of course, speaks more widely than just to those who took this view. Change the perfect tense to a future, and 33a becomes a Zealot war-cry: "we are the seed of Abraham, and we will never be slaves to anyone!"[49] For both sides, both the politically active and the quietist, the appeal to Abraham as a symbol of Israel's status was a central article of faith. And so it is not surprising that he features so prominently in this dialogue.[50] As we shall see, both sides are addressed by the development of the dialogue in 34-38.

7.2.4 *"There is no peace for the wicked" (34-36)*

Following the connotation of the various prescriptions for Israel's situation in 33, both the political and the spiritual, Jesus' response in 34-36 functions rather like the dramatic "There is no peace for the wicked!" in Isa 48:22. There, following the predictions of the return from exile in the preceding chapters, the problem of Israel's continuing sinfulness is raised: she will not be able to rest at peace, even if delivered from exile, until something is done about her wickedness. On this note, the ministry of the Servant is introduced as the answer to Israel's spiritual need.

So also here. Jesus' response
• (a) underlines the ineradicable nature of Israel's sin (34);
• (b) gently confirms that sin was the reason for the judgment, but in a way that gives hope (35); and
• (c) points to himself as the source of real freedom (36).

We will glance at each of these in turn:

(1) *Controlling the evil yetzer?* (34)[51] Several scholars point to the

---

49   Strathmann 149 finds in 8:33 "an echo of Maccabean faith, ready for martyrdom. So [the Jews] indignantly reject Jesus' offer of freedom".

50   The extraordinary disinterest in history which marks a particular stream of German scholarship is vividly illustrated here by Lona *Johannes 8* 318f: he suggests that 8:33 probably reflects the attitude of the Pharisees at the time of writing the Fourth Gospel, but argues that there is no intention to engage with them or with any particular group. They are used just as literary foil.

51   τῆς ἁμαρτίας ("of sin") is omitted from 8:34 by some Western texts (including Bezae), some bohairic MSS, and Clement of Alexandria. Several have supported the omission on the ground that it is a "western non-interpolation" (so e.g. Bartholomew *Sermon-Drama* 15; Lindars *Behind* 81 n. 2 and "Discourse" 100 n. 16). Sanders 228 argues for the shorter text on the ground that omission would have been most improbable. But *TextComm* 224 argues for inclusion, on the ground that

relevance of rabbinic (and earlier) teaching about the 'evil *yetzer*' for the interpretation of this verse.[52] Was it possible to control it? We find a wide variety of answers to this question. Sir 15:11-20 is a basic passage in this respect:

> He made humankind from the beginning, and left us to our own counsel. So if you want to, you will keep his commandments, and faithfully do his good will. He has set before you fire and water: you will stretch out your hand to whichever you want. Before us lie life and death: whatever we desire will be given to us (15:14-17, my trans.).

This passage allows full freedom to the human will. But such optimism was not universal. *Testaments of the 12 Patriarchs* provides several fascinating parallels to John 8, none more so than *T. Jud.* 19:4-20:5, where a statement of freedom closely akin to that in Sir 15 has been rather radically modified. At first sight *T. Jud.* 20:2 expresses the same complete freedom:

> ... and in the middle [*i.e. between the spirits of truth and error*] lies the spirit of the understanding of the mind, which inclines whichever way it likes.

But Judah has just provided a powerful gloss to this 'freedom', by describing the sins of greed, idolatry and fornication into which he himself fell, concluding with the explanation,

> for the prince of deception blinded me, and I did not know, as a fleshly human being, that I was destroyed in sins. I recognised my weakness, for I thought I was invincible (19:4).[53]

In four respects this passage parallels the pessimism of John: in (a) the notion of a *false sense* of freedom, (b) the idea of the devil as a *deceiver*, (c) the use of "blindness" as a metaphor for this deception, and (d) "dying in sins" as a metaphor.

Similarly at Qumran there was a strong sense of the power of human sinfulness,[54] and as we have seen, this view received a boost

---

its omission can be explained as a stylistic improvement to avoid repetition and to bring 34 into close connection with 35.

52   So e.g. Odeberg 297-300; Barrett 345; Manns *Vérité* 79

53 This translation differs significantly from that offered by H.C. Kee in *OTP* 1:800. Cf also *T. Iss.* 7:7, *T. Zeb.* 9:8, *T. Ash.* 3:2.

54   See the material gathered by Schnackenburg 2:208.

through the events of the Jewish War — as evidenced particularly in 4 Ezra, for whom the evil *yetzer* seems to be the final victor:

> The world to come will bring delight to few, but torments to many. For an evil heart has grown up in us, which has alienated us from God, and has brought us into corruption and the ways of death, and has shown us the paths of perdition and removed us far from life — and that not just a few of us but almost all who have been created! (4 Ezra 7:[48])

4 Ezra's pessimism seems to have been extreme, but many shared his basic sense that Israel — or at any rate certain parts of her — had been overwhelmed by sin, and the disaster showed it. The fact that the disaster had occurred *in spite of* the presence of many 'righteous' in Israel (2 Baruch's particular agony) could have opened many hearers to accept Jesus' judgment here: "doing sin" creates a horrible momentum, beyond the capacity of humankind to avert, even of the most righteous. And by putting it in this gnomic form, Jesus implicitly assaults prescriptions which were essentially just a reaffirmation of the failed formula (Torah will restore Israel and avert further disaster).

Yet such prescriptions became orthodoxy, as the Targums attest. Here we find a strong emphasis on human freedom to obey the law. For instance,

> He established the garden of Eden for the just and Gehenna for the wicked ... for the Law is the tree of life for all who study it and anyone who observes its precepts lives and endures as the tree of life in the world to come.[55]

The just and the wicked are free to decide their destiny. Even Cain is told,

> If you make good your work in this world it will be remitted and pardoned you in the world to come, but if you do not make good your work in this world until the day of the great judgement your sin is kept, and at the door of your heart your sin crouches, but into your hand I have given the dominion of the evil inclination and you have power over it for justification or for sin.[56]

---

55   *Tg. Neof.* Gen 3:24, trans. Díez Macho 505. Le Déaut comments, "That Israel's prosperity is conditional on her faithfulness to the Torah is a doctrine held in common by the Targum and the rabbinic writings" (*Targum* 94 n. 10).

56   *Tg. Neof.* Gen 4:7, trans. Díez Macho 506. "Make good" here does not mean

But John 8 addresses an earlier situation in which this simple confidence has received a severe blow. Because the connection between sin and disaster was universally acknowledged and has been unequivocally accepted in 5:14,[57] Jesus' words in 34 have a hopeless ring. Since none would claim sinlessness, what hope of averting further disaster remains? 35-36 express the johannine Gospel for his age.

(2) *Who may dwell in your house? (35).*The gnomic style continues, with a remarkable kaleidoscope of allusions and evocations. Some are inclined to regard this verse as a foreign body within its co-text here,[58] but from a 'hearing' perspective it coheres forcefully.

"House" as an image for the Temple is well attested. According to McCaffrey "house of God" is "the fixed and common [expression] for the Jerusalem temple in the Jewish tradition".[59] And so a reference to the 'expulsion' of Israel from the Temple would certainly be felt here.[60]

Yet the language is allusive and evocative, and scholars offer quite a range of comments:

• Several discern an echo of the story of Isaac and Ishmael.[61]

• Others interpret "house" as "household" and treat it as a semantic equivalent of "kingdom" or "people of God".[62] "House" is quite a frequent metaphor for Israel in the Qumran texts,[63] and it seems likely that such a connotation could readily be heard here.

• Others emphasise the parabolic quality of this saying,[64] and

"redeem" or "make up for": the Aramaic just means "do good work" (Kdbw(by+t).

57   Hahn "Prozeß" 80 n. 61 makes a connection between 5:14, 9:2 and 8:34.

58   E.g. Brown 1:355; Barrett 346; Dodd *Tradition* 380-2; Dozeman "Sperma" 354f; Ibuki *Wahrheit* 90f; Strathmann 150

59   McCaffrey *House* 30 n. 7

60   Although he emphasises the importance of this meaning of "house" for the interpretation of John 14:2-3, strangely McCaffrey does not discuss this possibility for 8:35, but understands it "in a spiritual sense of personal intimacy with the Father" (*House* 183). Those who find an allusion to the Temple here include Aker *Merits* 141f and Manns "12:1-11" 101f.

61   So Braun "Traditions" 443; Manns *Vérité* 76f; Reim *Hintergrund* 98; Barrett 346; Sanders 228; Bartholomew *Sermon-Drama* 44f; Neyrey "Process" 521-3, 525f

62   So Schlatter 213; Aalen "House" 237 (he finds a specific allusion to 1 Chron 17:13f); Reim *Hintergrund* 74 n. 190; Leroy *Rätsel* 68 n. 5.

63   E.g. 1QS 5:6, 8:5-9, CD 3:19

64   Dodd *Tradition* 380-2; Schnackenburg 2:209; Lindars *Behind* 44f, "Discourse" 91f

Lindars in particular makes it structurally important for the whole chapter: he argues that its meaning is left deliberately unclear, until (a) "freedom" has been redefined as "eternal life" (8:51), (b) Jesus has been identified as the Son (8:49, 54), and (c) the punch-line has been reached, with the assertion of the pre-existence of Jesus in 8:56ff (the inevitable implication of his status as the Giver of Life).

Schnackenburg points in a helpful direction by referring to the ordinary process of manumission in the first century, and in particular to the special conditions governing the manumission of Jewish slaves.[65] Provided the legislation of Exod 21:2-6 and Deut 15:12-18 was observed, then it was true for every Jewish slave that "the slave does not continue in the house for ever". They were supposed to be released after six years, *although they could stay if they wanted to*. This humanitarian freedom of will has now been denied to Israel. Because they have become slaves to *sin*, they have forfeited their right to remain and have been expelled from the "house" — that is, both from the Temple (the 'house of God') and from the people (the 'household of God'). The right to remain is enjoyed not by slaves, but by *sons* (35b).

By its ambiguous use of "house", this verse radicalises the alienation experienced in the loss of the Temple. Membership of *the people* has also been lost. The Rabbis later debated the conditions on which sin would lead to non-participation in the age to come, and, generally speaking, took a very lenient view. Virtually all sins could be atoned for, and suffering or death could atone for sins even in the absence of repentance. The basic principle, therefore, was that "all Israelites have a share in the world to come" (*m. Sanh.* 10:1), the only exceptions being cases of gross and unrepentant rebellion.[66] This represents the opposite end of the spectrum from the pessimism of 4 Ezra, where *any* sin is sufficient to lead to death.[67] The Fourth Gospel stands with 4 Ezra in this respect, but adds the message of hope that "the son remains for ever".[68]

---

65   Schnackenburg 2:209, 490 n. 79. But what follows is not his exposition of the idea. He does not draw out the significance of the right to remain.

66   See the material gathered and discussion in Sanders *PPJ* 147-182.

67   However, the difference between 4 Ezra and later rabbinism should not be exaggerated. In 4 Ezra, too, repentance will make atonement for sin (e.g. 7:[82]). The difference lies not in the respective understanding of atonement, but in their *breadth of concern:* 4 Ezra bewails the lot of *mankind*, not just of Israel; Israel shares the lot of the world, and has proved herself as unrepentant as the Gentiles.

68   The omission of 35b by) W Γ 33 and one or two versions gives pause for thought. However its omission can easily be explained either by haplography (εἰς τὸν αἰῶνα) or "because of the difficulty of this verse when read in its present context" (Brown 1:356). Its insertion is hard to account for.

To some extent Lindars' view, that 35 sets the agenda for the rest of the chapter, may be endorsed. "The son" is indeed unclear. A debate will immediately ensue, as to whether Jesus or "the Jews" can legitimately claim this sonship. Each will deny it to the other, but both will accept the premiss that 'the son of God' has a right to residence in 'the house of God'. Jesus claims this sonship for himself immediately in 36.

But the generic "son" in 35 opens the way for it to be true of others, too, and the Prologue has already pointed the reader in this direction (1:12f). The fact that the physical "house" is no more, at the time of reading, points to a different kind of "abiding" in 35b, and paves the way for 14:2-3, where Jesus claims not only to have the right of residence "in the house of my father", but also to be able to prepare "dwellings" for his disciples within it.[69] They obtain rights of residence through him.

(3) *True freedom (36).* This line of thought is extended with a claim that Jesus alone can give *real* freedom. The political force of this claim is underlined by "really" or "indeed" (ὄντως): the freedom Jesus gives is in contrast to another, illusory freedom which needs to be unmasked. This point is drawn out by Leroy. He rightly comments that the "free" who are not *really* free must be the slaves of 35,[70] but unfortunately offers no further suggestions about their identity, and does not discuss the function of this text in the late first century.

Illusory freedom is sought *either* by those who focus their desire on political independence and the restoration of the theocracy and its institutions, *or* by those who prize Torah as providing a spiritual liberty compatible with political subjugation. Either 'freedom' would leave Israel in slavery to sin, because both prescriptions have already been found wanting. The Temple left the spiritual needs of many untouched — as illustrated by the Samaritans and the lame man. Torah likewise, as the special possession of "the Jews" ("our law", 7:51), offered freedom only to those who agreed to be bound by the interpretative authority of the regulatory body, the Sanhedrin. The *real* freedom is that supplied by Jesus, whose disciples hear "the truth" from him and are set free by that knowledge (32).

This freedom is illustrated in the case of the blind man in ch. 9.

---

69   McCaffrey *House* rightly points to the double meaning of οἰκία in this passage, with an allusion to the Jerusalem Temple resting upon a reference to the heavenly dwelling of God.

70   Leroy *Rätsel* 69

His expulsion from the synagogue is the moment when he is released from bondage to that authority. No longer is he bound by the
judgment that he is irretrievably sinful (9:34), and he is free to
discover a whole new worship, outside the synagogue, and focused
upon Jesus. He symbolises the appeal of the Gospel, that Jews
should turn the tragedy of their enforced expulsion from the
"house" into a chance to discover a "real freedom" which successfully addresses Israel's need of moral and spiritual reformation.

7.2.5 Murder — obedience to Torah? (37-38)

It must have been possible for many of those whom Bornhäuser
calls the "Torah-fanatics" in the post-70 situation to do what
Josephus does and place the blame for the disaster squarely on the
Zealots. The traditions concerning the role of Yohanan ben Zakkai
during the War point in this direction. When an accommodation
with the Romans became impossible, he escaped from Jerusalem on
a funeral bier and went to express his loyalty to Vespasian the
Roman general (later Emperor), who permitted him to settle at
Yavneh which was already under Roman control.[71] It is not clear
from the rabbinic sources whether Yohanan opposed the War
completely, or just the murderous policies of the warring factions in
Jerusalem — but either way it was possible for the Yavneh sages to
argue that political quietism and the study of Torah would deliver
Israel in future, precisely because it was the *rejection* of these which
had caused the disaster in the first place. All sources agree that
political murder had become a fine art in Jerusalem in the two years
before the Romans took the city.

Against this background, Jesus' accusation that "you seek to kill
me, because my word finds no place in you" (37) breathes a
particular atmosphere — one in which the unacceptable policies of
an opponent make him fair game for an assassin's knife. The action
of those who brought about the death of Jesus — essentially, "the
Jews" as the Judean upholders of Torah-rectitude and the Jerusalem
authorities — is being compared to a kind of behaviour from which
the post-70 heirs of these groups wished to distance themselves very
firmly.

John does not use φονεύειν, the usual word for "murder" (used
in the sixth commandment both in Exod 20:13 and in Deut 5:18), but
this does not undermine this perspective on the text. Brooke comments that the sixth commandment is connoted by the repeated

---

71   See Neusner *Yohanan2* 157-166

references to killing Jesus, even though John uses the more general word ἀποκτείνειν. He suggests that John's choice of verb deliberately widens the perspective, so that the issue is not just casuistical:

> The deliberate avoidance of *phoneuo* takes the reader to the heart of the matter: he or she is involved in life or death, not in deciding between murder and manslaughter.[72]

Probably we should qualify this with the amendment, "not *just* in deciding ...". The reader certainly has to decide whether the death of Jesus was *murder* — and therefore whether the upholders of Torah were involved in just the kind of action which they deplored as causing the disaster — or whether it was *obedience* to Torah, the justified execution of a false prophet. The fact that ἀποκτείνειν is used of the penalty prescribed for the false prophet in Deut 13:10 is probably another factor here. The view of the narrator is clear: it was murder. And thus, for him, the moral distinction between the upholders of Torah and the Zealots evaporates.

The basic claim of 33, "we are Abraham's seed!", is granted in 37a, but it is then implied that their action in killing Jesus is incompatible with that claim (37b). Their opposition to Jesus is then traced back to different parentage (38): whereas Jesus reports to them a heavenly vision — something which many longed to have — they are not willing to receive it, because they are acting under obedience to "your father". In this allusive way the ground is laid for two developments in the next two exchanges:

- (a) the contention that, while they are certainly Abraham's σπέρμα ("seed"), they are not his τέκνα ("children", 39f), and
- (b) the charge that they are living by another obedience, signalled by their violation of Torah in the case of Jesus (42ff).

Heavenly visions could only be received by the obedient, according to 2 Baruch 54:4f:

> You are the one who reveals to those who fear that which is prepared for them so that you may comfort them ... You pull down the enclosure for those who have no experience and enlighten the darknesses, and reveal the secrets to those who are spotless, to those who subjected themselves to you and your Law in faith.

So when Jews refuse to accept the word of a prophet, their whole standing before God is called into question. Behind the intratextual

---

72   Brooke "Law" 105f

addressees here, we may discern the character of the 'implied reader', who though co-operative may not yet have accepted Jesus' prophetic status. For him, this dialogue poses the issue of faith very sharply. There is plenty of Old Testament precedent for Jews refusing to hear the words of a prophet — even for rejecting a prophet violently. Has the same thing happened in the case of Jesus? How are the rival responses to the destruction of Jerusalem to be evaluated? Is there any substance in Jesus' claim to give freedom *from sin*, which all acknowledge to be Israel's basic problem? The whole Gospel addresses these questions in different ways, I believe, but this particular dialogue focuses on the quality of the action which led to Jesus' death: was it rebellion against God, or obedience?

7.2.6 Conclusion

Reading 8:31-38 in this way reveals how fundamentally wrong is the contention of Lona that no real dialogue takes place here. He maintains that Jesus simply does not address the Jews' objection that, as Abraham's seed, they need no liberation: and draws the conclusion that Jesus is operating with a different linguistic "code".[73] Quite apart from the linguistic confusion in this argument,[74] Lona's view simply fails to cohere with the facts of the text when it is 'heard' in the way proposed here. These thoughts will be of importance in the understanding of 8:43, on which Lona lays some emphasis in arguing for his view.

In fact, we may even question the widespread view that "misunderstanding" is a dominant feature of this exchange. 8:31-33 is one of Leroy's eleven cases of misunderstanding in John, and Carson also calls this a case of "unambiguous misunderstanding", even though he is in several respects sharply critical of Leroy's analysis.[75] To some extent this is a matter of definition, because Jesus certainly *clarifies* 32 in his response in 34ff. But the Jews' "How can you say ...?" in 33 points not so much to misunderstanding as to a sharp rejection of something clearly understood — the suggestion that they need liberation. Of course, as we have seen, this reaction would be regarded by many other Jews — as it is by Jesus — as a fundamental nonsense which does not properly address Israel's

---

73   Lona *Johannes 8* 391

74   He employs the notion of "code" illegitimately. The shared linguistic "code" which is essential in order to enable communication to take place is Saussure's "langue" — in this case first-century koine Greek as employed within Jewish culture. When breakdowns in communication ("parole") occur, this does not mean that a different "langue" is being employed. See above, p 112 n. 21.

75   Leroy *Rätsel* 67ff, Carson "Misunderstandings" 91

situation. But this does not amount to making their reaction a *misunderstanding*.

The concept of 'discontinuous dialogue' helps here. Jesus' contributions are not so much incomprehensible as *unexpected*. The last thing these 'believing Jews' expect the Prophet to do is to oppose the power and validity of Torah, to assert that Torah has left them slaves to sin, and to accuse them of sharing their fellow-Jews' desire to kill him just because they object to this! But these discontinuities serve the presentation of a forceful case to the 'implied reader', who realises what a radical step it will be, to accept that Jesus was a prophet from God. It will mean commitment to *Jesus' words alone* as the means of liberation from sin.

7.3 8:39-47, the second and third exchanges: freedom from the devil

The third exchange brings us face to face with "the most anti-Jewish saying in the New Testament by far",[76] the "negative climax" of all the "anti-Jewish expressions" in John,[77] to which "there is no defamation of comparable severity of one religion by another".[78] Though we can offer no excuse for the use to which 8:44 has been put in the sad history of Christian anti-Judaism, we can at least try to determine how this text would have been heard by our 'implied reader' within late first-century Judaism.

7.3.1 *Structure*

The whole paragraph (39-47) is prompted by the undefined reference to the Jews' "father" in 37. The identity of this "father" is left unclear both in 38 and in 41a, and in each case prompts a response from Jesus' interlocutors, trying to clarify the allusion. In both cases he denies their claim — first that Abraham is their father, and then that *God* is their father. Both ideas were such deeply rooted aspects of Jewish self-consciousness[79] that Jesus' denial of them constitutes two sharp discontinuities in the dialogue.

---

76 Becker 1:304

77 Wengst *Gemeinde* 60

78 R.L. Rubinstein & J.K. Roth, *Approaches to Auschwitz. The Legacy of the Holocaust* (London; SCM, 1987), 43

79 'Children of Abraham' hardly requires illustration. 'Children of God': in addition to the Old Testament texts where this thought is expressed (e.g. Exod 4:22, Deut 14:1, Hos 11:1: cf Schnackenburg 2:212), we may point to *Sib. Or.* 3:702; Ps.-Philo *Bib. Ant.* 32:10,16; *m. 'Abot* 3:19 (a saying ascribed to Akiba).

In both cases, the denial is expressed through an 'unfulfilled condition' (39b,[80] 42a), and is based on a judgment about the behaviour of "the Jews" towards Jesus. They cannot be the children of Abraham, because they are seeking to kill him (39f), and they cannot be the children of God, because they do not receive his "word" (42f). Whose children are they, then? The second denial is followed by the answer: Jesus reveals that the "father" alluded to in 38b and 41a is the devil, from whom, as his children, "the Jews" have learned both aspects of behaviour just mentioned: murder, and denial of the truth (44).[81]

The prolonged build-up to the revelation in 44 is one of several arguments against the proposal of Dahl (strongly supported by Reim) that the "father" in 44 is not the devil, but Cain.[82] The motivation behind this proposal is laudable: it blunts the sharpness of the charge, so that instead of being the "most anti-Jewish" expression in the New Testament, it is rather the "most misunderstood and mis-used".[83] But the proposal collapses under several objections:

• (a) It depends upon a textual emendation for which there is no manuscript support.[84]

---

80   39b is strictly a mixed condition, fulfilled in the protasis (ἐστε), and unfulfilled in the apodosis (ἐποιεῖτε): "since you are Abraham's children, you would do Abraham's works". The strangeness of this has produced textual variants, one of which is supported by Dodd "Behind" 50 n. 1: the imperative ποιεῖτε (p⁶⁶ B*, some old Latin, Origen) is read in the apodosis, giving "since you are Abraham's children, do Abraham's works". Undoubtedly, however, the more difficult 'mixed' reading (which is overall the best attested) is the original (so *TextComm* 225).

The 'fulfilled' protasis arises from the fact that Jesus has just *granted* the claim of "the Jews" to be σπέρμα Ἀβραάμ (37). But the effect of the whole sentence, with its unfulfilled apodosis, is to withdraw this concession just made: "If you are really Abraham's children, you would be doing works worthy of Abraham" (trans. Brown 1:352). For Dodd, this apparent contradiction is sufficient reason to support the originality of the alternative text, but it is just another example of the *discontinuity* which marks the whole dialogue.

81   These 'delaying tactics' are emphasised by Lindars *Behind* 44f, who holds that the whole dialogue is an exploration of the possible identity of "the son" of 8:35. Cf Duke *Irony* 76.

82   Dahl "Erstgeboren"; Reim "Teufelskinder". Meeks expresses support ("Man From Heaven" 67).

83   Reim "Teufelskinder" 624: he interacts specifically with the judgment of Becker, quoted above. For a review of the role of Cain in contemporary texts, see the discussion in R.E. Brown *The Epistles of John* (AB; London, Geoffrey Chapman, 1983), 442f.

84   Dahl emends the beginning of the verse to read either ὑμεῖς ἐκ τοῦ πρωτοτόκου τοῦ διαβόλου ἐστέ ("you are of the first-born of the devil"), or ὑμεῖς ἐκ

• (b) While an *allusion* to Cain is quite possible in 44,[85] a *reference* to him as the "murderer" without specifically naming him (cf 1 John 3:11f) is surely unlikely, especially after the build-up to this revelation.

• (c) The 'anti-Judaism' of the charge can be defused without emending the text and introducing Cain, as we shall see.

• (d) The present tense "truth *is* not in him" is problematic on this view; and

• (e) "Cain" would be something of an anticlimax: we expect something more dramatic, and "of your father — the devil!" certainly provides this.

That this is no throw-away assertion is confirmed by the *inclusio* which frames the third exchange: "we have one father, God" (41) is picked up and finally denied by "you are not of God!" (47). Jesus' whole speech (42-47) — at 135 words the longest contribution in the dialogues of chs. 7-8 — is devoted to disproving the Jews' claim to have God as their father, and to proving the alternative asserted in 44.

Structurally, therefore, the charge in 44 is climactic and clear. But what exactly does it assert?

7.3.2 The ethical nature of the charge

It is vital to recognise that "you are of your father the devil", and its negative counterpart "you are not of God" (47), have an *ethical* and not an *ontological* force. Much exegesis has sought to distinguish between "you do the *works* of your father" (41a) and "you are *of* your father" (44), with the latter expressing the "origin" (Grässer) or the "essential nature" (Wengst) which underlies and gives rise to the "works". As we saw above (6.3.2), the tendency to interpret this verse in sharply dualistic terms is widespread. The argument is that here the *real nature* of "the Jews" is revealed, that which *makes* them irretrievably unbelieving opponents of Jesus.

8:44 was read in this way even in the second century, by the earliest Gnostic interpreters of the Fourth Gospel.[86] And we must grant that the expressions formulated with ἐκ ("of") in this passage ("of God", "of your father" etc — and cf 8:23) are certainly not

τοῦ πατρὸς τοῦ ἐκ τοῦ διαβόλου ἐστέ ("you are of your father who was of the devil").

85   So also Bowman "Samaritan Studies" 307, Brown 1:358, Manns *Vérité* 87f, Neyrey "Process" 532, Hengel "OT" 26, Grässer "Teufelssöhne" 166, Hahn "Prozeß" 78 n. 55, Le Déaut *Message* 41, "Targumic" 280f, Michaels 139

86   See Pagels *Gnostic Exegesis* 98-104.

synonymous with parallel expressions like "do the works of" and "will to do the desires of" (a point to which we will return). *But it must seriously be doubted whether our 'implied reader' would 'hear' this dualism in the way favoured by so many modern commentators, who perpetuate a Gnostic reading in this respect.*[87] Three arguments support this contention:

(1) *Ethical dualism in contemporary texts.* A full review of dualism and demonology in Second Temple Judaism is out of place here, but a brief survey is vital.

(a) At *Qumran* we find the doctrine of the two spirits, of truth and falsehood, both created by God but having dramatically different effects on mankind:

> Those born of truth spring from a fountain of light, but those born of falsehood spring from a source of darkness ... All the children of falsehood are ruled by the Angel of Darkness and walk in the ways of darkness.[88]

The angel of darkness is clearly Satan, and the idea of being his children is here implied.[89] However, although this dualism reflects the social distinction between the Qumran community and the rest of the world,[90] there is a remarkable absence of the kind of absolute determinism typical of later Gnosticism. Rather, there is a sense of freedom to belong to whichever source one wills. Allegiance to *both* spirits is the usual lot of mankind:

> The nature of all the children of men is ruled by these (two spirits), and during their life all the hosts of men have a portion in their divisions and walk in (both) their ways. And the whole reward for their deeds shall be, for everlasting ages, according to whether each

---

87   Meeks "Man From Heaven" 67f draws an explicit link with later Gnosticism,quoting from the third-century (Robinson *Library* 161) *Hypostasis of the Archons* 87:17-20: "Beings that merely possess a soul cannot lay hold of those that possess a spirit — for they were from below, while it was from above". Cf also Bultmann 318.

88   1QS 3:19-21 (*Vermes* 75)

89   It is expressed explicitly elsewhere (see next note). Schnackenburg 2:214f reviews the Qumran parallels impressively. He observes that the dualism at Qumran and in John "never becomes a metaphysical one; it shows itself in moral behaviour" (215). Hengel "OT" 26 regards these Qumran texts as "the closest Jewish parallels" to the language of 8:44.

90   In 4QFlor 1:8 the "sons of Belial" are the enemies who seek to fulfil "the plan of Belial" to destroy "the sons of light". The persecutors of the community seem to be in mind (so *Lohse* 297 n. 4), who could of course be fellow-Jews.

man's portion in their two divisions is great or small. For God has established the spirits in equal measure until the final age (1QS 4:15-16).

In line with this it is open to any to "freely pledge themselves to holiness" (1QS 5:6), which of course means joining the community. Being a "son of falsehood" ruled by the angel of darkness is by no means therefore a final judgment. The dualism is essentially ethical.

(b) A similar point may be made from earlier texts. At the beginning of *Jubilees* Moses prays,

> O Lord, let your mercy be lifted up upon your people, and create for them an upright spirit. And do not let the spirit of Beliar rule over them to accuse them before you and ensnare them from every path of righteousness ... Do not let them be ensnared by their sin henceforth and forever.[91]

The connection between being ensnared by sin and being under the rule of the devil resonates with John 8. In *Jub.* 15:33-34 Moses reveals what sort of thing this 'ensnaring' might be: there will come a time when

> the sons of Beliar will leave their sons without circumcising just as they were born. And great wrath from the Lord will be upon the sons of Israel because they have left his covenant and turned aside from his words ... because they have made themselves like the gentiles to be removed and be uprooted from the land.

Without hesitation such covenant unfaithfulness means that "the sons of Israel" become "sons of Beliar" and will lose all their covenant privileges. In Jubilees, as in John 8, the alternative to being sons of God is being under the rule of the devil, and obedience to the commandments is the hallmark of the children of God.

In Jubilees, too, we observe the connection between *the devil, murder and error/falsehood* which reappears in several later texts, including John 8:44. For instance, Noah says to his sons,

> For I see, and behold, the demons have begun to mislead you and your children. And now I fear for your sakes that after I die, you will pour out the blood of men upon the earth (*Jub.* 7:27).

---

91   *Jub.* 1:20, 21 (*OTP* 2:53f)

He has just made the shedding of blood the supreme sin of the Watchers and their offspring in the pre-flood period (*Jub.* 7:23-25). In *Jub.* 12 Abraham rejects idolatry (which is enforced by the devil, *Jub.* 11:4f) in favour of worshipping the God of heaven, and prays,

> Save me from the hands of evil spirits which rule over the thought of the heart of man, and do not let them lead me astray from following you, O my God; but establish me and my seed for ever, and let us not go astray henceforth and forever (*Jub.* 12:20).

The possibility of falling under the rule of 'Mastema' and his forces is a real threat for the author of Jubilees.

(c) The same ideas and connections are developed in the *Testaments of the 12 Patriarchs*, where 'Beliar' makes frequent appearances, and the material shows many contacts of thought with John 8. The devil is especially associated with error and falsehood,[92] and can "rule" over people, enslaving them to sin,[93] and gaining power over them especially through evil ἐπιθυμίαι (desires),[94] through πορνεία (sexual deviance),[95] and through murder and anger.[96]

The special connection between Beliar and murder has a political dimension in *T. Benj.* 7:1-5: Beliar "offers a sword to those who obey him" (7:1), and this sword brings the seven judgments of Cain with it (7:3), which include αἰχμαλωσία (captivity) and ἐρήμωσις (desolation, 7:2). These two terms — especially the first — are used typically of the captivity of Jerusalem: together in *T. Levi* 17:9-10 and *Jud.* 23:3-5, and αἰχμαλωσία alone in e.g. *T. Zeb.* 9:8, *Dan* 5:8, and *Naph.* 4:2. So the *personal* enslavement to sin which Beliar may produce is cognate with the *political* enslavement of Jerusalem. The remedy to all this is (of course) to pay careful heed to the teaching of the patriarchs, and especially to the law.[97]

(d) Manns suggests that the *Palestinian Targums* on Gen 3 shed

---

92   E.g. *T. Reu.* 2:1, 3:2; *Lev.* 3:3; *Jud.* 19:4f, 25:3; *Dan* 2:1, 3:6, 5:1,6

93   *T. Zeb.* 9:8; *Ash.* 3:2; *Jud.* 19:4. To give in to the evil inclination is to submit to the mastery of Beliar: *T. Ash.* 1:8f. We have already noted Dan's sobering word, ὁ ἄρχων ὑμῶν ἐστὶν ὁ Σατανᾶς ("your ruler is Satan", *T. Dan.* 5:6): the present tense here expresses the sad conviction of *T. Dan.* 5:1-6 — in the tradition of Deut 32 — that Israel is bound to go astray, because she is too prone to disobedience.

94   *T. Ash.* 1:8f, 3:2, 6:5

95   *T. Reu* 4:7,11; *Sim.* 5:3

96   *T. Dan* 1:7f, 5:1 ("depart from anger, and hate lying, so that the Lord may dwell in your midst and Beliar may flee from you"); *Benj.* 7:1.

97   *T. Reu.* 6:8; *Lev.* 19:1; *Dan* 5:1; *Naph.* 2:6; *Gad* 4:7

light on John 8.[98] Two points seem of particular significance:

• (i) The Targums too emphasise that the devil is a liar and a murderer (e.g. *Tg. Ps.-J.* Gen. 3:6 calls the serpent "Shammael, the angel of death").

• (ii) They provide clear background to the idea of being "sons" of the devil. The Hebrew (rz ("seed") in Gen 3:15 is translated with "son" (both Nyb and rb are used). So perpetual enmity between the "sons" of the woman and of the serpent is predicted, until "peace" comes "at the end, on the day of the Messiah-King".[99]

So Jesus' accusation that the Jews have the devil for father is *cognate* with the charge that they are breaking the law, specifically the law against murder — for all their desire to be loyal to it. If we may use these contemporary texts to reconstruct the hearing of John 8 by our 'implied reader', then we must at the least say that a Gnostic reading would be a clear novelty. The 'hearing' of ἐκ τοῦ θεοῦ / ἐκ τοῦ πατρός ("of God/of your father") which lies closest to hand understands the ἐκ as designating *ethical influence and power*.[100] This reading would be reinforced by the phrase ἐκ τῶν ἰδίων in 44, for which a paraphrase like "out of his own nature" suggests itself.[101] This ἐκ can only have an ethical force, and this creates a presumption for the others also.

Not all were ready to ascribe the foibles and tragedies of human-kind to the agency of the devil. As we saw above (3.2.2), some traditions clearly avoided 'devil' language. But the Fourth Gospel belongs in the tradition represented also by the *Apocalypse of Abraham*, where 'Azazel' is one of the primary actors in the drama, responsible for the idolatry which causes the disaster, if not for the destruction itself (which is ascribed to God). The Qumran sect went further: they ascribed large-scale human tragedies to the agency of 'Belial', even though God was ultimately in charge.[102] We shall consider under

98 *Vérité* 152-176. Manns' own observations and conclusions are rather weak: the material is more suggestive than he realises, I believe.

99 The relevance of this to the New Testament is amply demonstrated by Matt. 13:36-43, where "the sons of the kingdom" and "the sons of the evil one" are pictured as occupying the world in opposition to each other until the day of harvest when the latter will be destroyed. Here too the ethical force of the "of" is clear: "the sons of the evil one" are described as "those who do lawlessness" (Matt. 13:41).

100 — though I shall argue under 7.3.3 below that there is more to hear than just this, because of the way in which Jesus uses ἐκ τοῦ θεοῦ ("of God") of himself in 42, 47a.

101 The various English translations offer such paraphrases: "according to his own nature" (NRSV), "speaks his native language" (NIV, Brown 1:353), "drawing on his own store" (JB).

7.3.4 below how 8:44 would address readers who had lived through the 70 AD disaster.

(2) *Ethical kinship with Abraham.* Abraham was valued, not just as the "father", the recipient of the covenant promises on which Israel's existence rested, but as the supreme example of righteousness to which Jews aspired.[103] Manns *Vérité* 91f points out how common-place is the theme 'like father, like son' in rabbinic piety, especially in connection with Abraham.

The dominant presentation of Abraham in the literature of the late Second Temple period is of one who kept the law perfectly: who "was unequalled in glory ... kept the law of the Most High" (Sir 44:19f), "careful to do the will of the one who created" him (*Jub.* 21:3), who "was found faithful in trial, and it was reckoned to him as righteousness" (1 Macc 2:52). He resists and rejects idolatry (*Apoc. Abr.* 1-8), is not touched by the fire because of his sinlessness (Ps.-Philo *Bib. Ant.* 6), "was accounted friend of God because he kept the commandments of God and did not choose his own will" (CD 3:2f), was "above all others ... righteous in all goodness, having been hospitable and loving to the end of his life" (*Test. Abr.* 1:5), the recipient of great rewards for his "virtue" and "good deeds" (Josephus *Ant.* 1:183). Examples of such praises can be multiplied from the literature of the period. Sometimes the praise of Abraham's righteousness is explicitly related to an exhortation to be like him,[104] but this is usually implicit.

This laudatory tradition provides the interpretative frame for "if you are the children of Abraham, you would do the works of Abra-ham" (39b). Jewish readers could not 'hear' this except as a challenge to reproduce the great qualities for which Abraham was praised — most notably his faithfulness under trial, his hospitality, and his single-minded and pure worship of God. And such a challenge would be no novelty, but part of the basic ethical outlook of every Jew. This is rhetorically very significant: faith in Jesus is made a natural expression of Abraham-piety, and conversely rejection of Jesus is treated as a denial of it.

The particular power of this argument appears in v. 40, where the plot to kill Jesus is related to a particular 'deed' of Abraham, conno-

---

102   Cf 1QS 3:21-24, 1QH 3:23-33

103   A useful survey of "Abraham in Jewish Literature" is provided by G.W. Hansen in *Abraham in Galatians. Epistolary and Rhetorical Contexts* (JSNTSup 29; Sheffield Academic Press, Sheffield 1989), 175-199.

104   E.g. 1 Macc 2:50-52, CD 16:4-6

ted by the aorist ἐποίησεν ("did"). Scholars differ about the identity of this deed, as about that of the "works" in 39. A company of German scholars interprets the "works" as *faith*:[105] but this is quite impossible from a 'hearing' perspective. Should our 'implied reader' find Abraham's faith connoted here, it would be his faithfulness under trial, rather than faith in a more abstract (or Lutheran) sense. The suggestion of Brown has much to commend it, now taken up by Neyrey, that this 'work' is the hospitality shown to the three visitors in Genesis 18.[106] Neyrey summarises the force of the allusion thus:

> If Abraham were the father of Jesus' present audience, they would do what Abraham did, viz., show hospitality to the present heavenly visitor who has come into their midst, even Jesus. But as the text indicates, hospitality is far from their minds, which are set on murder ...

That such an allusion might be heard is supported by the prominence given to Abraham's hospitality in contemporary texts. In the *Testament of Abraham* it is the supreme virtue for which he is praised, and Neyrey cites Philo, Josephus and 1 Clement.[107] In addition to the contrast between hospitality and murder we may point to the fact that Jesus here pointedly — and uniquely — calls himself "a man", just as the messengers are "men" (Gen 18:2,16),[108] who likewise are charged with speaking the truth they have heard from God, about the coming birth of Isaac (Gen 18:10).

With such an echo, the text acquires considerable rhetorical power. Abraham welcomed the messengers and accepted their message, even though they appeared just as "men" and their message seemed so unlikely that Sarah "laughed".[109] So why have Abraham's children not given the same open, welcoming treatment to another "man" who claims to bring truth from God? In seeking to *kill* such a person, they are violating the Abraham-piety at the heart of Jewish life, and doing "the works" of another father, who is "a

105 So Schlatter 214, Bultmann 442 n. 6, Blank *Krisis* 236, Ibuki *Wahrheit* 96, Schnackenburg 2:211, Lona *Johannes 8* 321

106 Brown 1:357; Neyrey "Process" 524

107 "Process" 524 n. 31: "Philo ... praises Abraham over and over for his hospitality".

108 — although here in John 8:40 we have the generic ἄνθρωπος, while LXX uses the sex-specific ἄνδρες.

109 It is interesting that, although both Abraham and Sarah "laugh" at the news in Genesis (17:17, 18:12), from an early date Abraham's laughter was interpreted as *rejoicing* (cf John 8:56), while generally Sarah's was treated as cynicism: so e.g. *Jub.* 15:17, cf Reim *Hintergrund* 101.

murderer from the beginning" and never receives the truth (44).

The charge directed at "the Jews" in 39-40, therefore, is thorough-ly ethical and could speak with some force to Jewish readers. It points to a discrepancy between their claim and their behaviour, and suggests that the discrepancy arises from the influence of the devil.

(3) *The role of the law.* The third argument which supports an ethical, rather than an ontological, 'hearing' of the statements of origin in this passage takes us back to the observation above (5.2.2) that the decalogue plays an implicit role here. We observed that four of the ten commandments put in an unobtrusive appearance in the third exchange, three of them in v. 44: *murder* (40, 44b), *adultery* (41), *false witness* (44c) and *coveting* (44a). In addition 'honour your father' appears in 49.

In the case of each, "the Jews" are accused implicitly of breaking them, because of their connection with the devil, who is the law-breaker *par excellence*. Amongst these, the charge of *murder* is central, and the others all depend on it. If Jesus was murdered, then the claim that he was executed in obedience to the law is a *falsehood* (44c), and a question-mark is set against the motives of those who did it: they were *desiring* something contrary to the will of God, and in accordance with the demonology outlined above, this desire is traced back to the influence of the devil (44a).[110]

Engagement with the law in this passage is both positive and negative:

(a) *Positively*, the law is used as testimony to Jesus, both by undermining the action of his opponents as lawlessness, and by testifying to his own rightness.

Jesus throws down a legal challenge, one to which the reader must also respond: "which of you convicts me of sin?" (46a). Once again, our 'hearing' method requires us to recognise that, within the setting we are proposing, this would certainly be heard as a chall-enge to convict Jesus of *law-breaking*. Bultmann resists this reading strongly, because, for him, the Revealer cannot submit himself to human judgment: "the character of his word ... forbids all critical

---

110 In the case of πορνεία (fornication, 41b), the implicit accusation depends upon its metaphorical use to designate unfaithfulness to God (cf Brooke "Law" 107). If like their "father" they break the commandments, they are certainly guilty of πορνεία.

The thinking is illustrated by *Apoc. Abr.* 24:5, where the visionary sees "Adam and Eve ... and with them the crafty adversary and Cain, who had been led by the adversary to break the law". Here Cain 'does the desires' of the devil, and thus exemplifies the charge laid against "the Jews" in 8:44.

questions".[111] We may simply respond that the text does nothing to defend itself against *inevitably* being heard as an *invitation* to critical questioning — although not in the way Bultmann imagined. He is right to argue that the sinlessness of Jesus, here asserted by implication, is not that of his "personality". It is a more objective *legal* unimpeachability. The challenge is to *prove* that he has broken the law, to turn accusation into conviction.[112]

This relates to the broad concern of John 5-12 to claim the law as a witness to Christ, one which will be recognised by all who exercise the "right judgment" for which Jesus calls in 7:24 in relation to the Sabbath. It *looks* as though Jesus breaks the Sabbath law — but does he? This is precisely the dilemma which is explicitly posed in 9:16, and it is implicit here.[113]

(b) *Negatively*, we see Jesus setting himself in the place of the law here. John distances himself completely from the understanding of the law which we encountered above in (for instance) 2 Baruch 85, where obedience will enable all that has been lost to be regained. This is shown clearly by the allusions to the Shema in 41b-42a.[114] "We have one Father, God" (41b) and "he is our God" (54b) connote the central Jewish confession of faith, with its accompanying command to "love the Lord your God with all your heart ..." (Deut 6:4f). Jesus' response to the Jews' allusion to the Shema is very pointed: "If God were your father, you would love *me*" (42a).

Le Déaut notes that the Neofiti Targum systematically replaces the expression "love the Lord" in Deuteronomy with the formula "love the teaching of the law of the Lord".[115] The motivation for loving the law was, of course, precisely that it had "come from God" (42b): love for God was not *replaced* by loving the law, but *expressed* by it. Jesus makes precisely this claim in relation to himself, stepping into the place of the law as the self-expression of God.

The charge directed at "the Jews" in 8:44 is thus thoroughly *ethical*. Warning his sons against hatred, the patriarch Gad illustrates this kind of dualism:

For the spirit of hatred works together with Satan in all things,

---

111 Bultmann 323. Cf also Schnackenburg 2:216.

112 So e.g. Bruce 202, Carson 354

113 Beasley-Murray 136 suggests that the "sin" is some inconsistency between Jesus' message and his conduct. But this skirts the obvious meaning of "sin". Godet 2:350 and Westcott 137 find implicit reference to the law here.

114 Noted by Blank *Krisis* 237, Beasley-Murray 135 in relation to 41b.

115 E.g. in Deut 6:5, 10:12, 11:1, 13, 22 etc: noted by Le Déaut *Message* 42

through impatience, to men's death, but the spirit of love works together with the law of God, in longsuffering, to men's salvation.[116]

This is a "dualism of decision" — an expression typical of Bultmann's approach to johannine theology, expressing his emphasis on the free decision of faith or unbelief in response to the word of the Revealer.[117] But, because he also wanted to interpret johannine dualism in Gnostic terms, Bultmann insisted that at the moment of decision the *origin* of the decider, and not just his *destiny*, is determined:

> The decision of faith or unbelief deprives man of his ability to calculate his actions; since it is a decision for this or that origin, an origin which completely determines him, so that nothing that he does can ever be done if it be not done in God or the Devil ... This is what is meant when the Jews in v. 44 are denounced as children of the Devil.[118]

This rather tortuous piece of logic arises, I believe, from conflicting impulses — on the one hand rightly emphasising the *personal responsibility* which is implicit in "you are of your father the devil", but on the other inappropriately seeking to fit this into a basically Gnostic dualism.

To be fairer to John, we should abandon talk of "origin", lessen the focus on the *moment* of decision, and broaden it out to encompass the whole life-style of "the Jews" so addressed. At the moment, their action in desiring to kill Jesus shows that they are "of" (ἐκ) a power other than the love of God and obedience to him.

This should certainly not be understood as a final "judgment" on Judaism (Strathmann, Ibuki), nor as a "defamation" of one religion by another (Rubinstein & Roth). Here "the Jews" are merely "seeking" to kill Jesus, "willing" to do the desire of the devil. *It falls to one of Jesus' own disciples actually to become an instrument of Satan in turning 'seeking' into 'doing'*: cf 13:27. This remarkable fact should weigh heavily in judgments about the anti-Judaism of the Fourth Gospel. In 13:2 Judas is in the same state as "the Jews" of 8:44, with an *idea* firmly planted in his mind. But with the actual *entry* of Satan into him, the die is cast, and he becomes "the son of perdition" (17:12). The Jews are *not* portrayed in these terms in 8:44.

Before we consider the actual function of this charge (7.3.4), we

---

116 T. *Gad* 4:7, trans. Hollander/de Jonge 324f
117 It has been picked up by others: e.g. Grässer "Teufelssöhne" 164.
118 Bultmann 318

touch on a further dimension of meaning in the contrasting phrases ἐκ τοῦ θεοῦ / ἐκ τοῦ ... διαβόλου ("of God / of the devil").

7.3.3 The language of revelation

As we have seen, "I have come from God" (42) sets Jesus implicitly in the place of the law. This statement of heavenly origin relates to and draws on the other material in John which would have spoken to the *longing for heavenly revelation* felt so keenly in the years after 70 AD. The Fourth Gospel emphatically claims that *Jesus alone* is the source of such revelation (1:17f, 1:51, 3:13f, 6:62f). In all probability "you are from below, I am from above" (8:23) should be heard against this background. The recognition of Jesus as Prophet (8:31) is precisely the faith that he can bring words from God.

This sheds light on 8:47. Here "he who is of God hears the words of God" refers primarily to Jesus, who alone has direct auditory contact with God. 47b therefore ("this is why you do not hear his words, because you are not of God"), is not just a judgment on the *spiritual state* of "the Jews" — spiritually deaf, under the devil's power and influence rather than God's — but is also a comment on their *spiritual capacity*, in line with 5:37b, "you have never heard his voice nor seen his form".

The imperceptibility of God is a common Old Testament theme. But there are famous exceptions: behind 5:37b we may discern Moses in Num 12:8,[119] or Ezekiel's inaugural vision,[120] or Israel at Sinai in Deut 4:12.[121] This last seems particularly close:

> And the Lord spoke to you out of the midst of the fire. You heard the voice of his words, but you did not see his form; only his voice ...

But that which Moses and Ezekiel enjoyed, and Israel experienced at Sinai, is denied to first-century Jews in John 5:37 and 8:47. To some extent this simply reflects the feeling of the age, that such experiences are granted to very few: unlike their fathers at Sinai, the vast majority of Jews "do not hear" God.[122] But John makes christological capital out of this feeling.

In 5:37 the imperceptibility of God is related to the Father's witness on behalf of Jesus: he testifies, but how can they appreciate his testimony when they cannot hear his voice? This has the effect of

---

119 Kittel *TDNT* 2:374
120 Vawter "Ezek & John" 454
121 Dahl "History" 133; Meeks *Prophet-King* 299f
122 See above, 3.2.3 (2)

throwing the testimony of *Moses* into emphatic relief (5:39ff): *his* voice is audible.[123] But in 8:47, and especially 8:43, the same idea is applied to the audibility of *Jesus'* teaching. Like the Sinai fathers, whose response to hearing "the voice" was *fear* and a request that Moses listen on their behalf (Exod 20:18f, Deut 18:16), so too "you cannot hear my word" (43b).

This incapacity is partly ethical (they are "of the devil"), but also partly constitutional (they are "of this world", 8:23). On both grounds they are unable to "recognise my speech" (43a) as that of one who is "of God". We may compare 4 Ezra, where the fundamental dualism of heaven and earth is what makes the ways of God so puzzling and inaccessible,[124] but where also the relationship between mankind and God has been deeply scarred by sin. We find both ideas expressed together in 4 Ezra 4:10f, 21:

> He said to me, 'You cannot understand the things with which you have grown up *[fire, wind and time]*; how then can your mind comprehend the way of the Most High? And how can one who is already worn out by the corrupt world understand incorruption?' ... 'Those who dwell upon earth can understand only what is on earth, and he who is above the heavens can understand what is above the height of the heavens.'

An earth-bound existence and a corrupt nature conspire to make God inscrutable.

Conversely, the possibility of speaking "from the devil" (NB "when he speaks", 44c) is real, according to CD 12:2-3:

> Every man who is under the dominion of the spirits of Belial and preaches rebellion shall be judged according to the law relating to those possessed by a ghost or familiar spirit.[125]

The argument runs from the activity (preaching rebellion) to the diagnosis (under the dominion of Belial). This is the line of reasoning followed by Jesus in 8:44 (intention to murder prompts the same diagnosis), and by "the Jews" in 8:48: Jesus' unacceptable teaching indicates demon-possession. In 8:59 they seek to carry out the penalty prescribed for satanic speech.[126]

---

123 So Odeberg 222 and Lindars 229f analyse the train of thought.

124 See above, pp. 102-104

125 Cf also CD 5:11-6:1 (Jannes and Jambres were "raised up by Satan" to preach rebellion).

126 *Vermes* 113 and *Lohse* 290 n. 76 cite Lev 20:27 as the "law" to which CD

So, faced with these matching accusations (44a, 48), our 'implied reader' has to decide for herself *which* voice is that of the devil: that of "the Jews", who represent the Torah- and Temple-centred piety which received such a blow in 70 AD, but is now resurgent at Yavneh, or that of Jesus, who claims to stand in the position of both Torah and Temple?

The problem is that Jesus does not bring words like those provided by the apocalypses, words which affirm the continuity of the covenant despite its apparent breach (chiefly by predicting an *eschaton* which will reverse the damage). Instead he offers new "words of God", a new Exodus from *sin*, and deliverance from *death* (8:51). In the long run the reader can only decide if his is the voice of God by following the blind man and committing herself to discipleship *outside* the traditional parameters of Torah and Temple.

7.3.4 The rhetoric of the charge

These thoughts have already led us to ask about the *function* of this passage for the reader. We must reflect further on this, for 8:39-47 is frequently regarded as fatal to the overall view of the Gospel for which I have argued. As we noted earlier (p 62), it is suggested that the hostility to "the Jews" here makes it impossible that the Gospel could be intended to convert Jews to faith in Jesus.

I have carefully avoided judgments about the *intention* of the evangelist, and have focused instead upon the function of the text in the setting it seems to address. This approach is of considerable help in weighing this question. Instead of speculating whether "You are of your father, the devil" is compatible with an *intention* to convert, we may ask more concretely about the reactions of readers in the setting in late first-century Judaism.

Undoubtedly, convinced supporters of Yavneh would feel themselves directly vilified by 8:44, and would take offence. It is unlikely, however, that such people would read (or listen) this far through a Gospel so inimical to their theology! But, as we have seen, the reaffirmation of Torah associated with Yavneh was only one of several responses in this period. We may realistically imagine hearers of many hues, some of them quite hostile to the theology of "the Jews".

In any case, we have posited a reader who *co-operates* with this

12:3 refers: "A man or woman who is a medium or spiritist among you must be put to death. You are to stone them". We may connect with this the prescription of stoning for the false prophet who "preaches rebellion against the Lord" (Deut 13:10 — also cited by *Lohse*), and for the blasphemer (Lev 24:16).

text, that is, who attends to it sympathetically, and who is thus open to the possibility that its presentation of Jesus may be true. For such a reader, there will be a measure of alienation from the narrative. He constitutes a third party, a tacit participant in these exchanges, the very sharpness of which serves to raise issues and to pose dilemmas about which he *must* decide. We have noticed several of these in 8:31ff:

* Has 70 AD discredited Torah-piety as the answer to Israel's moral need?

* Was the rejection of Jesus a fundamental breach of hospitality?

* Was Jesus a law-breaker? Or did "the Jews" break the law in killing him?

* Is it possible that "the Jews" were acting under the direction of the devil when they killed Jesus?

* Above all, was Jesus "from God", or was he a false prophet?

* Could the 'Prophet like Moses' call people to follow himself rather than Moses, as Jesus does?

* He called God to witness, and judgment is promised to those who fail to "hear" the Prophet: so was his death God's judgment on him for false prophecy, or was the destruction of Jerusalem God's judgment for rejecting the true Prophet?

Once the reader is conceived as a third party, distinct from the text, then he is not bound to reproduce any of the reactions of the intra-textual characters, but these reactions will prompt him in the formulation of his own. This is very sharply the case in 8:59, where he *must* react to the violence of "the Jews". Does he reproduce it, or react against it? The text presses its reasons for the latter response, by making murder the work of the devil (8:44) — something with which many readers who had lived through the War would quickly agree.[127]

This one passage within the Gospel is merely part of an overall case urging faith in Jesus. It is certainly not inimical to that case, when viewed in this way. It functions as a warning against the power and influence of the devil, in continuity with many similar warnings in the literature of Second Temple Judaism, and one which gains extra force after the disaster; and it takes the presentation of Jesus forward by making the highly topical "freedom" claim, and by posing some vital questions to which all readers must make a

---

127 Some were ready to see the agency of the devil in such disasters, as we saw above. In the next section we will consider the significance of the War for understanding the theme of *death* in John.

response, even if it is not a believing one.[128]

7.4 8:48-59, the fourth, fifth, and sixth exchanges: freedom from Death

The change of interlocutor in 48 moves the dialogue into a new phase. As with Nicodemus, the "faith" of the Jews in 31 is left hanging: the reader is not told their response to Jesus' shocking words. We noted above Jouette Bassler's analysis of the rhetorical force of Nicodemus' "indeterminacy" (4.4.2, pp 118f): it compels the reader "to wrestle with the contours of Johannine faith".[129] So here too the reader asks: have the believing Jews changed sides, and joined their unbelieving colleagues? Or have they just moved in perplexity to the back of the crowd? As they slip into the background of the narrative they move alongside the 'implied reader', and stand together in uncertainty. How will they react to the violence of their fellow-Jews?

7.4.1 Structure

These three exchanges are even more closely bound together than exchanges 1-3. Violent language in 48 is matched by violent action in 59, but the dominant structural pattern is not concentric[130] but sequential: the pattern of the fourth exchange is repeated in exchanges five and six, taken together, so that 52-58 elaborates and amplifies 48-51. The main features of this sequence are:

(1) The accusation of demon-possession is made in 48 and reiterated with emphasis in 52. On the second occasion it could be just the equivalent of "you're mad" (cf 7:20), but following 48 it would more likely be heard with full force, "you are a false prophet, speaking by satanic inspiration".[131]

(2) In both cases Jesus' reply focuses

• (a) on his refusal to glorify himself (i.e. to respond directly to the charge), because God will do that for him (50, 54), and

---

128 Dunn moves in the direction of this interpretation in *Partings* 159f. He emphasises that John's dualism is not ontological but *rhetorical*, "deepened precisely in order to emphasise the scope of God's saving purpose through his Son", as part of "a contest for the minds and hearts of the Jewish people" (159). Unfortunately he does not explore the *ethical* dimension of the dualism in his brief treatment.

129 Bassler "Nicodemus" 644

130 Contra Kern "Aufbau" 452

131 Enslin "Perfect" 127: ἐγνώκαμεν is an "intensive perfect", emphasising the action: "Now we *are* sure of it".

• (b) on the fact of coming judgment, which will decide who is speaking the truth, himself or "the Jews" (50, 55).[132]

(3) The exchanges both conclude with dramatic "truly, truly, I say to you" sayings (51, 58), which have more in common than appears at first sight. 51 looks forward to the age to come (αἰών), 58 back to creation. 51 promises victory over death to Jesus' disciples, and 58 (together with 56) asserts that Abraham did *not* die, but was sustained in life by the 'I Am' who existed before him. 58 thus gives climactically the ontological basis on which Jesus is able to make the offer of 51.[133]

The reappearance of Abraham is significant. Lona points out that a statement about the relationship between Jesus and Abraham is needed, following 33ff where Jesus has denied the Jews' claim to have him as their father.[134] Jesus might be expected to claim him as father, too! Again, however, expectation is dramatically breached.

The three responses of "the Jews" in this section (48, 52f and 57) are of a different kind from those in 33, 39 and 41. As we saw above (7.2.7), the earlier ones are genuine *objections* from the perspective of Abraham-theology, and are inappropriately called 'misunderstandings'. However these later responses contain a clear element of misunderstanding, which enables an ironic dialogue to take place between implied author and reader. The bold charge "you are a Samaritan" (48) is so wildly wrong, and so out of tune with the Pharisees' and the crowd's recognition of Jesus' Galilean origin in 7:41, 52, that "and you have a demon" is ironically undermined — all the more so since their charge is put in a form which requires an answer: "do we not rightly say ...?" No, you do not!

There are similar elements of misunderstanding and irony in 52f and 57 which we will explore below.

---

132 That judgment is future here is denied by Blank *Krisis* 243, who interprets "there is one who ... judges" (50) in line with his theory about the *present realisation* of judgment in the Fourth Gospel. But even though "judges" (κρίνων) is a present participle, the movement of the statement is forward-looking, because Jesus is referring judgment to God as a reason for *not* engaging in judgment now (cf 8:15). In any case, as we shall argue below, "judgment" would have a very clear future referent for readers.

133 Lindars 331 brilliantly draws out the connection between 51 and 58. He develops this point further in *Behind* 44f and in his articles "Discourse" and "Slave".

134 Lona *Johannes 8* 327. Lona maintains that Abraham is treated simply as a witness to Jesus, and that there is no salvation-historical dimension in the treatment of him here. But salvation-history is implied simply by the appellation "Abraham your father" (56). The covenant significance of Abraham is crucial for the readership.

7.4.2 Death and Judgment

Lindars rightly brings the "truly, truly" saying in 51 into close connection with the offer of 'freedom' in 31f, not just because of the parallel "if" clauses ("abide in my word" // "keep my word"), but because of the semantic overlap between *freedom from sin* and *deliverance from death*.[135] The connection between the two is well illustrated by the rabbinic discussion about the meaning of "engraved" (**tw.rfx**) in Exod 32:16. This was read as **tw.ry"x**, "freedom", and the discussion then concerned "freedom from what?" The view was that Israel had three "freedoms" when she came out of Egypt — from death, from suffering and from political domination — but she lost them all when she made the Golden Calf:

> It is now clear why, after their exodus from Egypt, the Israelites once again came under the rule of foreign nations. If they had waited patiently for Moses and had not made the golden calf for themselves, the first tablets would not have been destroyed and neither oppressors nor the angel of death would have gained power over Israel.[136]

Hengel *Zealots* 120 dates this discussion in the second century, but argues that it has first-century roots. A connection between sin, death and political enslavement would have been so topical in the late first century that we may well accept an early date for that connection, if not for the specific tradition about Israel's three-fold freedom at the Exodus.

So the offer of deliverance from death is not without political connotations — and this would be especially the case following a War in which, according to Josephus, 1,100,000 died, nearly all of them Jews.[137] This figure is undoubtedly exaggerated, but it attests a *sense* of horrifying, wholesale slaughter which transcends any particular figure, and which undoubtedly left a deep scar on the generation which experienced it, to say the least. Against this background, Jesus' offer in 51 takes on a very particular force: "anyone who keeps my word will not see death but attain the age to come" (ἐάν τις τὸν

---

135 E.g. Lindars "Slave" 274; also Bartholomew *Sermon-Drama* 77. In fact 8:51 stands out as the next in a sequence of crucial claim-sayings which usually involve Exodus symbolism and which function as way-markers or 'topic statements' within the narrative: cf 5:24, 6:51, 7:37f, 8:12, 8:31f.

136 *Exod. Rab.* 32:1; cf *m.* '*Abot.* 6:2.

137 *War* 6:420

ἐμὸν λόγον τηρήσῃ, θάνατον οὐ μὴ θεωρήσῃ εἰς τὸν αἰῶνα). We may make three points about it, all of which relate to its 'hearing' in the post-70 aftermath:

(1) *Restoration of Israel's loss?* If the rabbinic tradition cited above was current in the first century, then some at least will have heard this saying as a claim to restore to Israel the freedom from "the angel of death" which she lost through sin. This tradition has been felt by many to be important as background to John 10:34, and its very suitability there may itself be an argument for an early date. Several Rabbis interpreted "you are gods" in Ps 82:6 as addressed to Israel at Sinai, and therefore applied the following "you shall die like men" to the effect of the worship of the Golden Calf, through which Israel became subject again to death.[138] If "gods" was a suitable description for Israel at Sinai, receiving the word of God and enjoying freedom from death, then is it not a suitable title for Jesus? In 8:51 he claims to *give* freedom from death.

(2) *The struggle with death.* We may develop this point further. Jesus' offer was highly topical. There are inevitably times and places where the tragedy of death is more keenly felt, and where therefore the search for *answers to questions* and for *salvation* becomes especially acute. The apocalypses make it clear that the late first century was such a time.

The reaction of "the Jews" says it all. The offer seems totally unrealistic, in view of the universality of death. If even Abraham and the prophets died (52b), those who lived closest to God, then Jesus' offer must be ridiculous. Here we must point to some remarkable parallels with the *Testament of Abraham*, where the *inevitability* of death is a central theme. The work describes how even Abraham tried hard to avoid death, only to be tricked into it in the end. He has to be reminded by God through the Archangel Michael,

Do you not know that all those who spring from Adam and Eve die? And not one of the prophets escaped death (οὐδεὶς ἐκ τῶν προφητῶν τὸν θάνατον ἐξέφυγον), and not one of those who reign has been

---

138 This interpretation is ascribed to the first-century R. Joshua b. Hananiah in *Lev. Rab* 4:1; cf also *Exod. Rab.* 32:7, *Mek. Bahodesh* 9 (*Lauterbach* 2:272), *b. 'Abod. Zar.* 5a (cf Str-B 2:464). Scholars who interpret 10:34 against this background include Dahl "History" 133f, Manns "Jabné" 93f, Thyen "Johannes 10" 133f and 167 n. 49, Neyrey *Revolt* 221-4, Barrett 384f. On the other hand Ps 82:6 was interpreted of angelic beings at Qumran (11QMelch 11f), and this is the background favoured by Ashton *Understanding* 147-150.

immortal. Not one of the forefathers (προπατόρων) has escaped the mystery of death. All have died, all have departed into Hades ...[139]

The date and provenance of *Test. Abr.* is problematic, but Sanders makes a good case for a late first- / early second-century date in Egypt.[140] It is impossible to know how widespread was this legend about Abraham's tussle with death, but we can say with some certainty

• (a) that this is the kind of story which would have gained currency in the aftermath of a disaster (death is ὁ τὸν κόσμον λυμαίνων, the ravager of the world[141]); and

• (b) that the strange emphasis on Abraham's death in 52f (mentioned twice) could point to a situation in which "even Abraham died!" was a piece of popular consolation in the face of death. This would explain the remarkable parallel between these verses and the passage quoted above.[142]

The change of term in the Jews' repetition of Jesus' claim — they use "taste" instead of "see" (52b) — points to the fact that they understand "death" in a thoroughly physical way. So the reader is alerted to the possibility that this is not what Jesus meant.[143] In the legend just referred to, Abraham certainly "tastes" death, and even "sees" death in visionary form,[144] yet he does not finally "see" death in the sense of coming under its power. Throughout the book, he is protected by the power of God, and ultimately comes to Paradise. In fact, he "sees" many other things as he is led round heaven by the archangel, and "what Abraham saw" is introduced specifically into

---

139 *Test. Abr.* 8:9 (Recension A)

140 *OTP* 1:874f

141 *Test. Abr.* 17:5 (A)

142 Abraham's battle with death in *Test. Abr.* is strange. For when he eventually dies, angels escort "his precious soul" to heaven, where he worships God. He is then taken to Paradise, where the μοναί (dwellings, cf John 14:2) of the other patriarchs are, and where "there is no toil, no grief, no moaning, but peace and exultation (ἀγαλλίασις, cf John 8:56) and endless life" (*Test. Abr.* 20:12-14 (A)). We are left wondering why he avoided death with such determination. A very possible answer to this is that the *horror of death* which the book expresses with such power is actually that felt by the implied readers who have faced this horror directly and need to hear this encouragement.

143 Significance in the change is found by Barrett 350f, even though he regards the two verbs as synonyms; also by Neyrey "Process" 529 (*contra* Leroy *Rätsel* 75). The two terms are essentially synonymous as far as wider usage is concerned (e.g. Beasley-Murray 137 cites their use in parallel in the *Gospel of Thomas* logia 1, 18, 19), but the *alteration* points to a different signification in this case.

144 *Test. Abr.* 17:9ff (A): Death reveals himself to Abraham in all his "ferocity ... decay and bitterness".

the discussion by Jesus (56).

(3) *Judgment on Israel — but also hope.* It must be admitted that Jesus' claim in 51 is ambiguous, and the Jews' response understandable. It certainly sounds like an offer of freedom from death in *all* its forms. The offer has a distinct barb to it, because of the implied negative: what will happen to those who do *not* "keep my word"? — like "the Jews" who have just accused him of speaking by demonic inspiration, and to whom Jesus has replied that there is one who seeks his glory *and judges* (50)?

As we noted above, warnings of judgment gain considerable authenticity when they are read after judgment has fallen. It is scarcely avoidable, that 8:50-51 would be heard to claim that the *judgment* and *death* experienced by Israel in the catastrophe resulted from rejecting Jesus' word. A similar observation may be made about 3:18-19, where likewise the judgment of God is radically re-focused onto Jesus.

Later Christians did not hesitate to interpret the destruction of the Temple as a judgment for unbelief in Christ,[145] and this seems to be encouraged by this passage. The offer was scorned — as the reaction of "the Jews" so pointedly signals — and so freedom from death was *not* enjoyed. Far from it.

W.D. Davies argues that Jesus' departure from the Temple in 8:59 is a deliberate act of judgment, a final rejection of the Holy Place:

> For John, 'I am' has departed from the Temple, that 'holy space' is no longer the abode of the Divine Presence. The Shekinah is no longer *there*, but is now found wherever Christ is, because later (10:36 makes this probable, if not unmistakably clear) Christ himself is the Sanctified One, the altar and Temple, the locus of the Shekinah.[146]

There is much truth in this. That Jesus replaces the Temple for John, becoming "the locus of the Shekinah", is indicated by more than just 10:36. And it may be that some readers would hear echoes of Ezekiel's vision of the departure of the *merkabah* from Jerusalem, which heralded the destruction of the city in 587 BC (Ezek 10) — especially since an equivalent departure before the final destruction

---

145 So Justin *Dial.* 108:1-3; cf *Dial.* 16:2-3 (interpreting the Bar Kokba defeat in the same way). The Christian editing of *T. Levi* 16:3-5 makes this point also and must be early, because it antedates the whole extant MS tradition. So also Pseudo-Clement *Recognitions* 39:3.

146 Davies *Land* 295, his emph. The discussion occupies *Land* 290-6.

in 70 AD had become a matter of popular legend, finding its way even into the Roman historian Tacitus.[147]

However, also to describe Jesus' departure in 8:59 as a "definitive rejection of Judaism and its 'holy place'"[148] goes too far. Jesus leaves secretly, just as he came (7:14). There is no public act of rejection, and he *returns* to the Temple in 10:22.[149] "The Jews" have rejected him, but he immediately renews his claim to be the light of the world (9:5), and seeks out a Jew who is already alienated from the cult and from the Torah-loyal Jews who have rejected him — another man like the lame man in ch. 5, for whom cult and Torah offer no hope. Such a man would not normally (at all?) be found in the Temple;[150] so it is quite possible that Jesus' action in leaving the Temple is just the necessary (and pointed) step he must take in order to come into contact with the blind man.

If this is so, then the 'exile' experienced by the man in 9:34 is but an extension of an exile he has already undergone, by virtue of his disability. So 8:59 is not a rejection of Judaism, but a breach with some Jews; and readers already unsympathetic to the Torah-loyal Yavneh school could be further drawn towards Jesus, both by his rejection and by the action which he immediately takes towards the blind man.

As we have seen (5.4.3), the story of the blind man is told in such a way as to echo poignantly the issues of justice and theodicy with which many Jews wrestled after the War. If 8:31ff has effectively made the disaster a judgment *for the rejection of Jesus* (cf also 8:21,24), then ch. 9:

• (a) denies that apportioning blame is either possible or appropriate (9:3 — though the Pharisees do so, 9:34),

• (b) vividly presents Jesus' ministry as "the works of God" (9:3) to bring restoration to those who have been exiled from their place of worship, and

• (c) proclaims a new cult- and Torah-free worship in *the worship of Jesus as the Son of Man* (9:35-38). As we noted above, this brings a

---

147 *Histories* 5:13; cf Josephus *War* 5:412, 6:297-300, 2 Baruch 8:1-5. There were widespread legends about the portents that preceded and warned of the coming judgment: *b. Yoma* 39b records the tradition that Yohanan b. Zakkai saw the doors of the Temple opening by themselves and took this as a sign of coming destruction (cf Neusner *Yohanan2* 64f). Cf also Josephus *War* 6:288ff.

148 Davies *Land* 291

149 Davies is at pains to explain this away, arguing that in 10:22ff Jesus "seems disengaged; he is at best an onlooker" (*Land* 292). But this is surely special pleading.

150 See above, ch. 5 n. 1 (p 123).

striking message of hope in the post-70 situation, which both builds
upon and balances the 'judgment' theme in ch. 8.

7.4.3 Abraham the visionary

"Abraham your father exulted that he was to see my day, and he
saw it, and rejoiced!"

8:56 has a climactic force in the structure of the paragraph. The
Jews object that Jesus' claim to give life apparently makes him
superior even to Abraham, who had to die: so "whom do you make
yourself?" (53b)? Jesus responds once again by referring judgment to
God (54), and then by denying the Jews' capacity to judge his answer
to the question (55). 55 is bitingly ironic: the false prophet is defined
in Deut 13:2 as one who calls Israel to "follow other gods, gods you
have not known". So, by their very rejection of him, "the Jews" are
granting the rightness of his accusation that they "do not know" the
God he calls his father. For this reason, they cannot 'hear' his answer
to the question "whom do you make yourself?" They should
"rejoice" over Jesus, like Abraham their father (56), instead of
accusing him of demon-possession.[151]

The point made by 56 is that, though he died, Abraham was able
to see beyond the grave: and in this vision he saw the "day" of Jesus,
and rejoiced at the sight. This engages with the strong tradition that
Abraham was given visionary knowledge of the world and the
future.[152] Granted that this was so (the argument runs), it is too
simple to say just "Abraham died". He died having received a vision
which gave him hope of victory over death, and indeed in the vision
itself he had already transcended death: and Jesus boldly portrays
himself as the content of that vision.[153]

The tradition of Abraham's vision was widespread among the
Rabbis.[154] On the basis of the rabbinic material alone, Str-B 2:526

---

151 The *imitation* of Abraham is implicit in the progression of thought here —
carried through from 8:39f.

152 So e.g. Schlatter 220; Barrett 351f; Lona *Johannes 8* 292-313 (a whole section
devoted to exploring this background); Brown 1:359f; Leroy *Rätsel* 83 n. 2, 86;
Lindars 334; Schnackenburg 2:221f; Beasley-Murray 138f

153 It is worth speculating whether there is any contact here with the synoptic
debate with the Sadducees about the resurrection (Mk 12:18-27 *par.*), in which Exod
3:6 is quoted ("I am the God of Abraham, and the God of Isaac, and the God of
Jacob") and the comment added, "He is not God of the dead but of the living" (Mk
12:27). The point there seems to be that the covenant relationship in itself implies
transcendence over death. In John we find this same thought *christologised* and
linked to the Abraham vision-tradition. Because of the covenant relationship,
Abraham was given visions which assured him of his place in the future of God's
people, and *Jesus Christ* is set at the centre of this hope.

comment that "Jesus could reckon with a certain understanding among his hearers". According to *Gen. Rab.* 44:22,[155] Yohanan ben Zakkai and Akiba discussed exactly what Abraham saw: was it is just this world (Yohanan), or also the world to come (Akiba)? The first-century sources reveal why this question was raised, because of the sheer variety of objects proposed. In *Apoc. Abr.* 12:10 he sees

what is in the heavens, on the earth and in the sea, in the abyss, and in the lower depths, in the garden of Eden and in its rivers, in the fullness of the universe.

In 4 Ezra 3:14 he sees "the end of the times"; in 2 Baruch 4:4 he sees the heavenly Temple "which will be revealed" when "it will be restored forever" (4:3, 6:9); in Ps.-Philo *Bib. Ant.* 23:6 he sees the place of judgment; in *Test. Abr.* 9:8 (A) he sees "all the inhabited world", and then sees the judgment of souls at the gate of heaven (chs. 11-14 (A)). In the midst of all this variety, it is certainly a moot point whether he sees just this world or also the world to come!

The theme of Abraham's rejoicing has an equally strong pedigree. As noted above, Abraham's "laughter" in Gen 17:17 was interpreted as genuine rejoicing as early as *Jubilees*, where there are no fewer than twelve references to his "rejoicing", nearly all of them over the promise of "seed".[156] Similarly in *Apoc. Abr.* 10:15:

Stand up, Abraham, go boldly, be very joyful and rejoice ... for a venerable honour has been prepared for you by the Eternal One.

The "honour" is the nation and the land which God will give him.

Lona searches in vain for a text apart from John 8:56 where the two ideas of Abraham's *vision* and his *rejoicing* appear together. It is true that there seems to be no parallel to this. But this is hardly significant, for both ideas form the presupposition-pool from which the hearers of this text would draw. Against this background, Jesus' claim is dramatic indeed. He, rather than Isaac or Israel, is the "seed" over which Abraham rejoiced, and his "day", rather than the secrets

---

154 Str-B 2:525f; Beasley-Murray 138

155 This reference is wrongly given as 44:25 by Lindars, and as 44:28a by Beasley-Murray.

156 Abraham rejoices over *Isaac* or his "seed" generally: *Jub.* 14:21, 15:17, 16:19; 17:2, 3; 22:1; over *Jacob*: 22:26, 28; over *Tabernacles* (although this is clearly connected with the rejoicing over the gift of sons): 16:20, 25, 27 (cf also 16:31); over *Weeks:* 18:18.

of the universe or Israel's final vindication and salvation, is what Abraham was glad to see.

The reaction of "the Jews" (57) reveals their continuing conviction that Jesus is demon-possessed, so that his claims are completely irrational. They misunderstand, in that they do not appear to realise that Jesus is drawing on the Abraham-vision tradition.[157] Jesus' response in return (58) is not calculated to reassure them about his sanity: he unmistakably applies the divine name to himself, and claims to pre-exist Abraham (and thus also to be the giver of life to Abraham).

The background to this use of the 'I Am' has been widely explored,[158] but I believe that John Ashton has added a significant new dimension to our understanding by pointing to *Apoc. Abr.* and the figure of Iaoel, Abraham's angelic guide.[159] The fact that Iaoel bears the name of God himself is deliberate:

> While I was still face down on the ground, I heard the voice speaking, "Go, Iaoel of the same name, through the mediation of my ineffable name, consecrate this man for me and strengthen him against his trembling."[160]

Without proposing a direct relationship between *Apoc. Abr.* and the Fourth Gospel, Ashton suggests that this divine messenger-figure, who bears the name of God, acts as a model for the christology of John 8:58. His case would have been strengthened, had he drawn upon the material gathered and impressively assessed by Larry Hurtado in his 1988 monograph, *One God, One Lord.* Hurtado includes a consideration of Iaoel in *Apoc. Abr.*[161] in a wide-ranging survey of the different types of 'divine agent' in Jewish thinking at this time. He makes a strong case for the view that Judaism was consistently monotheistic throughout this period, even while it allowed agents to bear the name and attributes of God, and

---

157 It is not impossible that we should read "has Abraham seen you?" rather than "have you seen Abraham?" The textual evidence in favour of the former is not inconsiderable, including p[75] and)*. Bernard 2:321 makes a good case for it, and indeed scribal error could easily have produced ἑώρακας out of ἑώρακέ σε by haplography. The possibility is rejected by Brown 1:360, is not considered in *TextComm* 226f, and is not accepted by any other commentator, so far as I am aware. But "Has Abraham seen you?" is given as a marginal alternative in the *New Revised Standard Version.*

158 See now the study by David Ball, *'I AM' in John's Gospel.*

159 Ashton *Understanding* 142-5

160 *Apoc. Abr.* 10:3; cf 10:8, 17:13

161 *One God, One Lord* 87-89

points to the significance of the *worship* of Jesus as the vital point of "mutation" which moved early christology decisively away from its Jewish roots.[162]

Hurtado aids considerably the analysis of the 'hearing' of John 8:58 (though he does not refer to it). It would *not* be heard as a claim to *be God*. It *would* be heard as a claim to be a divine agent, anointed with the name and powers of God, and (in this case) active in the *genesis* of Abraham. The decisive new step occurs in 9:38, when the rejection of Jesus by "the Jews" in the temple is balanced by the *worship* of Jesus by the (ex-)blind man outside the synagogue. That is a crucial moment in the development of the narrative force of the Gospel, which faces the reader with a dramatic decision.

But here in 8:56-59 things have not developed so far — though they are dramatic enough. The four closing verses of the chapter deal successive hammer-blows to the reader. Jesus' claim to be the object of Abraham's vision and a bearer of the divine name face the reader with the necessity of choice. Will she move towards acceptance of the claim, or approve of the action taken by "the Jews" in 59 — the response appropriate to a false prophet and blasphemer? Soon, she will have to decide.

7.5 Conclusion

Our discussion has shown that, far from being heard as insulting and denigrating, this passage would have served as a powerful appeal to Jews in the late first century to believe in Jesus the Christ. Its rhetoric coheres with other examples from the period and earlier, which show that "you are of your father the devil" would not have been heard as a designation of Jewish ontology, but as a serious *warning* about the real nature of a certain course of action (executing Jesus). Hearing such a warning, the late first-century reader must decide what attitude she will take to the Christ-faith which is quite possibly being vigorously canvassed and debated in her environment.

At point after point we have seen how the dialogue engages quietly with themes or slogans from the period, so that it exercises its effect by extra-textual reference, sometimes ironic. Such quiet, unsignalled allusions are a regular part of the johannine stock-in-trade, so

---

162 *One God, One Lord* 99f. Hurtado's monograph has sparked considerable discussion and response, which we do not review here because our point simply draws on the 'agency' background which he displays.

we should not be surprised to have found them. Some have been observed before, and some have not.

The argument from 'fit' needs to be employed carefully, but it has validity. It is the argument on which Martyn's appeal rests, as we noted above (p 14). We suggested that, in Martyn's case, the 'fit' was illusory because it built on an insufficient assessment of both the internal and the external evidence. We have done our best to make good this deficiency in the reading presented here. As fully as possible, we have sought to hear this text with ears attuned to first-century issues and thought-patterns. And it fits! The issues of sin, death and judgment, freedom and slavery, Abraham and the covenant, vision and eternal life, all so vital to late first century Jewish self-consciousness, are also the vital moving themes of this passage. The argument from 'fit' prompts enthusiastically to affirm that we have heard the authentic voice of this text, as it testifies to Jesus, the 'I Am' of God.

8

Conclusions

As outlined in the Introduction, this study has had three inter-locking aims:[1]
- (1) We have sought to understand the Gospel's anti-Judaism,
- (2) by focusing on the way this text would have been *heard* by Jews in the late first century. In order to facilitate this we have
- (3) explored a method of interpretation which holds together a narrative and a historical approach, and have attempted an outline justification of this method.

What conclusions may we draw from our study?

8.1 The sting has been drawn from the charge of hostile anti-Judaism

The Fourth Gospel may certainly be called 'anti-Jewish', if this is defined as a motivation to prove the illegitimacy of the ways in which various Jewish groups sought to be faithful to their heritage. But this statement needs to be qualified in several ways, not least in that, on our analysis, this motivation is *not at all hostile* towards the groups concerned. This conclusion, like every secure support, rests on three points:

8.1.1 The nature of first-century polemic

We pointed to the work of Luke Johnson, who shows how 'normal' and acceptable polemical language was in first-century debate: reveals, in fact, that the language of the Fourth Gospel is comparatively mild according to both Graeco-Roman and Jewish standards.[2] But this explanation purely in terms of convention is not sufficient to excuse the Fourth Gospel, in the light of its claim to teach a *new* ethic of love (13:34). Even if mild by comparison with other examples, Johnson still locates the Gospel's polemic in the

---

1   See above, p 6.
2   Johnson "Polemic" 441

adversarial tradition of the Greek philosophical schools.[3] This is one reason why it is vital to see this polemic against the *prophetic* background which we have outlined. In the tradition of a Hosea — but using a different literary genre — the evangelist calls to his nation to turn again, by issuing threats and warnings in God's name.

Within the tradition of prophetic polemic, 'hostility' is not an appropriate description of the prophet's attitude. The prophet acts out of a total commitment to Israel's good, ready to endure great hardship and persecution in order to obey his call (e.g. Jer 20:8, Ezek 2:6f, Hos 3:1). Predictions of judgment and warnings are issued so that they might *not* be fulfilled. The prophet "intensifies the alternative in order to provoke a decision".[4] He shocks in order to deter.

Interpreted against this background, even "you are of your father, the devil" becomes, in its context, a passionate appeal to change direction — not to be rebellious children who do not know or understand (Isa 1:2f), but to be "willing and obedient" (Isa 1:19); not to reject and murder Jesus as a blasphemer, but to confess him as the Christ. The polemic of John 8 serves not merely to *denounce* but more particularly to *warn*, to *persuade*, in fact to *prompt its own negation*.

8.1.2 A debate within family

Ashton effectively employs the notion of 'family' to illumine the particularly 'Jewish' quality of the arguments in John 5, 8 and 10. But for Ashton (working within the Martyn tradition), these are "fierce family rows ... which so astonish the outsider by their vehemence and bitterness".[5] The thesis defended here retains the 'family' idea but drops the "vehemence and bitterness". The parallels with the contemporary apocalypses allow the Fourth Gospel to be heard as *a Jewish Christian response to the very issues over which all Jews, including Christian Jews, agonised in the period after 70 AD*. It is a Christian contribution to the melting-pot of answers and responses, made at a time of confusion, when relationships were fluid and later lines of demarcation had not yet been drawn. Here is Jew speaking to Jew, in just the same way as the authors of 4 Ezra and 2 Baruch tried to minister to the needs of their fellow-Jews by publishing their own solutions in written form.

The diversity of this 'family' has been an essential feature of our

---

3   "Polemic" 428-30

4   Dunn *Partings* 159 — although he does not employ a comparison with Old Testament prophetic polemic.

5   Ashton *Understanding* 137

answer to the problem. "The Jews" is not a global designation of all Abraham's descendants. We have suggested that the lexicography of this word is complex, but that in essence it would be heard — and its usage in the Gospel reinforces this — to refer to a distinct group within Judaism, the Judea-based, Torah-loyal adherents of the Yavneh ideals, the direct heirs of pre-70 Pharisaism. This view has the advantage of covering virtually all the occurrences of οἱ Ἰουδαῖοι in the Fourth Gospel — all except the handful of places where it has a purely ethnic force, particularly in the phrase "King of the Jews".[6]

Certainly the Fourth Gospel would be heard to be strongly inimical to the Yavneh programme, the renewed emphasis on Torah lifestyle as the answer to Israel's need. But by no means all were sympathetic to this programme; and John is not *merely* polemical towards it, but also addresses the concerns of its sympathisers by the emphatic presentation of Jesus as the Mosaic Prophet who fulfils the promise of Deut 18. If he really is, then one's view of Torah needs revision simply as part of the package.

In any case, these "Jews" are by no means tarred with a black brush throughout. It is true that, finally, "the Jews" are closely associated with "the chief priests" in seeking Jesus' death (e.g. 18:12, 19:6f,14f).[7] But they are treated warmly in the Lazarus episode (11:19, 31, etc), and Jesus allows himself to be identified as one by the Samaritan woman (4:9, 20). The positive "salvation is of the Jews" (4:22), and the thoroughly sympathetic portrayal of Nicodemus (who shows by coming to Jesus that his "deeds have been done in God", 3:21), also serve to unmask as a caricature the picture of unrelieved hostility often drawn.

Dunn effectively brings out the dividedness of "the Jews" in his treatment of the issue,[8] although he makes the expression relate to distinct groups: *qua* crowd, "the Jews" are open to Jesus, but *qua* the Jerusalem authorities, they are hostile. This distinction does not do justice to the linguistic facts, however: no markers signal such a distinction in *reference*, although the distinction in *response* is clear. Since the definition defended here allows the term to bear the same *sense* throughout, with a *reference* which covers all but a handful of exceptions, it may be deemed to fit the data better than its rivals.

---

6   See 18:20,33,35; 19:3,19,21.

7   But as we saw (2.4.4, pp 51f), it is unwise to infer a *semantic identity* between these terms. Even here, the particular connection between "the Jews" and matters of legal observance is clear: 18:28-31; 19:7,31,42.

8   *Partings* 156ff

8.1.3 A commitment to rebuilding

Our proposal explains Ashton's puzzle (above, p 14): "why is the Gospel at once so Jewish and yet so anti-Jewish?"[9] In the Fourth Gospel we encounter a passionate commitment to the rebuilding of Israel, an intense longing to see the people rise again from the ashes of Jerusalem. But there is only one way! And that way does not point to a future restoration, as the Apocalypses do, but has *already* been provided in Jesus, whose crucifixion at the hands of the Jerusalem authorities is already the means of life for Israel. In that action they foreshadowed all the later murders which would so deface God's people, but at the same time ironically they opened the way to the Father — if only they could see!

By ironic allusions to the destruction, the Gospel initiates a hidden conversation with the reader, a secret communication which depends on shared knowledge of the disaster to which open reference is never made. The great issues are tackled — sin, death, resurrection, covenant; and the appeal is made, Don't put faith in the failed formula, the illusory promise that the Torah life-style can still bring freedom! There is no deliverance from sin and death by that way.

As part of this appeal, 8:31-59 plays a distinctive role. Our passage contains the sharpest, most poignant polemic against that failed formula. The claim to freedom in 8:33 is agonizingly ironic, in its expression of childlike confidence which is blind to the obvious. Many Jews would be willing to agree that *slavery to sin* had led to the disaster. And to such the Gospel addresses its presentation of the Christ who provides *real freedom*, by his death and resurrection which portend the rebuilding of the Temple, through the reformation of the scattered people of God around him (11:52), the rerooting of the Vine (15:1-10).

That Vine is already growing again in the company of those who confess this Christ, as they experience together the inner, spiritual reality of all that Israel thought she had and now has lost. So far as I am aware, no one has yet suggested that the realised eschatology of the Fourth Gospel owes its *raison d'être* to the fact that it was addressing a widespread conviction among Jews that *the judgment of God is now past* — in fact, just experienced in the destruction of Jerusalem. Josef Blank does not exploit this line of thought at all in his magisterial study of the judgment theme in John, even though he wants to emphasise the realised quality ("Vergegenwärtigung") of

---

9   Ashton *Understanding* 109

judgment. He feels that this quality derives straight from the christology of the Gospel, so that "the Jews" quickly become universal
'types' of unbelief, hardened under judgment.

So there are no historical overtones when Blank writes, "John saw
in the judgment of Israel a 'sign' and exemplar of universal judgment".[10] "The judgment of Israel" has no particular historical
location for him — even though, as we saw, he resists Bultmann's
total abstraction of "the Jews" from history and suggests that they
are "the Jerusalem Temple-party".[11] But it was supremely in the
dreadful events of the Jewish War that "the Jerusalem Temple-party"
experienced the judgment of God.

Employing a reading-centred hermeneutic, there can be no doubt
that these are the historical points of reference which would be
sensed by Jewish readers of the late first century. It would not be
hidden from them that the Gospel announces a rebuilding programme.

8.2 New arguments now support the 'evangelistic' view of the Gospel

We must be careful not to claim too much here. We have based
our argument on function, and not on speculations about intention.
All that we claim, therefore, is that it is far from unrealistic to
imagine that this Gospel could have been effective in convincing
Jews that Jesus is the Christ, and indeed that its structure and
content *seems* to be designed to achieve this goal. Of course, for a
full assertion of 'fit', our theory would need to be tested against the
whole Gospel, rather than just against chs. 5-12. But I believe (a) that
such a test would not produce evidence seriously to undermine the
picture painted here, and (b) that the way in which the picture 'fits'
even 8:31-59, apparently so inimical to it, is strong testimony to its
basic truth.

We have presupposed the inaccessibility of authorial (or editorial)
intention, but it may nonetheless be a focus of speculation! For if we
find a substantial 'fit' between the text and the *first* context in which
it functioned in its final form, then it seems reasonable to suppose
that this was at least foreseen by the final author / editor, if not
directly intended. This is especially the case since in 20:30f we have a
statement of intention in relation to which there does not seem to be

---

10   "Johannes sah in der Krisis Israels ... ein 'Zeichen' und Musterbeispiel für
die Krisis überhaupt", *Krisis* 313

11   "Die Jerusalemer Kultgemeinde", *Krisis* 247: see above, p 54.

any *necessity* to distinguish sharply between narrator and (real) author / editor, and this statement strongly 'fits' the overall picture we have painted. According to Martin de Boer, J.L. Martyn has given his support to this line of argument in an unpublished paper read in 1990:

> On the way toward ascertaining the intention of an early Christian author, the interpreter is *first* to ask how the original readers of the author's document understood what he had said in it.[12]

This is what we have attempted to do. Is there any evidence that the Fourth Gospel actually worked in this way? All we know of its life during its first century is that it was hijacked by Gnostic Christianity, which began the interpretative tradition we have opposed here.[13] It is interesting that quotations and allusions to the synoptics and Acts are clearly present in the Pseudo-Clementine *Recognitions*, but not to the Fourth Gospel.[14]

From a later period, however, comes the story of Josephus told by Epiphanius, which there is no reason to doubt in its fundamentals. Josephus, a fourth-century leader of the synagogue in Tiberias, became a Christian in part through reading a Hebrew translation of the Fourth Gospel which he found, with a similar translation of Matthew, in the synagogue treasury.[15] The presence of such a translation in such a place attests a remarkable openness and readiness to 'own' such literature as belonging within the orbit of Judaism, even though baptism was a socially difficult step to take — and even though both these Gospels are renowned for their 'vilification' of the Jews. The presence of 8:44 in John's Gospel certainly did not deter Josephus.

---

12   Martyn, "How I Changed My Mind": paper read at the Annual Meeting of the SBL, New Orleans, November 1990: quoted by de Boer "Narrative Criticism" 40 n. 25.

13   Irenaeus reports that the Valentinians made "copious use" of John (*Adv. Haer.* 3.11.7). This popularity seems to have rested largely on their use of the Prologue. However this meant that from the start the Fourth Gospel was used to support an ahistorical understanding of the heart of Christian faith — completely contrary to its fundamental engagement, not just with the history of Jesus but also with that of first-century Judaism. See Pagels *Gnostic Exegesis* 12-16.

14   Martyn "Persecution" 63-80 considers the relationship at length. He finds (very slim) evidence of "some kind of specific connection" but the difference between John and the Synoptics (and Acts) in this respect is very striking.

15   Epiphanius *Panarion* 30:6:7-9

8.3 There is a common way forward for 'narrative' and 'history'

The methodological proposal I have made has been essential to this study, because of the *priority* it suggests for the *original* reading of the Gospel. A text as powerful and suggestive as the Fourth Gospel can suggest all sorts of responses — quite apart from its vital use in liturgy and devotion by Christians. Such a 'classic' can speak compellingly quite apart from any awareness of the circumstances of its composition. It is in part this feature which has fuelled recent ahistorical readings, emphasising its narrative qualities.

It is not difficult to feel the force of the argument which suggests that investigating the origins of such a text is a dry exercise in literary archaeology, far less compelling than an appropriation of its present literary power. I agree that an *exclusive concentration* on literary origins, as though this were the only access to meaning, has professionalised biblical interpretation in a manner to which the fourth evangelist would strongly object![16] But the nature of this text is such that ultimately it *calls* for attention to be paid to its origins. The "you" of 20:31 ensures this. The argument I have mounted, both in chapter 4 above and in the related article,[17] suggests that the 'implied readers' of the Fourth Gospel have an historical character, so that finally the meaning of this text is shaped by the contours of the relationship between it and them — whatever further meaning and significance it may have accrued during its long *Wirkungsgeschichte.*

The techniques of narrative criticism have much to offer historical critics, as I hope this study has shown. A *rapprochement* is certainly possible, and indeed *necessary*, I maintain. If my argument is allowed force, then I have grounds for speaking out, on behalf of the implied readers of this text, against all appropriations of it which violate its fundamental commitment to the well-being of Israel and its heart of love for Jews.

8.4 The Fourth Gospel may be rescued as Word of God for today

For many Christians, of course, the status of John as word of God was never in doubt. But we faced in the Introduction a serious challenge to the moral and theological integrity of this sacred Christian text. Is it guilty of an anti-Judaism which all right-thinking

---

16   See above, 6.4 (pp 176-8).
17   See ch. 4 n. 4 (p 106).

Christians would heartily repudiate?

As we saw, this agonising question required us to examine the dominant consensus on the origins of the Gospel, for the 'Martyn hypothesis' suggests that hostility between Jews and Christians conditioned its very genesis. But we have found the hypothesis wanting in many respects, and have been led by a broad analysis of the evidence to a much more positive understanding of the relationship. For this discovery to contribute to the *theological* rehabilitation of the text, however, it must be accepted that such historical analysis has a right to speak in the theological arena. As we put it in the Introduction (p 4), the older sister has a right to regulate the behaviour of her younger sibling! As long as the words of this text are just launched on the world without any qualification, they will serve the purpose of the moment, whatever that is.

Christian theology has usually admitted the validity of this partnership between theology and history. But at various times it has been denied. The early church faced just such a denial in second-century Gnosticism. As Elaine Pagels puts it,

> Gnostic theologians do not necessarily *deny* that the events proclaimed of Jesus have occurred in history. What they deny is that the actuality of these events matters *theologically*. Heracleon claims, for example, that those who insist that Jesus, a man who lived "in the flesh", is "Christ" fail to distinguish between literal and symbolic truth ... Heracleon goes on to say that those who take the events concerning Jesus "literally" — as if the events *themselves* were revelation — have fallen into "flesh and error".[18]

We have seen a revival of this theological distrust of history in the 20th century, especially in the theology of Rudolph Bultmann and those influenced by him. And it is notable that Gnostic exegesis originated, and Bultmann perpetuates, the view that the Jews are ontologically demonised in the Fourth Gospel. In both approaches it is their value as 'symbols' which matters.

It is my contention that we need to fall into "flesh and error" again: not just in an affirmation of the theological importance of Christ's flesh-and-blood incarnation, but more especially (for our purposes) in a recognition of the incarnation of this particular word, the Fourth Gospel, in its originating historical setting, the late first-century trauma of shattered Judaism. If this is allowed — and all who deny a Gnostic dualism of flesh and spirit will want to allow it — then this Gospel will be able to speak in its own authentic tones.

---

18   Pagels *Gnostic Exegesis* 13, 14, her emph.

But this will not solve the problem completely. For Ruether the anti-Judaism of John is found supremely in its *christology*, rather than in any particular anti-Jewish sayings. She regards its *replacement theology* as a fundamental affront to Judaism, especially because it involves a claim to the sole authentic interpretation of the Scriptures. As Gregory Baum puts it in his introductory essay in Ruether's *Faith and Fratricide,*

> As long as the Christian Church regards itself as the successor of Israel, as the new people of God substituted in the place of the old, and as long as the Church proclaims Jesus as the one mediator without whom there is no salvation, no theological space is left for other religions, and, in particular, no theological validity is left for Jewish religion.[19]

But our historical analysis allows us to see that there is no *clash of religions* in the Fourth Gospel. As we commented above, here Jew speaks to Jew in a situation in which *all* are confused and seeking answers. Only an anachronistic imposition of later conditions can read the replacement theology of the Fourth Gospel in this way. But having said this, the Fourth Gospel certainly makes an exclusive claim for its answer to the agony. The reader cannot fudge the issue: either Jesus is the Christ, or the new Torah-obedience taught by Yavneh is the way forward, or the *sicarii* represent the best option in a violent re-establishment of what is lost, or perhaps the covenant should be dramatically reinterpreted in terms of universal 'piety'. But then the reader knew that she could not fudge the issue, anyway. She was surrounded by exclusive claims to know the answer. They could not be blurred into an amorphous amalgam.

Theologically, this leaves modern readers with a similar challenge. The exclusive claim of the Fourth Gospel is as clear now as it was then. If it is to remain a pillar of Christian sacred literature, then Christians cannot deny something so fundamental to its nature. We will deny *our* nature, too, if we start to accept that there are other mediators, apart from Christ.

But this does not entail rejection of others in a spirit of theological superiority. We, too, live in an age in which Israel has endured a physical and theological trauma of enormous proportions. The Holocaust must shape Christian relationships with Jewish people as fundamentally as the Jewish War shaped the way in which the fourth evangelist expressed the Good News to his own people. He

---

19   *Fratricide* 5

stood alongside them, sharing their pain. And with great creativity he carved a Gospel which not only recorded the story as he understood it, but told it in a way which brought out its deep relevance for Israel in her need, and as passionately and attractively as possible. He offers a model for Christians today.

Abbreviations and Bibliography

Commentaries are usually cited simply by the name of the author. Commonly used reference works, monographs and articles are usually cited with an appropriate abbreviation of name and title. Occasionally full bibliographical details are given at the place of citation, and these works are not listed again below.

Abbreviations of the titles of biblical books and other ancient Jewish and Christian works, and of the titles of periodicals and serials, follow the conventions prescribed for contributors to the *Journal of Biblical Literature* (*JBL* 107 (1988), 584-96), except that I have generally referred to 2 Baruch as '2 Baruch'! — and with the following additions:

BibRes	Biblical Research
IRM	International Review of Mission
JChSt	Journal of Church and State
JSPSup	Journal for the Study of the Pseudepigrapha, Supplement Series
JTSA	Journal of Theology for Southern Africa
LitTh	Literature and Theology
SBFLA	Studium Biblicum Franciscanum, Liber Annuus
SNTU	Studien zum Neuen Testament und seiner Umwelt
StPh	Studia Philonica

Works of Reference

[Abbreviation if applicable]

APOT

R.H. Charles (ed.) *The Apocryph and Pseudepigrapha of the Old Testament* (2 Vols; Oxford, Clarendon Press, 1913)

I. Epstein (ed.) *The Babylonian Talmud: translated into English with notes etc* (18 Vols; London, Soncino, 1938-1948)

Daniélou, *Theology*

J. Daniélou, *The Theology of Jewish Christianity* (London; Darton, Longman & Todd, 1964)

Díez Macho

A. Díez Macho, *Neophyti 1. Targum Palestinense MS de la Biblioteca Vaticana* (Madrid / Barcelona; Consejo Superior de Investigaciones Científicas, 1968)

Hollander/de Jonge

H.W. Hollander & M. de Jonge, *The Testaments of the Twelve Patriarchs. A Commentary* (Leiden; Brill, 1985)

JE

The Jewish Encyclopaedia (12 vols; New York, Funk and Wagnells, 1901-1906)

Lauterbach

Jacob Z. Lauterbach, *Mekilta de Rabbi Ishmael. A Critical Edition etc* (3 vols; Philadelphia, Jewish Publication Society of America, 1933)

Le Déaut, *Targum*

R. Le Déaut, *Targum du Pentateuque. Traduction des deux Recensions Palestiniennes Complètes avec Introduction etc* (SC; Paris, Éditions du Cerf, 1978)

Lohse

E. Lohse (ed.), *Die Texte aus Qumran: Hebräisch und Deutsch etc* (Darmstadt; Wissenschaftliche Buchgesellschaft, 1981)

MR

H. Freedman & M. Simon (edd.), *The Midrash Rabbah: translated into English with notes etc* (5 Vols; London etc, Soncino, 1977)

Neusner, *Tosefta*

Jacob Neusner (ed. & trans.), *The Tosefta: translated from the Hebrew* (6 vols; New York, KTAV, 1977ff)

Nickelsburg	George W.E. Nickelsburg, *Jewish Literature Between the Bible and the Mishnah. A Historical and Literary Introduction* (London; SCM, 1981)
OTP	James H. Charlesworth (ed.), *The Old Testament Pseudepigrapha* (2 Vols; London, Darton Longman & Todd, 1983 & 1985)
Robinson, *Library*	J.M. Robinson, *The Nag Hammadi Library in English* (Leiden; Brill, 1988/3)
Sanders, *Judaism*	E.P. Sanders, *Judaism. Practice and Belief, 63 BCE — 66 CE* (London / Philadelphia; SCM / TPI, 1992)
Sanders *PPJ*	E.P. Sanders, *Paul and Palestinian Judaism. A Comparison of Patterns of Religion* (London; SCM, 1977)
Schürer	Emil Schürer, *The History of the Jewish People in the Age of Jesus Christ (175 B.C. - A.D. 135)*: 3 Vols, revised and edited by G. Vermes, F. Millar & M. Goodman (Edinburgh; T. & T. Clark, 1973-1987)
Stone	M.E. Stone (ed.), *Jewish Writings of the Second Temple Period: Apocrypha, Pseudepigrapha, Qumran Sectarian Writings, Philo, Josephus* (Assen/Philadelphia; Van Gorcum/Fortress, 1984)
Str-B	H.L. Strack & Paul Billerbeck, *Kommentar zum Neuen Testament aus Talmud und Midrasch* (4 Vols; München, C.H. Beck, 1926)
TextComm	Bruce M. Metzger, *A Textual Commentary on the Greek New Testament* (London, New York; United Bible Societies, 1971)
Urbach, *Sages*	E.E. Urbach, *The Sages. Their Concepts and Beliefs* (Jerusalem; Magnes Press, 1979/2)
Vermes	G. Vermes, *The Dead Sea Scrolls in English* (Harmondsworth; Penguin, 1968)
Williams, *Panarion*	F. Williams (trans.), *The Panarion of Epiphanius of Salamis, Book 1 (Sects 1-46)* (NHS 35; Leiden, E.J. Brill, 1987)

Commentaries

Barrett	C.K. Barrett, *The Gospel According to John. An Introduction with Commentary etc* (London; SPCK, 1978/2)
Beasley-Murray	G.R. Beasley-Murray, *John* (WBC 36; Waco, Word, 1987)
Becker	Jürgen Becker, *Das Evangelium nach Johannes* (2 vols, Ökumenischer Taschenbuchkommentar zum Neuen Testament 4; Gütersloh, Gerd Mohn, 1985/2)
Bernard	J.H. Bernard, *A Critical and Exegetical Commentary on the Gospel According to St John* (ICC; Edinburgh, T. & T. Clark, 1928)
Brown	R.E. Brown, *The Gospel According to John* (2 vols, AB 29; London etc, Geoffrey Chapman, 1966)
Bruce	F.F. Bruce, *The Gospel of John. Introduction, etc* (Basingstoke; Pickering, 1983)
Bultmann	R. Bultmann, *The Gospel of John: A Commentary* (Oxford; Blackwell, 1971)
Carson	D.A. Carson, *The Gospel According to John* (Leicester / Grand Rapids; IVP / Eerdmans, 1991)
Ellis *Genius*	Peter F. Ellis, *The Genius of John: A Composition-Critical Commentary on the Fourth Gospel* (Collegeville; The Liturgical Press, 1984)
Dodd *Interpretation*	C.H. Dodd, *The Interpretation of the Fourth Gospel* (Cambridge; CUP, 1953)
Godet	F. Godet, *Commentary on the Gospel of St John* (3 vols, Clark's Foreign Theological Library 4/51, 53, 56; Edionburgh, T. & T. Clark, 1888-9)
Haenchen	Ernst Haenchen, *A Commentary on the Gospel of John* (2 vols, Hermeneia Commentary; Philadelphia,

Fortress, 1984)

Holtzmann — H.J. Holtzmann, *Evangelium, Briefe und Offenbarung des Johannes* (Hand-Commentar zum NT 4; Tübingen, J.C.B. Mohr, 1908/3)

Hoskyns — E.C. Hoskyns, *The Fourth Gospel* (ed. F.N. Davey; London, Faber & Faber, 1947/2)

Lagrange — M.-J. Lagrange, *Évangile Selon Saint Jean* (Paris; Librairie Victor Lecoffre, 1925/2)

Lindars — B. Lindars, *The Gospel of John* (NCB; London, Oliphants, 1972)

Michaels — J. Ramsey Michaels, *John* (Good News Commentary; San Francisco etc, Harper & Row, 1984)

Odeberg — H. Odeberg, *The Fourth Gospel. Interpeted in relation to Contemporary Religious Currents in Palestine and the Hellenistic-Oriental World* (Amsterdam; B.R. Grüner, 1974. First published Uppsala 1929)

Sanders — J.N. Sanders & B.A. Mastin, *The Gospel According to St. John* (Black's New Testament Commentary; London, A & C Black, 1968)

Schlatter — Adolph Schlatter, *Der Evangelist Johannes. Ein Kommentar zum vierten Evangelium* (Stuttgart; Calwer Verlag, 1975/4)

Schnackenburg — R. Schnackenburg, *The Gospel According to St John* (HTKNT; Vols 1 & 2, London, Burns & Oates, 1968 & 1980)

Strathmann — Hermann Strathmann, *Das Evangelium nach Johannes* (NTD 4; Göttingen, Vandenhoeck & Ruprecht, 1955/3)

Westcott — B.F. Westcott, *The Gospel According to St. John* (London; James Clarke, 1958. First published London, 1880)

Articles and Monographs

Aalen, S.

"'Reign' and 'House' in the Kingdom of God in the Gospels", *NTS* 8 (1962), 215-240

Aker, Benny C.

The Merits of the Fathers: An Interpretation of John 8:31-59 (PhD Dissertation, Univ. of St Louis, 1984)

Ashton, John

"The Identity and Function of the ʹΙΟΥΔΑΙΟΙ in the Fourth Gospel", *NT* 27 (1985), 40-75

Ashton, John

Understanding the Fourth Gospel (Oxford; Clarendon Press, 1991)

Aune, David E.

The Cultic Setting of Realised Eschatology in Early Christianity (Leiden; E.J. Brill, 1972)

Austin, J.L.

How To Do Things with Words (Oxford; Clarendon Press, 1962)

Ball, David M.

'I AM' in John's Gospel. Literary function, background and theological implications (JSNTSup 124; Sheffield, Sheffield Acad. Press, 1966)

Ball, David M.

"'My Lord and My God': the Implications of 'I Am' Sayings for Religious Pluralism", in A.D. Clarke & B.W. Winter (edd.) *One God, One Lord in a World of Religious Pluralism* (Cambridge; Tyndale House, 1991), 53-71

Barclay, John M.G.

"Mirror-Reading a Polemical Letter: Galatians as a Test Case", *JSNT* 31 (1987), 73-93

Bartholomew, G.L.

An Early Christian Sermon-Drama: John 8:31-59. (PhD Dissertation, Union Theological Seminary, 1974)

Bassler, Jouette M.

"The Galileans: A Neglected Factor in Johannine Community Research", *CBQ* 43 (1981), 243-257

Bassler, Jouette M.

"Mixed Signals: Nicodemus in the Fourth Gospel", *JBL* 108 (1989), 635-646

Baumbach, G. "Gemeinde und Welt im Johannesevangelium", *Kairos* 14 (1972), 121-136

Beasley-Murray, G. R. *Word Biblical Themes: John* (Dallas, etc; Word Publishing, 1989)

Becker, Jürgen "Das Johannesevangelium im Streit der Methoden 1980-1984", *TRu* 51 (1986), 1-78

Becker, Jürgen "Wunder und Christologie. Zum literarkritischen und christologischen Problem der Wunder im Johannesevangelium", *NTS* 16 (1969-70), 130-148

Beilner, W. *Christus und die Pharisäer. Exegetische Untersuchung über Grund und Verlauf der Auseinandersetzungen* (Wien; Herder, 1959)

Berger, P. L. & Luckmann, T. *The Social Construction of Reality. A Treatise in the Sociology of Knowledge* (Harmondsworth; Penguin, 1967)

Berger, Klaus "Die impliziten Gegner. Zur Methode des Erschließens von 'Gegnern' in neutestamentlichen Texten", in D. Lührmann & G. Strecker (edd.) *Kirche. Festschrift für Günther Bornkamm zum 75. Geburtstag* (Tübingen; J.C.B. Mohr, 1980), 373-400

Bisnauth, Dale "A Re-reading of John in the Struggle for Liberation", *IRM* 79 (1990), 325-330

Blank, Josef *Krisis. Untersuchungen zur johanneischen Christologie und Eschatologie* (Freiburg im Breisgau; Lambertus-Verlag, 1964)

Boers, Hendrikus *Neither on This Mountain Nor in Jerusalem. A Study of John 4* (SBLMS 35; Atlanta, Scholars Press, 1988)

Borgen, Peder "God's Agent in the Fourth Gospel", in J. Neusner (ed.) *Religions in Antiquity* (Leiden; Brill, 1968), 137-148

Bornhäuser, Karl *Das Johannesevangelium. Eine Missionsschrift für Israel* (BFCT 2:15; Gütersloh, C. Bertelsmann, 1928)

Bowman, J "Samaritan Studies", *BJRL* 40 (1958), 298-327

Braun, F.-M.   "L'Évangile de saint Jean et les grandes traditions
                       d'Israël", *RevThom* 59 (1959), 421-450; 60 (1960), 165-
                       184, 325-363

Brooke, George J.   "Christ and the Law in John 7-10", in B. Lindars (ed.)
                       *Law and Religion: Essays on the Place of Law in Israel
                       and Early Christianity* (Cambridge: James Clarke,
                       1988), 102-112, 180-184

Brown, R.E.   *The Community of the Beloved Disciple. The Life, Loves
                       and Hates of an Individual Church in New Testament
                       Times* (New York; Paulist Press, 1979)

Brown, R.E.   "'Other Sheep Not of This Fold': The Johannine
                       Perspective on Christian Diversity in the Late First
                       Century", *JBL* 97 (1978), 5-22

Bühner, Jan-A.   *Der Gesandte und sein Weg im 4. Evangelium. Die
                       kultur- und religionsgeschichtlichen Grundlagen der
                       johanneischen Sendungschristologie sowie ihre
                       traditionsgeschichtliche Entwicklung* (WUNT 2:2;
                       Tübingen, J.C.B. Mohr, 1977)

Bultmann, R.   *Theology of the New Testament* (2 Vols; London, SCM,
                       1952, 1955)

Caroll, K.L.   "The Fourth Gospel and the Exclusion of Christians
                       from the Synagogue", *BJRL* 40 (1957-8), 19-32

Carson, D.A.   "John and the Johannine Epistles", in D.A. Carson &
                       H.G.M. Williamson (edd.) *It is Written: Scripture
                       Citing Scripture* (FS B. Lindars; Cambridge, CUP
                       1988), 245-264 [Carson"OT"]

Carson, D.A.   "The Purpose of the Fourth Gospel: John 20:31
                       Reconsidered", *JBL* 106 (1987), 639-651

Carson, D.A.   "Understanding Misunderstandings in the Fourth
                       Gospel", *TynB* 33 (1982), 59-91

Chatman, Seymour   *Story and Discourse. Narrative Structure in Fiction and
                       Film* (Ithaca & London; Cornell Univ. Press, 1978)

Chernus, Ira   *Mysticism in Rabbinic Literature: Studies in the History of Midrash* (Berlin etc; de Gruyter, 1982)

Coetzee, J.C.   "Jesus' Revelation in the *EGO EIMI* Sayings in Jn 8 and 9", in J.H. Petzer & P.J. Hartin (edd.) *A South African Perspective on the New Testament* (Leiden; E.J. Brill, 1986), 170-177

Cohen, Shaye J.D.   "Yavneh Revisited: Pharisees, Rabbis, and the End of Jewish Sectarianism", (SBLASP; Chico, Scholars Press, 1982), 45-61

Cook, Michael J.   "The Gospel of John and the Jews", *RevExp* 84 (1987), 259-271

Cotterell, Peter & Turner, Max *Linguistics and Bibilical Interpretation* (London; SPCK, 1989)

Cripps, F.L   "A Reassessment of the Date of Origin and the Destination of the Gospel of John", *JBL* 89 (1970), 38-55

Crossan, D.M.   "Anti-Semitism and the Gospel", *TS* 26 (1975), 189-214

Culpepper, R. Alan   *Anatomy of the Fourth Gospel. A Study in Literary Design* (Philadelphia; Fortress, 1983)

Culpepper, R. Alan   "The Gospel of John and the Jews" *RevExp* 84 (1987) 273-288

Culpepper, R. Alan   "The Pivot of John's Prologue", *NTS* 27 (1981), 1-31

Culpepper, R. Alan   "The Theology of the Gospel of John", *RevExp* 85 (1988), 417-432

Dahl, Nils A.   "Der Erstgeborene Satans und der Vater des Teufels (Polyk. 7.1 und Joh. 8.44)", in W. Eltester (ed.) *Apophoreta* (BZNW 30; Berlin, Töpelmann, 1964), 70-84

Dahl, Nils A.   "The Johannine Church and History", in W. Klassen and G.F. Snyder (edd.) *Current Issues in New Testament Interpretation: Essays in Honor of Otto A. Piper* (New York; Harper, 1962), 124-142

Davies, W.D.	*The Gospel and the Land: Early Christianity and Jewish Territorial Doctrine* (Berkeley, etc; Univ. of California Press, 1974)
Davies, W.D.	*The Setting of the Sermon on the Mount* (Cambridge; Cambridge University Press, 1964)
De Boer, Martin	"Narrative Criticism, Historical Criticism, and the Gospel of John", *JSNT* 47 (1992), 35-48
De Jonge, M.	"Jesus as Prophet and King in the Fourth Gospel", *ETL* 49 (1973), 160-177
De Jonge, M.	*Jesus: Stranger From Heaven and Son of God. Jesus Christ and the Christians in Johannine Perspective* (Missoula; Scholars Press, 1977)
De Jonge, M.	"Jewish Expectations about the 'Messiah' According to the Fourth Gospel", *NTS* 19 (1972-73), 246-270
Derrett, J. Duncan M.	"Circumcision and Perfection: A Johannine Equation (John 7:22-23)", *EvQ* 63 (1991), 211-224
Dodd, C.H.	"Behind a Johannine Dialogue", *More New Testament Studies* (Manchester; Manchester University Press, 1968), 41-57
Dodd, C.H.	"The Dialogue Form in the Gospels", *BJRL* 37 (1954), 54-67
Dodd, C.H.	*Historical Tradition in the Fourth Gospel* (Cambridge; CUP, 1963)
Domeris, William R.	"Christology and Community: A Study of the Social Matrix of the Fourth Gospel", *JTSA* 64 (1988), 49-56
Dozeman, T.B.	"*Sperma Abraam* in John 8 and Related Literature: Cosmology and Judgment", *CBQ* 42 (1980), 342-358
Du Rand, J. A.	"A Syntactical and Narratological Reading of John 10 in Coherence with Chapter 9" in J. Beutler and R.T. Fortna (edd.), *The Shepherd Discourse of John 10 and its Context. Studies by members of the Johannine Writings Seminar* (SNTSMS 67; Cambridge, CUP, 1991), 94-115

Duke, Paul D.   *Irony in the Fourth Gospel* (Atlanta; John Knox, 1985)

Dunn, J.D.G.   "Let John Be John: A Gospel for Its Time" in P. Stuhlmacher (ed.) *Das Evangelium und die Evangelien. Vorträge vom Tübinger Symposium 1982* (Tübingen; J.C.B. Mohr, 1983), 309-339

Dunn, J.D.G.   *The Partings of the Ways Between Christianity and Judaism and their Significance for the Character of Christianity* (London; SCM, 1991)

Eckardt, A. Roy   "The Nemesis of Christian Antisemitism", *JChSt* 13 (1971) 227-244

Elliott, J.H.   *A Home for the Homeless: A Sociological Exegesis of 1 Peter, its Situation and Strategy* (London; SCM, 1982)

Ellis, Peter F.   *The Genius of John. A Composition-Critical Commentary on the Fourth Gospel* (Collegeville, Minnesota; Liturgical Press, 1984)

Enslin, M.S.   "The Perfect Tense in the Fourth Gospel", *JBL* 55 (1936), 121-131

Eslinger, Lyle   "The wooing of the woman at the well: Jesus, the reader, and reader-response criticism", *LitTh* 1 (1987) 167-183

Evans, Craig A.   "Obduracy and the Lord's Servant: Some Observations on the Use of the Old Testament in the Fourth Gospel", in Craig A. Evans and W.F. Stinespring (edd.) *Early Jewish and Christian Exegesis: Studies in Memory of William Hugh Brownlee* (Atlanta; Scholars Press, 1987), 221-236

Fortna, R. T.   *The Fourth Gospel and Its Predecessor. From Narrative Source to Present Gospel* (Edinburgh; T & T Clark, 1989)

Fortna, R.T.   *The Gospel of Signs: A Reconstruction of the Narrative Source underlying the Fourth Gospel* (SNTSMS 11; Cambridge, CUP, 1970)

Fortna, R.T.   "Theological Use of Locale in the Fourth Gospel", *ATR* Supplementary Series 3 (March 1974), 58-94

Freed, E.D.   "Did John Write His Gospel Partly to Win Samaritan Converts?" *NovT* 12 (1970), 241-256

Freed, E.D.   "Who or What was Before Abraham in John 8:58?", *JSNT* 17 (1983) 52-59

Freyne, Sean   "Vilifying the Other and Defining the Self: Matthew's and John's Anti-Jewish Polemic in Focus", in J. Neusner and E.S. Frerichs (edd.), *"To See Ourselves as Others See Us": Christians, Jews, "Others" in Late Antiquity* (Chico; Scholars Press, 1985), 117-143

Gemser, Berend   "The rîb- or controversy-pattern in Hebrew mentality", in M. Noth & D. Winton Thomas (ed.) *Wisdom in Israel and in the Ancient Near East, Essays presented to H.H. Rowley on his 65th birthday* (VTSup 3; Leiden, Brill, 1955), 120-137

Geyser, A.S.   "Israel in the Fourth Gospel", *Neot.* 20 (1986), 13-20

Glasson, T.F.   *Moses in the Fourth Gospel* (London; SCM, 1963)

Goulder, Michael   "Nicodemus", *SJT* 44 (1991), 153-168

Gräßer, Erich   "Die antijüdische Polemik im Johannesevangelium", *NTS* 11 (1964-5), 74-90

Gräßer, Erich   "Die Juden als Teufelssöhne in Johannes 8, 37-47", in W.P. Eckert et al. (edd.), *Antijudaismus im Neuen Testament? Exegetische und systematische Beitrage* (Abhandlungen zum christlich-judischen Dialog 2; Munich, Chr. Kaiser, 1967), 157-170

Gryglewicz, Feliks   "Die Pharisäer und die Johanneskirche", in A. Fuchs (ed.), *Probleme der Forschung* (SNTU A.3; Wien / München, Herold Verlag, 1978), 144-158

Hahn, Ferdinand   "'Die Juden' im Johannesevangelium", in P.-G. Mueller and W. Stenger (edd.) *Kontinuität und Einheit* (FS Franz Mussner; Freiburg etc, Herder, 1981), 430-438

Hahn, Ferdinand   "Der Prozeß Jesu nach dem Johannesevangelium",

EKKNT *Vorarbeiten Heft* 2 (Zürich / Neukirchen; Benziger / Neukirchener Verlage, 1970), 23-96

Halperin, David J.   *The Merkabah in Rabbinic Literature* (AOS 62; New Haven Connecticut; American Oriental Society, 1980)

Harvey, A.E.   *Jesus on Trial. A Study in the Fourth Gospel* (London; SPCK, 1976)

Hellig, Jocelyn   "The Negative Image of the Jew and its New Testament Roots", *JTSA* 64 (1988), 39-48

Hengel, Martin   *The Charismatic Leader and his Followers* (New York; Crossroad, 1981)

Hengel, Martin   *The Johannine Question* (London; SCM, 1989)

Hengel, Martin   "The Old Testament in the Fourth Gospel", *HBT* 12 (1990), 19-41

Hengel, Martin   *The Zealots* (Edinburgh; T.&T. Clark, 1989)

Hickling, C.J.A.   "Attitudes to Judaism in the Fourth Gospel", in M. de Jonge (ed.) *L'Évangile de Jean: sources, rédaction, théologie* (BETL 44; Leuven, Leuven Univ. Press, 1977), 347-354

Hooker, M.D.   "The Johannine Prologue and the Messianic Secret", *NTS* 21 (1975), 40-58

Horbury, William   "The Benediction of the *Minim* and Early Jewish-Christian Controversy", *JTS* 33 (1982), 19-61

Horsley, R.A. & Hanson, J.S. *Bandits, Prophets and Messiahs. Popular Movements at the Time of Jesus* (Minneapolis; Winston, 1985)

Hurtado, Larry W.   *One God, One Lord. Early Christian Devotion and Ancient Jewish Monotheism* (London; SCM, 1988)

Ibuki, Yu   "'Viele glaubten an ihn' — Auseinandersetzung mit dem Glauben im Johannesevangelium", *AJBI* 9 (1983), 128-183

Ibuki, Yu   *Die Wahrheit im Johannesevangelium* (BBB 39; Bonn,

Peter Hanstein, 1972)

Jasper, David   *The New Testament and the Literary Imagination*
                    (London; Macmillan, 1987)

Jocz, J.   "Die Juden im Johannesevangelium", *Judaica* 9
                   (1953) 129-142

Johnson, E. E.   "Jews and Christians in the New Testament: John,
                   Matthew and Paul", *Reformed Review* 42 (1988), 113-
                   128

Johnson, Luke T.   "The New Testament's Anti-Jewish Slander and the
                   Conventions of Ancient Polemic", *JBL* 108 (1989),
                   419-441

Judge, Edwin A.   "Response to Bruce Malina" in H.C. Waetjen (ed.)
                   *Protocol of the 48th Colloquy of the Center for
                   Hermeneutical Studies in Hellenistic and Modern
                   Culture* (Berkeley, California; Graduate Theological
                   Union & University of California-Berkeley, 1985), esp
                   24-29 [but further responses are given in the
                   following verbatim record of the colloquy]

Katz, Steven T.   "Issues in the Separation of Judaism and Christianity
                   after 70 C.E.: A Reconsideration", *JBL* 103 (1984), 43-
                   76

Kee, H.C.   *Community of the New Age: Studies in Mark's Gospel*
                   (London; SCM, 1977)

Kemper, Friedmar   "Zur literarischen Gestalt des Johannesevangeliums",
                   TZ 43 (1987), 247-264

Kermode, Frank   "John", in R. Alter and F. Kermode (edd.), *The
                   Literary Guide to the Bible* (London; Collins, 1987),
                   440-466

Kern, W.   "Die symmetrische Gesamtaufbau von Jo 8, 12-58",
                   ZKT 78 (1956), 451-454

Kimelman, Reuven   "*Birkat Ha-Minim* and the Lack of Evidence for an
                   Anti-Christian Jewish Prayer in Late Antiquity", in
                   E.P. Sanders (ed.), *Jewish and Christian Self-Definition
                   Volume Two: Aspects of Judaism in the Graeco-Roman*

Period (London; SCM, 1981), 226-244

Knight, G.A.F.   "Antisemitism in the Fourth Gospel", *Reformed Theological Review* 27 (1968), 81-88

Koenig, John   *Jews and Christians in Dialogue: New Testament Foundations* (Philadelphia; Westminster Press, 1979)

Koester, Craig R.   *Symbolism in the Fourth Gospel. Meaning, Mystery, Community* (Minneapolis; Fortress, 1995)

Kurz, William S.   "The Beloved Disciple and Implied Readers", *BTB* 19 (1989), 100-107

Kysar, Robert   *The Fourth Evangelist and his Gospel. An Examination of Contemporary Scholarship* (Minneapolis; Augsburg, 1975)

Lategan, B.C.   "The Truth that sets Men Free: John 8:31-36", *Neot* 2 (1968), 70-80

Le Déaut, R.   *The Message of the New Testament and the Aramaic Bible (Targum)* (trans. S. F. Miletic; Rome, Biblical Institute Press, 1982)

Le Déaut, R.   "Targumic Literature and New Testament Interpretation", *BTB* 4 (1974), 243-289

Leibig, Janis E.   "John and 'the Jews': Theological Antisemitism in the Fourth Gospel", *JES* 20 (1983), 209-234

Leistner, Reinhold   *Antijudaismus im Johannesevangelium? Darstellung des Problems in der neueren Auslegungsgeschichte und Untersuchung der Leidensgeschichte* (Bern/Frankfurt; Herbert Lang, 1974)

Leroy, Herbert   *Rätsel und Missverständnis: Ein Beitrag zur Formgeschichte des Johannesevangeliums* (BBB 30; Bonn, Peter Hanstein, 1968)

Limburg, James   "The Root byr and the Prophetic Lawsuit Speeches", *JBL* 88 (1969), 291-304

Lindars, B.   *Behind the Fourth Gospel* (London; SPCK, 1971)

Lindars, B.   "Discourse and Tradition: the Use of the Sayings of Jesus in the Discourses of the Fourth Gospel", *JSNT* 13 (1981), 83-101

Lindars, B.   "The Persecution of Christians in John 15:18-16:4a", in W. Horbury and B. McNeil (edd.), *Suffering and Martyrdom in the New Testament. Studies presented to G.M. Styler by the Cambridge New Testament Seminar* (Cambridge; CUP, 1981), 48-69

Lindars, B.   "Slave and Son in John 8:31-36", in W.C. Weinrich (ed.), *The New Testament Age. Essays in Honor of Bo Reicke* (Macon; Mercer Univ. Press, 1984), 1:269-286

Lona, H.E.   *Abraham in Johannes 8. Ein Beitrag zur Methodenfrage* (Europäische Hochschulschriften 23/65; Bern/Frankfurt, Peter Lang, 1976)

Longenecker, Bruce   *Eschatology and the Covenant: A Comparison of 4 Ezra and Romans 1-11* (JSNTSup 57; Sheffield, JSOT Press, 1991)

Louw, Johannes   "A Semiotic Approach to Discourse Analysis with reference to Translation Theory", *BT* 36 (1985), 101-107

Lowe, Malcolm   "Who Were the ΙΟΥΔΑΙΟΙ?", *NovT* 18 (1976), 101-130

Lowry, Richard   "The Rejected-Suitor Syndrome: Human Sources of the New Testament 'Antisemitism'", *JES* 14 (1977), 219-232

Lütgert, Wilhelm   "Die Juden im Johannesevangelium", in *Neutestamentliche Studien fur Georg Heinrici zu seinem 70. Geburtstag* (UNT 6; Leipzig, J.C. Hinrichs, 1914), 147-154

Lyons, George   *Pauline Autobiography: Towards a New Understanding* (SBLDS 73; Atlanta, Scholars Press, 1985)

McCaffrey, James   *The House with Many Rooms. The Temple Theme of Jn. 14,2-3* (Rome; Editrice Pontificio Istituto Biblico, 1988)

MacRae, George W. "Theology and Irony in the Fourth Gospel", in R.J.

Clifford and G.W. MacRae (ed.), *The Word in the World: Essays in Honor of F.L. Moriarty* (Cambridge, Mass.; Weston College Press, 1973), 83-96

Malina, Bruce   "The Gospel of John in Sociolinguistic Perspective", in H.C. Waetjen (ed.), *Protocol of the 48th Colloquy of the Center for Hermeneutical Studies in Hellenistic and Modern Culture* (Berkeley, California; Graduate Theological Union & Univ. of California-Berkeley, 1985), 1-23

Manns, F.   "L'Évangile de Jean, Réponse Chrétienne aux Décisions de Jabne", *SBFLA* 30 (1980), 47-92 [Manns "Réponse"]

Manns, F.   "L'évangile de Jean, réponse chrétienne aux décisions de Jabne. Note complémentaire", *SBFLA* 32 (1982), 85-108 [Manns "Jabne"]

Manns, F.   "Lecture symbolique de Jean 12:1-11", *SBFLA* 36 (1986), 85-110

Manns, F.   *"La Vérité vous fera libres": Etude exégétique de Jean 8/31-59.* Studium Biblicum Franciscanum, Analecta 11 (Jerusalem; Franciscan Printing Press, Imprimatur 1976)

Mantel, Hugo   "The Causes of the Bar Kokba Revolt" *JQR* 58 (1968) 224-242, 274-296

Martyn, J. Louis   "Glimpses into the History of the Johannine Community From its Origin through the Period of Its Life in Which The Fourth Gospel Was Composed", in M. de Jonge (ed.), *L'Évangile de Jean: sources, rédaction, théologie* (BETL 44: Leuven; Leuven Univ. Press, 1977), 149-175

Martyn, J. Louis   *History and Theology in the Fourth Gospel* (Nashville; Abingdon, 1968/1, 1979/2)

Martyn, J. Louis   "Persecution and Martyrdom: A Dark and Difficult Chapter in the History of Johannine Christianity", in *The Gospel of John in Christian History. Essays for Interpreters* (New York, etc; Paulist Press, 1978), 55-89

Mattill, A.J., Jr.   "Johannine Communities Behind the Fourth Gospel:
                          Georg Richter's Analysis", *TS* 38 (1977), 294-315

Meeks, Wayne A.   "'Am I a Jew?' Johannine Christianity and Judaism",
                          in J. Neusner (ed.), *Christianity, Judaism, and Other
                          Graeco-Roman Cults: Studies for Morton Smith at Sixty*
                          (SJLA 12; Leiden, E.J. Brill, 1975) I:163-186

Meeks, Wayne A.   "Breaking Away: Three New Testament Pictures of
                          Christianity's Separation from the Jewish
                          Communities", in J. Neusner and E.S. Frerichs (edd.),
                          *"To See Ourselves as Others See Us": Christians, Jews,
                          "Others" in Late Antiquity* (Chico; Scholars Press,
                          1985), 93-115

Meeks, Wayne A.   "The Man From Heaven in Johannine Sectarianism",
                          JBL 91 (1972), 44-72

Meeks, Wayne A.   "Moses as God and King", in J. Neusner (ed.),
                          *Religions in Antiquity. Essays in Memory of Erwin
                          Ramsdell Goodenough* (Studies in the History of
                          Religions 14; Leiden, Brill, 1968), 354-371

Meeks, Wayne A.   *The Prophet-King. Moses Traditions and the Johannine
                          Christology* (NovTSup 14; Leiden, Brill, 1967)

Mlakuzhyil, George   *The Christocentric Literary Structure of the Fourth
                          Gospel* (AnBib 117; Rome, Pontifical Biblical Institute,
                          1987)

Moule, C.F.D.   "The Intention of the Evangelists", in *The
                          Phenomenon of the New Testament* (London; SCM,
                          1967), 100-114

Mueller, James R.   "The Apocalypse of Abraham and the Destruction of
                          the Second Jewish Temple", SBLASP (Chico; Scholars
                          Press, 1982), 341-349

Murphy F.J.   "*2 Baruch* and the Romans", *JBL* 104 (1985), 663-669

Murphy, F.J.   *The Structure and Meaning of Second Baruch* (SBLDS
                          78; Atlanta, Scholars Press, 1985)

Murray, Robert "'Disaffected Judaism' and Early Christianity: Some Predisposing Factors", in J. Neusner and E.S. Frerichs (edd.), *"To See Ourselves as Others See Us": Christians, Jews, "Others" in Late Antiquity* (Chico; Scholars Press, 1985), 263-281

Neusner, Jacob "The Formation of Rabbinic Judaism. Methodological Issues and Substantive Theses", in *Formative Judaism: Religious, Historical and Literary Studies, Third Series: Torah, Pharisees, and Rabbis* (BJS 46; Chico, Scholars Press, 1983), 99-144

Neusner, Jacob *Jews and Christians. The Myth of a Common Tradition* (London; SCM, 1991)

Neusner, Jacob "Judaism after the Destruction of the Temple: An Overview", in *Formative Judaism: Religious, Historical and Literary Studies, Third Series: Torah, Pharisees, and Rabbis* (BJS 46; Chico, Scholars Press, 1983), 83-98

Neusner, Jacob *A Life of Rabban Yohanan ben Zakkai Ca. 1-80 C.E.* (Leiden; Brill, 1962/1, 1970/2)

Neyrey, Jerome H. *An Ideology of Revolt. John's Christology in Social-Science Perspective* (Philadelphia; Fortress Press, 1988)

Neyrey, Jerome H. "Jesus the Judge: Forensic Process in John 8,21-59", *Bib* 68 (1987) 509-541

Nickelsburg, G.W.E. "Revealed Wisdom as a Criterion for Inclusion and Exclusion: From Jewish Sectarianism to Early Christianity", in J. Neusner and E.S. Frerichs (edd.), *"To See Ourselves as Others See Us": Christians, Jews, "Others" in Late Antiquity* (Chico; Scholars Press, 1985), 73-91

Nicol, W. *The Semeia in the Fourth Gospel: Tradition and Redaction* (NovTSup 32; Leiden, Brill, 1975)

O'Day, Gail R. "Narrative Mode and Theological Claim: A Study in the Fourth Gospel", *JBL* 105 (1986), 657-668

O'Day, Gail R. *Revelation in the Fourth Gospel: Narrative Mode and Theological Claim* (Philadelphia; Fortress, 1986)

Okure, Teresa   *The Johannine Approach to Mission. A Contextual Study of John 4:1-42* (WUNT 2.31; Tübingen, J.C.B. Mohr, 1988)

Onuki, Takashi   *Gemeinde und Welt im Johannesevangelium. Ein Beitrag zur Frage nach der theologischen und pragmatischen Funktion des johanneischen "Dualismus"* (WMANT 56; Neukirchen-Vluyn, Neukirchener Verlag, 1984)

Onuki, Takashi   "Zur literatursoziologischen Analyse des Johannes-evangeliums: auf dem Wege zur Methodenintegration", *AJBI* 8 (1982), 162-216

Osborne, Grant R.   *The Hermeneutical Spiral: A Comprehensive Introduction to Biblical Interpretation* (Downers Grove; IVP, 1991)

Østenstad, Gunnar   "The Structure of the Fourth Gospel: Can it be Defined Objectively?" *ST* 45 (1991), 33-55

Pagels, Elaine H.   *The Johannine Gospel in Gnostic Exegesis. Heracleon's Commentary on John* (SBLMS 17; Nashville, Abingdon, 1973)

Painter, John   "Christ and the Church in John 1, 45-51", in M. de Jonge (ed.), *L'Évangile de Jean: sources, rédaction, théologie* (BETL 44: Leuven; Leuven Univ. Press, 1977), 359-363

Painter, John   *The Quest for the Messiah. The History, Literature and Theology of the Johannine Community* (Edinburgh; T.& T. Clark, 1991)

Painter, John   "Text and Context in John 5", *AusBR* 35 (1987), 28-34

Pancaro, Severino   *The Law in the Fourth Gospel. The Torah and the Gospel, Moses and Jesus, Judaism and Christianity According to John* (Leiden; Brill, 1975)

Plescia, J.   "On the Persecution of the Christians in the Roman Empire", *Latomus* 30 (1971), 120-132

Polhill, John B.   "John 1-4: The Revelation of True Life", *RevExp* 85 (1988), 445-457

Pryor, John W.   "Jesus and Israel in the Fourth Gospel — John 1:11"

NovT 32 (1990), 201-218

Pryor, John W.   *John: Evangelist of the Covenant People. The Narrative &
                 Themes of the Fourth Gospel* (London; Darton,
                 Longman & Todd, 1992)

Rebell, Walter   *Gemeinde als Gegenwelt: zur soziologischen und
                 didaktischen Funktion des Johannesevangeliums* (BBET
                 20; Frankfurt, Lang, 1987)

Reim, G.   "Joh. 8.44 — Gotteskinder / Teufelskinder: wie anti-
                judaistisch ist 'Die wohl antijudaistischste Äusserung
                des NT'?", *NTS* 30 (1984), 619-624

Reim, G.   *Studien zum alttestamentlichen Hintergrund des Johan-
                nesevangeliums* (SNTSMS 22; Cambridge, CUP, 1974)

Rensberger, David *Johannine Faith and Liberating Community*
                   (Philadelphia; Westminster Press, 1988)

Richard, E.   "Expressions of Double Meaning and their Function
                in the Gospel of John", *NTS* 31 (1985), 96-112

Rissi, Mathias "Der Aufbau des vierten Evangeliums", *NTS* 29
                (1983), 48-54

Robert, René   "Le Malentendu sur le Nom divin au chapitre VIII du
                quatrième évangile", *RevThom* 88 (1988), 278-287

Robinson, J.A.T. "The Destination and Purpose of St John's Gospel", in
                  Twelve New Testament Studies (London; SCM, 1962),
                  107-125

Robinson, J.A.T. "The New Look on the Fourth Gospel", *Twelve New
                  Testament Studies* (London; SCM, 1962), 94-106

Robinson, J.A.T. *Redating the New Testament* (London; SCM, 1975)

Roth, Wolfgang "Scriptural Coding in the Fourth Gospel", *BibRes* 32
                (1987), 6-29

Ruether, R.R.   *Faith and Fratricide. The Theological Roots of Anti-
                Semitism* (Minneapolis; Seabury, 1974)

de Saussure, F. *Course in General Linguistics* (London; Collins, 1974)

Schäfer, Peter "Die sogenannte Synode von Jabne. Zur Trennung von Juden und Christen im ersten / zweiten Jh. n. Chr.", *Judaica* 31 (1975), 54-64, 116-124

Schenke, Ludger "Joh 7-10: Eine dramatische Szene", *ZNW* 80 (1989), 172-192

Schenke, Ludger "Der 'Dialog Jesu mit den Juden' im Johannes-evangelium: Ein Rekonstruktionsversuch", *NTS* 34 (1988), 573-603

Schiffman, Lawrence H. "At the Crossroads: Tannaitic Perspectives on the Jewish-Christian Schism", in E.P. Sanders (ed.), *Jewish and Christian Self-Definition Volume Two: Aspects of Judaism in the Graeco-Roman Period* (London; SCM, 1981), 115-156

Schoeps, H.-J. "Ebionite Christianity", *JTS* 4 (1953), 219-224

Siker, Jeffrey S. *Disinheriting the Jews: Abraham in Early Christian Controversy* (Louisville; Westminster / John Knox, 1991)

Smalley, Stephen S. "John's Revelation and John's Community", *BJRL* 69 (1986), 549-571

Smalley, Stephen S. *John: Evangelist and Interpreter* (Exeter; Paternoster Press, 1978)

Smith, D. Moody "The Life Setting of the Gospel of John", *RevExp* 85 (1988), 433-444

Smith, D. Moody "The Setting and Shape of a Johannine Narrative Source", in *Johannine Christianity: Essays on its Setting, Sources and Theology* (Edinburgh; T. & T. Clark, 1987), 80-93

Smith, Morton *Palestinian Parties and Politics That Shaped the Old Testament* (New York / London; Columbia Univ. Press, 1971)

Staley, Jeffrey Lloyd *The Print's First Kiss: A Rhetorical Investigation of the Implied Reader in the Fourth Gospel* (SBLDS 82. Atlanta; Scholars Press, 1988)

Stanton, Graham N.   *A Gospel for a New People. Studies in Matthew* (Edinburgh; T. & T. Clark, 1992)

Stibbe, Mark W.G.   "The Elusive Christ: A New Reading of the Fourth Gospel", *JSNT* 44 (1991), 19-37

Stibbe, Mark W.G.   *John* ('Readings' Commentary; Sheffield, Sheffield Acad. Press, 1993)

Stibbe, Mark W.G.   *John as Storyteller. Narrative Criticism and the Fourth Gospel* (SNTSMS 73; Cambridge, CUP, 1992)

Stone, Michael E.   "Reactions to Destructions of the Second Temple: Theology, Perception and Conversion", *JSJ* 12 (1981), 195-204

Strecker, G.   "On the Problem of Jewish Christianity", Appendix in Walter Bauer, *Orthodoxy and Heresy in Earliest Christianity* (London; SCM, 1972), 241-285

Suggit, J.N.   "Nicodemus — the True Jew", *Neot* 14 (1981), 90-110

Theissen, G.   *The First Followers of Jesus: a Sociological Analysis of Early Christianity* (London; SCM, 1978)

Thomas, J.C.   "The Fourth Gospel and Rabbinic Judaism", *ZNW* 82 (1991), 159-182

Thompson, Marianne M. *The Humanity of Jesus in the Fourth Gospel* (Philadelphia; Fortress, 1988)

Thyen, Hartwig   "'Das Heil kommt von den Juden'", in D. Lührmann & G. Strecker (edd.), *Kirche. Festschrift für Günther Bornkamm zum 75. Geburtstag* (Tübingen; J.C.B. Mohr, 1980), 163-183

Thyen, Hartwig   "Johannes 10 im Kontext des vierten Evangeliums", in J. Beutler and R.T. Fortna (edd.) *The Shepherd Discourse of John 10 and its Context. Studies by members of the Johannine Writings Seminar* (SNTSMS 67; Cambridge, CUP, 1991), 118-134

Townsend, John T.   "The Gospel of John and the Jews: The Story of a Religious Divorce", in A. Davies (ed.) *Antisemitism* and the *Foundations of Christianity* (New York; Paulist Press, 1979), 72-97

Trites, Allison A.   *The New Testament Concept of Witness* (SNTSMS 31; Cambridge, CUP, 1977)

Urban, L. & Henry, P.   "'BEFORE ABRAHAM WAS I AM': Does Philo Explain John 8:56-58?", *StPh* 6 (1979), 157-195

Van Unnik, W.C.   "The Purpose of St John's Gospel", *SE* I (= TU 73, 1959), 382-411

Vawter, B.   "Ezekiel and John", *CBQ* 26 (1964) 450-458

Vermes, G.   "The Decalogue and the Minim", in *Post-Biblical Jewish Studies* (SJLA 8; Leiden, Brill, 1975), 169-177

Vermes, G.   "Hanina ben Dosa", in *Post-Biblical Jewish Studies* (SJLA 8; Leiden, Brill, 1975), 178-214

Von Wahlde, U. C.   *The Earliest Version of John's Gospel* (Wilmington; Michael Glazier, 1989

Von Wahlde, U. C.   "The Johannine 'Jews': A Critical Survey", *NTS* 28 (1982), 33-60

Von Wahlde, U. C.   "Literary Structure and Theological Argument in Three Discourses with the Jews in the Fourth Gospel", *JBL* 103 (1984), 575-584

Vouga, Francois   *Le Cadre Historique et l'Intention Théologique de Jean* (Paris; Beauchesne, 1977)

Warner, Martin   "The Fourth Gospel's Art of Rational Persuasion", in M. Warner (ed.) *The Bible As Rhetoric. Studies in Biblical Persuasion and Credibility* (London etc; Routledge, 1990), 153-177

Wengst, Klaus   *Bedrängte Gemeinde und verherrlichter Christus. Der historische Ort des Johannesevangeliums als Schlüssel zu seiner Interpretation* (BTS 5; Neukirchen-Vluyn, Neukirchener Verlag 1981)

Whitacre, Rodney A. *Johannine Polemic. The Role of Tradition and Theology*

(SBLDS 67; Chico, Scholars Press, 1982)

Wiefel, Wolfgang "Die Scheidung von Gemeinde und Welt im Johannesevangelium auf dem Hintergrund der Trennung von Kirche und Synagoge", *TZ* 35 (1979), 213-227

Wind, A. "Destination and Purpose of the Gospel of John", *NovT* 14 (1972), 26-69

Wittenberger, W. "Judenpolemik und Liebesgebot im Johannes-Evangelium", *Zeichen der Zeit* 27 (1973), 321-327

Woll, D. Bruce *Johannine Christianity in Conflict: Authority, Rank, and Succession in the First Farewell Discourse* (SBLDS 60; Chico, Scholars Press, 1981)

Yee, Gale A. *Jewish Feasts and The Gospel of John* (Wilmington; Michael Glazier, 1989)

Indices

1. Citation Index

Inter-testamental and first-century literature

8:58   146, 158f, 200, *208f*
8:59   68, 135, 139, 141, 150, 151, 161, 196, 198, 199, 204, 205, 209

Early Christian sources

Nag Hammadi
Hypostasis of the Archons
87:17-20   186

2. Author / Subject Index

[More sustained interactions or treatments are indicated by italics]

Paternoster Biblical Monographs
(All titles uniform with this volume)

Joseph Abraham
Eve: Accused or Acquitted?
A Reconsideration of Feminist Readings of the Creation Narrative Texts in Genesis 1–3
Two contrary views dominate contemporary feminist biblical scholarship. One finds in the Bible an unequivocal equality between the sexes from the very creation of humanity, whilst the other sees the biblical text as irredeemably patriarchal and androcentric. Dr. Abraham enters into dialogue with both camps as well as introducing his own method of approach. An invaluable tool for anyone who is interested in this contemporary debate.
2002 / ISBN 0-85364-971-5 / xxiv + 272pp

Paul Barker
The Triumph of Grace in Deuteronomy
This book is a textual and theological analysis of the interaction between the sin and faithlessness of Israel and the grace of Yahweh in response, looking especially at Deuteronomy chapters 1–3, 8–10 and 29–30. The author argues that the grace of Yahweh is determinative for the ongoing relationship between Yahweh and Israel and that Deuteronomy anticipates and fully expects Israel to be faithless.
2004 / ISBN 1-84227-226-8 / xxii + 270pp

Jonathan F. Bayes
The Weakness of the Law
God's Law and the Christian in New Testament Perspective
A study of the four New Testament books which refer to the law as weak (Acts, Romans, Galatians, Hebrews) leads to a defence of the third use in the Reformed debate about the law in the life of the believer.
2000 / ISBN 0-85364-957-X / xii + 244pp

Mark Bonnington
The Antioch Episode of Galatians 2:11-14 in Historical and Cultural Context
The Galatians 2 'incident' in Antioch over table-fellowship suggests significant disagreement between the leading apostles. This book analyses the background to the disagreement by locating the incident within the dynamics of social interaction between Jews and Gentiles. It proposes a new way of understanding the relationship between the individuals and issues involved.
2004 / ISBN 1-84227-050-8 / approx. 350pp

May 2004

Mark Bredin
Jesus, Revolutionary of Peace
A Nonviolent Christology in the Book of Revelation
This book aims to demonstrate that the figure of Jesus in the Book of Revelation can best be understood as an active nonviolent revolutionary.
2003 / ISBN 1-84227-153-9 / xviii + 262pp

Daniel J-S Chae
Paul as Apostle to the Gentiles
His Apostolic Self-awareness and its Influence on the Soteriological Argument in Romans
Opposing 'the post-Holocaust interpretation of Romans', Daniel Chae competently demonstrates that Paul argues for the equality of Jew and Gentile in Romans. Chae's fresh exegetical interpretation is academically outstanding and spiritually encouraging.
1997 / ISBN 0-85364-829-8 / xiv + 378pp

Luke L. Cheung
The Genre, Composition and Hermeneutics of the Epistle of James
The present work examines the employment of the wisdom genre with a certain compositional structure and the interpretation of the law through the Jesus' tradition of the double love command by the author of the Epistle of James to serve his purpose in promoting perfection and warning against doubleness among the eschatologically renewed people of God in the Diaspora.
2003 / ISBN 1-84227-062-1 / xvi + 372pp

Andrew C. Clark
Parallel Lives
The Relation of Paul to the Apostles in the Lucan Perspective
This study of the Peter-Paul parallels in Acts argues that their purpose was to emphasize the themes of continuity in salvation history and the unity of the Jewish and Gentile missions. New light is shed on Luke's literary techniques, partly through a comparison with Plutarch.
2001 / 1-84227-035-4 / xviii + 386pp

May 2004

Andrew D. Clarke
Secular and Christian Leadership in Corinth
A Socio-Historical and Exegetical Study of 1 Corinthians 1–6
This volume is an investigation into the leadership structures and dynamics of first-century Roman Corinth. These are compared with the practice of leadership in the Corinthian Christian community which are reflected in 1 Corinthians 1–6, and contrasted with Paul's own principles of Christian leadership.

2004 / ISBN 1-84227-229-2 / xii + 188pp

Stephen Finamore
God, Order and Chaos
René Girard and the Apocalypse
Readers are often disturbed by the images of destruction in the book of Revelation and unsure why they are unleashed after the exaltation of Jesus. This book examines past approaches to these texts and uses René Girard's theories to revive some old ideas and propose some new ones.

2004 / ISBN 1-84227-197-0 / approx. 344pp

Scott J. Hafemann
Suffering and Ministry in the Spirit
Paul's Defence of His Ministry in II Corinthians 2:14–3:3
Shedding new light on the way Paul defended his apostleship, the author offers a careful, detailed study of 2 Corinthians 2:14–3:3 linked with other key passages throughout 1 and 2 Corinthians. Demonstrating the unity and coherence of Paul's argument in this passage, the author shows that Paul's suffering served as the vehicle for revealing God's power and glory through the Spirit.

2000 / ISBN 0-85364-967-7 / xiv + 262pp

Douglas S. McComiskey
Lukan Theology in the Light of the Gospel's Literary Structure
Luke's Gospel was purposefully written with theology embedded in its patterned literary structure. A critical analysis of this cyclical structure provides new windows into Luke's interpretation of the individual pericopes comprising the Gospel and illuminates several of his theological interests.

2004 / ISBN 1-84227-148-2 / approx. 400pp

Stephen Motyer
Your Father the Devil?
A New Approach to John and 'The Jews'
Who are 'the Jews' in John's Gospel? Defending John against the charge
of anti-semitism, Motyer argues that, far from demonizing the Jews, the
Gospel seeks to present Jesus as 'Good News for Jews' in a late first
century setting.
1997 / ISBN 0-85364-832-8 / xiv + 260pp

Esther Ng
Reconstructing Christian Origins?
The Feminist Theology of Elizabeth Schüssler Fiorenza: An Evaluation
In a detailed evaluation, the author challenges Elizabeth Schüssler
Fiorenza's reconstruction of early Christian origins and her underlying
presuppositions. The author also presents her own views on women's roles
both then and now.
2002 / ISBN 1-84227-055-9 / xxiv + 468pp

Robin Parry
Old Testament Story and Christian Ethics
The Rape of Dinah as a Case Study
What is the role of story in ethics and, more particularly, what is the role of
Old Testament story in Christian ethics? This book, drawing on the work
of contemporary philosophers, argues that narrative is crucial in the ethical
shaping of people and, drawing on the work of contemporary Old
Testament scholars, that story plays a key role in Old Testament ethics.
Parry then argues that when situated in canonical context Old Testament
stories can be reappropriated by Christian readers in their own ethical
formation. The shocking story of the rape of Dinah and the massacre of the
Shechemites provides a fascinating case study for exploring the parameters
within which Christian ethical appropriations of Old Testament stories can
live.
2004 / ISBN 1-84227-210-1 / approx. 350pp

David Powys
'Hell': A Hard Look at a Hard Question
The Fate of the Unrighteous in New Testament Thought
This comprehensive treatment seeks to unlock the original meaning of
terms and phrases long thought to support the traditional doctrine of hell. It
concludes that there is an alternative – one which is more biblical, and
which can positively revive the rationale for Christian mission.
1997 / ISBN 0-85364-831-X / xxii + 478pp

May 2004

Rosalind Selby
The Comical Doctrine
Can a Gospel Convey Truth?
This book argues that the Gospel breaks through postmodernity's critique of truth and the referential possibilities of textuality and its gift of grace. With a rigorous, philosophical challenge to modernist and postmodernist assumptions, it offers an alternative epistemology to all who would still read with faith *and* with academic credibility.
2004 / ISBN 1-84227-212-8 approx. 350pp

Kevin Walton
Thou Traveller Unknown
The Presence and Absence of God in the Jacob Narrative
The author offers a fresh reading of the story of Jacob in the book of Genesis through the paradox of divine presence and absence. The work also seeks to make a contribution to Pentateuchal studies by bringing together a close reading of the final text with historical critical insights, doing justice to the text's historical depth, final form and canonical status.
2003 / ISBN 1-84227-059-1 / xvi + 238pp

Alistair Wilson
When Will These Things Happen?
A Study of Jesus as Judge in Matthew 21–25
This study seeks to allow Matthew's carefully constructed presentation of Jesus to be given full weight in the modern evaluation of Jesus' eschatology. Careful analysis of the text of Matthew 21–25 reveals Jesus to be standing firmly in the Jewish prophetic and wisdom traditions as he proclaims and enacts imminent judgement on the Jewish authorities then boldly claims the central role in the final and universal judgement.
2004 / ISBN 1-84227-146-6 / xvi + 292pp

Lindsay Wilson
Joseph Wise and Otherwise
The Intersection of Covenant and Wisdom in Genesis 37–50
This book offers a careful literary reading of Genesis 37–50 that argues that the Joseph story contains both strong covenant themes and many wisdom-like elements. The connections between the two helps to explore how covenant and wisdom might intersect in an integrated biblical theology.
2004 / ISBN 1-84227-140-7 approx. 350pp

Stephen I. Wright
The Voice of Jesus
Studies in the Interpretation of Six Gospel Parables
This literary study considers how the 'voice' of Jesus has been heard in
different periods of parable interpretation, and how the categories of figure
and trope may help us towards a sensitive reading of the parables today.
2000 / ISBN 0-85364-975-8 / xiv + 280pp

May 2004

Paternoster Theological Monographs
(All titles uniform with this volume)

Emil Bartos
Deification in Eastern Orthodox Theology
An Evaluation and Critique of the Theology of Dumitru Staniloae
Bartos studies a fundamental yet neglected aspect of Orthodox theology: deification. By examining the doctrines of anthropology, christology, soteriology and ecclesiology as they relate to deification, he provides an important contribution to contemporary dialogue between Eastern and Western theologians.
1999 / ISBN 0-85364-956-1 / xii + 370pp

James Bruce
Prophecy, Miracles, Angels *and* Heavenly Light?
The Eschatology, Pneumatology and Missiology of Adomnán's Life of Columba
This book surveys approaches to the marvellous in hagiography, providing the first critique of Plummer's hypothesis of Irish saga origin. It then analyses the uniquely systematized phenomena in the *Life of Columba* from Adomnán's seventh-century theological perspective, identifying the coming of the eschatological Kingdom as the key to understanding.
2004 / ISBN 1-84227-227-6 / approx. 400pp

Colin J. Bulley
The Priesthood of Some Believers
Developments from the General to the Special Priesthood in the Christian Literature of the First Three Centuries
The first in-depth treatment of early Christian texts on the priesthood of all believers shows that the developing priesthood of the ordained related closely to the division between laity and clergy and had deleterious effects on the practice of the general priesthood.
2000 / ISBN 1-84227-034-6 / xii + 336pp

Iain D. Campbell
Fixing the Indemnity
The Life and Work of George Adam Smith
When Old Testament scholar George Adam Smith (1856–1942) delivered the Lyman Beecher lectures at Yale University in 1899 he confidently declared that 'modern criticism has won its war against traditional theories. It only remains to fix the amount of the indemnity.' In this biography, Iain D. Campbell assesses Smith's critical approach to the Old Testament and evaluates its consequences, showing that Smith's life and work still raises questions about the relationship between biblical scholarship and evangelical faith.
2004 / ISBN 1-84227-228-4 / approx. 276pp

Sylvia W. Collinson
Making Disciples
The Significance of Jesus' Educational Strategy for Today's Church
This study examines the biblical practice of discipling, formulates a definition, and makes comparisons with modern models of education. A recommendation is made for greater attention to its practice today.
2004 / ISBN 1-84227-116-4 / approx. 320pp

Stephen M. Dunning
The Crisis and the Quest
A Kierkegaardian Reading of Charles Williams
Employing Kierkegaardian categories and analysis, this study investigates both the central crisis in Charles Williams's authorship between hermetism and Christianity (Kierkegaard's Religions A and B), and the quest to resolve this crisis, a quest that ultimately presses the bounds of orthodoxy.
2000 / ISBN 0-85364-985-5 / xxiv + 254pp

Keith Ferdinando
The Triumph of Christ in African Perspective
A Study of Demonology and Redemption in the African Context
The book explores the implications of the gospel for traditional African fears of occult aggression. It analyses such traditional approaches to suffering and biblical responses to fears of demonic evil, concluding with an evaluation of African beliefs from the perspective of the gospel.
1999 / ISBN 0-85364-830-1 / xviii + 450pp

May 2004

Andrew Goddard
Living the Word, Resisting the World
The Life and Thought of Jacques Ellul
This work offers a definitive study of both the life and thought of the French Reformed thinker Jacques Ellul (1912-1994). It will prove an indispensable resource for those interested in this influential theologian and sociologist and for Christian ethics and political thought generally.
2002 / ISBN 1-84227-053-2 / xxiv + 378pp

Ruth Gouldbourne
The Flesh and the Feminine
Gender and Theology in the Writings of Caspar Schwenckfeld
Caspar Schwenckfeld and his movement exemplify one of the radical communities of the sixteenth century. Challenging theological and liturgical norms, they also found themselves challenging social and particularly gender assumptions. In this book, the issues of the relationship between radical theology and the understanding of gender are considered.
2004 / ISBN 1-84227-048-6 / approx. 304pp

Roger Hitching
The Church and Deaf People
A Study of Identity, Communication and Relationships with Special Reference to the Ecclesiology of Jürgen Moltmann
In *The Church and Deaf People* Roger Hitching sensitively examines the history and present experience of deaf people and finds similarities between aspects of sign language and Moltmann's theological method that 'open up' new ways of understanding theological concepts.
2003 / ISBN 1-84227-222-5 / xxii + 236pp

John G. Kelly
One God, One People
The Differentiated Unity of the People of God in the Theology of Jürgen Moltmann
The author expounds and critiques Moltmann's doctrine of God and high-lights the systematic connections between it and Moltmann's influential discussion of Israel. He then proposes a fresh approach to Jewish-Christian relations building on Moltmann's work using insights from Habermas and Rawls.
2004 / ISBN 0-85346-969-3 / approx. 350pp

May 2004

Mark F.W. Lovatt
Confronting the Will-to-Power
A Reconsideration of the Theology of Reinhold Niebuhr
Confronting the Will-to-Power is an analysis of the theology of Reinhold Niebuhr, arguing that his work is an attempt to identify, and provide a practical theological answer to, the existence and nature of human evil.
2001 / ISBN 1-84227-054-0 / xviii + 216pp

Neil B. MacDonald
Karl Barth and the Strange New World within the Bible
Barth, Wittgenstein, and the Metadilemmas of the Enlightenment
Barth's discovery of the strange new world within the Bible is examined in the context of Kant, Hume, Overbeck, and, most importantly, Wittgenstein. MacDonald covers some fundamental issues in theology today: epistemology, the final form of the text and biblical truth-claims.
2000 / ISBN 0-85364-970-7 / xxvi + 374pp

Gillian McCulloch
The Deconstruction of Dualism in Theology
With Reference to Ecofeminist Theology and New Age Spirituality
This book challenges eco-theological anti-dualism in Christian theology, arguing that dualism has a twofold function in Christian religious discourse. Firstly, it enables us to express the discontinuities and divisions that are part of the process of reality. Secondly, dualistic language allows us to express the mysteries of divine transcendence/immanence and the survival of the soul without collapsing into monism and materialism, both of which are problematic for Christian epistemology.
2002 / ISBN 1-84227-044-3 / xii + 282pp

Leslie McCurdy
Attributes and Atonement
The Holy Love of God in the Theology of P.T. Forsyth
Attributes and Atonement is an intriguing full-length study of P.T. Forsyth's doctrine of the cross as it relates particularly to God's holy love. It includes an unparalleled bibliography of both primary and secondary material relating to Forsyth.
1999 / ISBN 0-85364-833-6 / xiv + 328pp

May 2004

Nozomu Miyahira
Towards a Theology of the Concord of God
A Japanese Perspective on the Trinity
This book introduces a new Japanese theology and a unique Trinitarian formula based on the Japanese intellectual climate: three betweennesses and one concord. It also presents a new interpretation of the Trinity, a co-subordinationism, which is in line with orthodox Trinitarianism; each single person of the Trinity is eternally and equally subordinate (or serviceable) to the other persons, so that they retain the mutual dynamic equality.

2000 / ISBN 0-85364-863-8 / xiv + 256pp

Eddy José Muskus
The Origins and Early Development of Liberation Theology in Latin America
With Particular Reference to Gustavo Gutiérrez
This work challenges the fundamental premise of Liberation Theology, 'opting for the poor', and its claim that Christ is found in them. It also argues that Liberation Theology emerged as a direct result of the failure of the Roman Catholic Church in Latin America.

2002 / ISBN 0-85364-974-X / xiv + 296pp

Anna Robbins
Methods in the Madness
Diversity in Twentieth-Century Christian Social Ethics
The author compares the ethical methods of Walter Rauschenbusch, Reinhold Niebuhr and others. She argues that unless Christians are clear about the ways that theology and philosophy are expressed practically they may lose the ability to discuss social ethics across contexts, let alone reach effective agreements.

2004 / ISBN 1-84227-211-X / xvi + 320pp

Ed Rybarczyk
Beyond Salvation
Eastern Orthodoxy and Classical Pentecostalism on becoming like Christ
At first glance eastern Orthodoxy and Classical Pentecostalism seem quite distinct. This groundbreaking study shows that they share much in common, especially as it concerns the experiential elements of following Christ. Both traditions assert that authentic Christianity transcends the wooden categories of modernism.

2003 / ISBN 1-84227-144-X / xii + 356pp

May 2004

Signe Sandsmark
Is World View Neutral Education Possible and Desirable?
A Christian Response to Liberal Arguments
(Published jointly with The Stapleford Centre)
This book discusses reasons for belief in world view neutrality, and argues that 'neutral' education will have a hidden, but strong world view influence. It discusses the place for Christian education in the common school.
2000 / ISBN 0-85364-973-1 / xiv + 182pp

Hazel Sherman
Reading Zechariah
The Allegorical Tradition of Biblical Interpretation through the Commentaries of Didymus the Blind and Theodore of Mopsuestia
A close reading of the commentary on Zechariah by Didymus the Blind alongside that of Theodore of Mopsuestia suggests that popular categorising of Antiochene and Alexandrian biblical exegesis as 'historical' or 'allegorical' is inadequate and misleading.
2004 / ISBN 1-84227-213-6 / approx. 280pp

Andrew Sloane
On Being a Christian in the Academy
Nicholas Wolterstorff and the Practice of Christian Scholarship
An exposition and critical appraisal of Nicholas Wolterstorff's epistemology in the light of the philosophy of science, and an application of his thought to the practice of Christian scholarship.
2003 / ISBN 1-84227-058-3 / xvi + 274pp

Daniel Strange
The Possibility of Salvation Among the Unevangelised
An Analysis of Inclusivism in Recent Evangelical Theology
For evangelical theologians the 'fate of the unevangelised' impinges upon fundamental tenets of evangelical identity. The position known as 'inclusivism', defined by the belief that the unevangelised can be ontologically saved by Christ whilst being epistemologically unaware of him, has been defended most vigorously by the Canadian evangelical Clark H. Pinnock. Through a detailed analysis and critique of Pinnock's work, this book examines a cluster of issues surrounding the unevangelised and its implications for christology, soteriology and the doctrine of revelation.
2002 / ISBN 1-84227-047-8 / xviii + 362pp

May 2004

G. Michael Thomas
The Extent of the Atonement
A Dilemma for Reformed Theology from Calvin to the Consensus
This is a study of the way Reformed theology addressed the question, 'Did Christ die for all, or for the elect only?', commencing with John Calvin, and including debates with Lutheranism, the Synod of Dort and the teaching of Moïse Amyraut.
1997 / ISBN 0-85364-828-X / x + 278pp

Mark D. Thompson
A Sure Ground on which to Stand
The Relation of Authority and Interpretive Method in Luther's Approach to Scripture
The best interpreter of Luther is Luther himself. Unfortunately many modern studies have superimposed contemporary agendas upon this sixteenth-century Reformer's writings. This fresh study examines Luther's own words to find an explanation for his robust confidence in the Scriptures, a confidence that generated the famous 'stand' at Worms in 1521.
2004 / ISBN 1-84227-145-8 / xvi + 322pp

Graham Tomlin
The Power of the Cross
Theology and the Death of Christ in Paul, Luther and Pascal
This book explores the theology of the cross in St Paul, Luther and Pascal. It offers new perspectives on the theology of each, and some implications for the nature of power, apologetics, theology and church life in a postmodern context.
1999 / ISBN 0-85364-984-7 / xiv + 344pp

Graham J. Watts
Revelation and the Spirit
A Comparative Study of the Relationship between the Doctrine of Revelation and Pneumatology in the Theology of Eberhard Jüngel and of Wolfhart Pannenberg
The relationship between revelation and pneumatology is relatively unexplored. This approach offers a fresh angle on two important twentieth century theologians and raises pneumatological questions which are theologically crucial and relevant to mission in a post modern culture.
2004 / ISBN 1-84227-104-0 / xxii + 232pp

May 2004

Nigel G. Wright
Disavowing Constantine
Mission, Church and the Social Order in the Theologies of
John Howard Yoder and Jürgen Moltmann
This book is a timely restatement of a radical theology of church and state
in the Anabaptist and Baptist tradition. Dr Wright constructs his argument
in dialogue and debate with Yoder and Moltmann, major contributors to a
free church perspective.
2000 / ISBN 0-85364-978-2 / xvi + 252pp

The Paternoster Press
PO Box 300,
Carlisle,
Cumbria CA3 0QS,
United Kingdom
Web: www.paternoster-publishing.com

May 2004